Italian Villas and Gardens

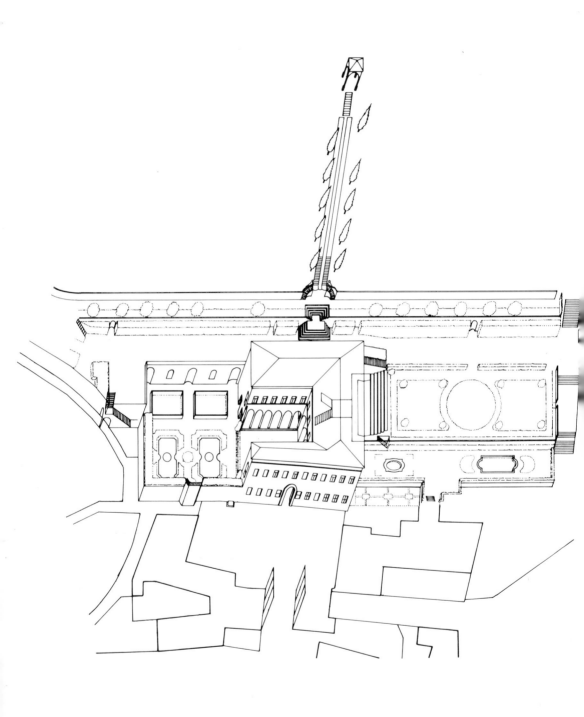

Italian Villas and Gardens

A corso di disegno by

Paul van der Ree

Gerrit Smienk *and*

Clemens Steenbergen

Prestel

This publication has been made possible by the financial support of the Faculty of Architecture of the Delft University of Technology, Architectura & Natura International Booksellers Amsterdam, and the Dutch Ministry of Welfare, Health and Cultural Affairs (wvc).

First published in the Netherlands by THOTH Publishers,
P.C. Hooftstraat 57-1, 1071 BN Amsterdam
Tel. 20: 673 23 27   Fax 20: 673 02 94

Cover illustration Villa Gamberaia (Gerrit Smienk)
Frontispice Villa Cicogna (Paul van der Ree)

Distribution outside the Netherlands and Belgium by
Prestel-Verlag, Mandlstrasse 26, D-8000 Munich 40, Germany
Tel. 89: 38 170 90   Fax 89: 38 170 935

Distributed in continental Europe by Prestel-Verlag
Verlegerdienst München GmbH & Co Kg
Gutenbergstrasse 1, D-8031 Gilching, Germany
Tel. 8105: 2110   Fax 8105: 5520

Distributed in the USA and Canada by te Neues Publishing Company
15 East 76th Street, New York, NY 10021, USA
Tel. 212: 288 0265   Fax 212: 570 2373

Distributed in Japan by YOHAN-Western Publications Distribution Agency
14-9 Okubo 3-chome, Shinjuku-ku, J-Tokyo 169
Tel. 3: 208 0181   Fax 3: 209 0288

Distributed in the United Kingdom, Ireland and all remaining countries by
Thames & Hudson Limited
30-34 Bloomsbury Street, London WC1B 3 QP, England
Tel. 71: 636 5488   Fax 71: 636 4799

Type setting Cédilles, Amsterdam
Production Haasbeek bv, Alphen aan den Rijn
Printed in the Netherlands

ISBN 3-7913-1181-6

Contents

Foreword   7

Introduction   9

Theoretical reconstruction   13

1 Tuscany   29

2 Rome   83

3 The Roman Campagna   121

4 Frascati   197

5 Veneto   227

6 North Italy   271

Bibliography   289

Index   293

ACKNOWLEDGEMENTS This book is the result of a decade of research. During this time we have inevitably incurred a debt to many individuals and institutions. It would be impossible to mention them all, but there are several whom we should especially like to thank here. Firstly, the departments of architecture and landscape design at the Delft University of Technology. It was in the department of landscape design, headed by Professor F. M. Maas, that the idea of analysing the architectural principles underlying villa and landscape design was born. We are grateful to Wilfried van Winden, Willem Heesen and Joris Molenaar, who, in the initial stages of the research, co-ordinated and directed a group of enthusiastic students who provided a challenging and stimulating forum in which many of the ideas presented in this book originated. These students also drew a number of the plans and axonometric projections included here. In this context we should like to extend our thanks to the following: Christian Bouma, Anoul Bouwman, Enno Ebels, Anthoni Folkers, Jeroen Geurst, Ingeborg Grandia, Jan Frederik Groos, Bernhard Heesen, Bert van den Heuvel, Heide Hintertür, Klaas Hofman, Susan Komossa, Mirjam Marijnissen, Lucas Reymer, Bart de Roos, Anton Ruigrok, Karin Theunissen, Rolf Tjerkstra, Christ Vanderheyden, Viktor van Velzen, Peter van Vlaardingen, Tom Voorsluys, Peter Witschey and Wim Woensdrecht. In addition, Wilfried van Winden, Willem Heesen and Joris Molenaar also wrote part of the introduction to the chapter on Palladio and provided several of the analyses and drawings.

We owe a special debt to the many villa owners who extended their hospitality to us during our visits, and in particular to Signora Anna Mazzini (Villa Medici Fiesole), the Contessa Cicogna Mozzoni (Villa Cicogna) and Professor Aldo Visalberghi (President of the Board of Directors of the CEDE, Villa Falconieri). Carla van Vlaanderen and Pia 't Lam, both of the Istituto Olandese in Rome, and A. Frangioni, the mayor of Fiesole, were helpful in providing us with an introduction to a number of villa owners.

Hans Krüse of the Delft University of Technology was responsible for some of the photographs reproduced in this book. W. H. Kempen and F. Vos of the Hogere Bosbouw en Cultuurtechnische School in Velp surveyed the Villa Medici in Fiesole. The architect E. Baldari provided us with useful geographical information on Rome.

Juliette Beckering and Christine Jonge Poering were helpful in translating Italian source material. José van Os and Gonnie van der Plas typed several of the early drafts of the book. Marja Kramp and Paul Willcox translated the original Dutch text. Rolf Bouwknegt, Nina Scheffers and Sarah Vernon-Hunt read through early versions of the manuscript and provided valuable comments and corrections. The final text was edited by Chris Gordon and Paul van der Ree.

We should like to express our special thanks to Alje Olthof for his valuable advice concerning the design of this book.

We are indebted also to the Faculty of Architecture of the Delft University of Technology and the Dutch Ministry of Welfare, Health and Cultural Affairs (WVC) for their financial support.

Finally, we owe a great debt to Guus Kemme, whose faith in this project has been constant throughout its transition from initial idea to publication.

Foreword

Over the years so many books have been written about the phenomenon of the Italian Renaissance villa that one could be forgiven for wondering whether another is necessary. If it were to be a systematic survey of Italian villas then this doubt would be justified. The villas in Italy have already been thoroughly documented. If, however, the book proposed to consider how the interaction between the architecture, the gardens and the landscape can be studied, then the reply would have to be that such a book has not yet appeared. Most of the well-known studies and guides to the Renaissance villa are concerned with their cultural-historical characteristics or the botanical and picturesque aspects of their gardens. There are a few exceptions to this: Bentmann and Müller, for example, have made the villa the subject of a socio-historical analysis; Wittkower has examined the architectural principles which lay behind Palladio's villa designs; and perhaps, above all, Franck's study of the typological arrangement of the Frascati villa is probably the one which has most in common with the intentions of the authors of this book, to explore and identify the specific relationship between the villa and its surroundings, between architecture and landscape.

Since the *villeggiatura* expressed the enjoyment of nature as compensation for the troubles of urban life and architecture was reputed to be a reflection of a cosmic plan, one should almost certainly be able to find indications in villa architecture of the inclusion of the landscape as a fundamental element in the formal plan of the architectural composition. The main aim of this book is to identify these indications and thereby discover an explicit and structural relationship between architecture and landscape. Almost at the same time, it was realized that a study of the *integrazione scenica* of the Renaissance villa would lead to a consideration of the extent to which the architectural features of the villa were determined by its location, and of peculiar local architectural characteristics, the inclusion or exclusion of topographical, situative or general local characteristics within the architectural scheme, in short the debate concerning the concept of the *genius loci*.

In this way, despite the historical nature of the subject, the theme of the relationship between architecture and landscape took on a timeless dimension, and slowly and gradually it was possible to make links between current architectural debates and how these relate to the continuity of traditions.

Ultimately, though, it is not the historicism of the subject but the pleasure of 'redesigning' the villas that the authors want to communicate to the reader through this *corso di disegno*.

GERRIT SMIENK

Introduction

The villa   10

The classification and typology of the villas   11

The villa as a *corso di disegno*   12

The villa

When the Italian villa and its relationship to the landscape is referred to here we have in mind a collection of objects sharing a number of common features. These features are those which lead an object to be designated as an element of landscape architecture and to be analysed as such. The villa as an object consists of a composition of buildings and gardens. The casino is the actual house or garden house.

Following the domestication of the countryside in the quattrocento the villa made its appearance in Italy as a country house of the urban aristocracy. Subsequently villa architecture developed through transformations of the *castello* and the *podere* (farm) into an independent genre. The ideological basis of villa architecture was the *villeggiatura*, the culture of country life, which can be regarded as both opposite and complementary to the culture of the ruling class determined by the city. Unspoilt nature was a prerequisite for the aristocracy's presence in the countryside and thus an essential part of the villa programme. The country villa-with-garden was, in fact, not a new phenomenon: the ancient world had long ago alternated its busy town existence with the restful one offered by the country. Pliny the Younger's letters about his Villa Tuscum in particular provided an important reference for the occupants of Renaissance villas.

The development of villa architecture spanned a period of several centuries and the villas therefore reflect a number of different building traditions. Nevertheless, the villas can be compared in terms of their formal characteristics. The relationship between house, garden and landscape is invariably organized within a single architectural scheme. The way in which this occurs differs from villa to villa, but it is always determined according to a system of formal rules. The differences in the finished product are less dependent on stylistic theories or different building traditions than on the precise way in which active interaction with the landscape is brought about in the plan. It is especially the differences in the programme, the nature of the landscape, or the situational conditions which determined the development of the plan and the way in which the ideal of the *villeggiatura* was expressed. To the Renaissance architect the coherent system of dimensions and relations formed a design model in which the spatial arrangement of elements enabled the landscape to be introduced into the architectural composition of the villa.

The classification and typology of the villas

For practical reasons the villas in this guide are classified historically and geographically. Tuscany, Rome, the Roman Campagna, Frascati and the Veneto district are reviewed successively. This classification corresponds to a broad, overall typology in as far as the villas are considered in their spatial relationship to the landscape. In this guide it has been decided not to give a general all-embracing architectural typology for all the villas. The analysis of the separate villas and their components does reveal the existence of typological interrelationships however.

In fifteenth-century Tuscany, especially in Florence, the Medici dynasty gave a considerable impetus to the revival of the classical *villeggiatura* ideal. In a long-lasting process of land purchase and building programmes a territorial system of villas came into existence along the sides of the Arno valley around the town. In these villas the transformation of *castello* and farm into places of enjoyment gave the *vita rustica* its first tentative form. The 'natural' landscape was brought into the visual range of the villa. In sixteenth-century Rome, during the period of the Counter-Reformation, this Florentine experiment evolved into the complete architectural scheme of the *integrazione scenica*. At the scale of the villa this is expressed in a complex interaction between topography, geometry and perspective. On the scale of the wider landscape the villas dominate the panorama as in an amphitheatre. In the second part of the sixteenth century Vignola and Ligorio built their large villas in the Roman Campagna. In their plans the natural panorama is put into perspective. They themselves restructured the panorama and introduced this in the form of an artificial landscape into the domain of the villa. At the same time, Palladio followed an entirely different approach. He was given the task by the large Venetian landowners of unifying the *comodità* with the *utilità*. In his Veneto villas roads or axes which belong to the rational agrarian infrastructure bring about a functional arrangement as well as an *integrazione scenica* of the (agrarian) villa in the landscape.

Finally, the early-seventeenth-century conversions of villas at Frascati show how villas, with their terraces and façades, were inflated to monumental proportions. Through similarity of orientation and axial organization they fix the point from which the panorama is viewed and impose a direction on it. The natural panorama begins to disintegrate as cosmic space, and it thereby loses its architectural relationship with the villa.

The villa as a *corso di disegno*

The intention of this guide is to be more than that of the average catalogue of places. Apart from being a vade-mecum this guide is also a *corso di disegno*, a course in design. With the help of an accompanying analysis each plan has been rendered 'transparent'. As in an anatomy lesson the architectural object is laid bare. The spatial concept, the way the programme is incorporated into the villa plan, and the way in which topography is interpreted in this plan are discussed.

As has been said previously, Italian villas were designed as architectural unities. They therefore lend themselves to such analytical research. House, garden and landscape form a coherent complex that is rationalized by the application of analogous rules of design to all its parts. Renaissance architecture is based on the idea of the existence of a universal regulating system. This system is reflected in formal rules which can be derived from geometrical shapes and dimensional proportions. The architect had a twofold task: in his designs he had to apply the rules, but, in addition, he was also forced to investigate this universal model because there were no handbooks in which the formal system was set down.

The most important consequence for villa architecture was not so much the belief that it was possible to deduce an ideal, proportional system, but rather that the relationship between villa and landscape or, in more general terms, man and nature, could reveal itself within this formal system of dimensions and proportions. The presence of unordered nature was a precondition for the construction of the country residence. The concern of the villa architect was to represent the natural landscape within the domain of the villa and, in addition, to elicit the hidden order from the chaos presented to him by nature.

The stage for this representation was the garden. Within the boundaries of the garden – the link between landscape and villa – the game played between the imitation of nature and its regulation could take place. As such, every villa can be regarded as a *corso di disegno*. In order to explain this the authors of this book will, as it were, redesign a selection of villas. By doing so we hope to elucidate the sometimes complicated rules according to which the complex was constructed and to illustrate how the villas can be compared and classified by, for example, the regular appearance of the same elements or structures. At the same time we hope to stimulate a much enhanced understanding of nature and landscape as expressed in villa architecture. The manipulation of this concept in particular forms a key for new ideas concerning the synthesis of architecture and landscape, for which this guide will be a *corso di disegno*.

Theoretical reconstruction

The cultural ideal of rural life   15

The sensualization of the landscape   17

The rationalization of the concept of nature   19

The objectification of space and horizon   22

The concept of stage-management   25

Introduction 1*a*

Introduction 1*b*

The cultural ideal of rural life

The possibility of erecting villas arose at the time when control of the hinterland by the cities rendered fortified rural settlements unnecessary. Existing country houses belonging to the large landowning town nobility could be converted, and newly-built villas did not need to be defensible. Both types, the agricultural farmhouse as well as the villa, which was built exclusively for the enjoyment of country life, represent the cultural ideal of rural life, the so-called *villeggiatura*. The start of this development, the transformation of *castello* and *podere* into villas, can be observed in fifteenth-century Tuscan villas. In the *villeggiatura*, as it matured in Italy from the quattrocento onwards, new life was breathed by a humanist élite into the classical ideal of *otium* as opposed to *negotium*, while remaining within the framework of Christian culture. In the villa one could recover from the fatigue and the obligations associated with a high social or ecclesiastical position.

One withdrew from the town, but not to turn one's back on it, and still less as a form of criticism. When Alberti deals in his treatises with the ideal location of a villa, he recommends sites from which there is, apart from a view of hills and plains and so forth, also a view of the town. The villa embodied the enjoyment of rural life, but this took place in an urban manner. Its construction was based on the idea of the town and the urban palazzo and was complementary to this. The artificial arrangement of nature was determined by rules which were part of the cultural world of a ruling class. Alberti linked the degree to which the villa remained utilitarian in character to the social and economic status of the owner.

During the course of the fifteenth century the villa became more and more a place for contemplation and sensuous pleasure. The Romans had already made a distinction between the *villa rustica* as a farm and the *villa urbana* as a spacious country house, to which, in the warm season, the owner would retreat from his urban *domus*. The letters of Pliny the Younger, with their extensive descriptions of his own villas and the landscapes in which they were situated, were among the most important classical sources to have had a direct influence on garden architecture in the Renaissance.

In classical times Cicero and Seneca associated a peaceful stay in the countryside with the urban culture of study and philosophy. In 1462 Cosimo de Medici wrote to his humanist friend Marsilio Ficino: 'Yesterday I went to my villa in Careggi, not to cultivate my land but my soul'. He also made his villa at Careggi the seat of the Academia Platonica, where the literature and philosophy of the ancient Greeks were studied.

Here the humanists tried, in fact, to combine two traditions: that of monastic contemplation and the classical tradition of pastoral seclusion. In Ficino's concept of contemplation nature takes up a central position. The outstanding place for contemplation was the garden, where geometry was a reflection of cosmic order and, therefore, of divine order. Since, according to Ficino and his associates, virtue is nothing other than nature transformed into perfection, the garden, in which nature was sublimated, was also the place in which virtue was nurtured. In Careggi, Ficino thought, young men could learn moral laws without any effort. Poetry and intellectual discipline were as established here as the sensuous enjoyment of nature. It was therefore in a villa, l'Albergaccio, that Machiavelli completed his *Il principe* (1513).

One of the books which had a great influence on garden architecture and on its acceptance by the cultural élite was the *Hypnerotomachia Poliphili*. Insight into Poliphilus' nature is identified in this with insight into the secrets of classical culture and, in particular, into those of classical architecture (fig. 1a, 1b). The development of the *villeggiatura* and the contrast between the *vita contemplativa* and the *vita activa*, the need for pastoral seclusion coupled with an active involvement in (church) politics, went together with such a cultural reorientation towards classical literature. Humanist poets, and Petrarch in particular, referred to Arcadia (Virgil) and the mythical gardens of the gods.

In association with specific topoi of classical literature, nature 'in the wild' was also introduced into the villa. This occurred especially in such elements as the *bosco*, the grotto and the nymphaeum. Ovid's *Metamorphoses* formed an important source by means of which the hidden meaning of such elements was revealed to the initiated.

The sensualization of the landscape

The Renaissance villa substitutes the sensuous pleasure of tangible nature for the symbolic medieval representation of worldly paradise. In medieval thought the distinction between celestial and worldly spheres was discernible in the Creation. The cyclical movement of the celestial bodies referred to the perfection of the original creation, while in the terrestrial domain the results of the Fall had an appreciable effect on the unpredictable and chaotic movements of nature.

The attitude of men towards nature was influenced by the awareness that the latter had been perverted by the sin of Adam and Eve. In art and architecture there was no question of the sensuous enjoyment of nature, but rather of the representation of the lost perfection symbolized in the portrayal of the Garden of Eden. The archetype of the paradise garden consists of a square plan with a centrally placed tree or spring. From there four streams flow towards each of the four points of the compass. They can be regarded as an iconographic representation of the four Evangelists, with Christ in the middle.

The decorative elements are not placed in a spatial relationship but are parts of a fragmented, additive composition. The place of the object in the representation gives a more specific definition or is an attribute of that same object. The elements have a mystical significance (the Tree of Knowledge, the *fons salutis*, for example) and are linked in a symbolic-anecdotal manner. The garden is a representation in miniature of God's Creation. The representation of nature in art and architecture is therefore distinct and separate from real nature.

One of the most important written sources concerning garden architecture in the late Middle Ages is the *Liber ruralium commodorum* of Pietro de Crescenzi (1305). He does not refer, either directly or indirectly, to the environment or to the landscape. His representation of a farmyard with, on the outside, a dovecote and an orchard is even more the evocation of a harmonious closed life cycle. Although the idea of the *hortus conclusus* was preserved in an aspect of the Renaissance garden, the so-called *giardino segreto*, the villa concept nevertheless reflects a fundamental change in attitude towards nature. The landscape itself is given meaning in relation to the ideal of the *vita rustica*. Unspoilt nature was an essential part of the villa programme as a setting for the sojourn of the aristocracy in the countryside. At the same time, the significance of the elements established in the matrix of the garden changed during the Renaissance.

In the thirteenth and fourteenth centuries there were Persian and Arab influences as a result of Islamic expansion and the Crusades. The Islamic garden, like the European medieval garden, is arranged geometrically, but is, in its layout, more oriented towards sensual enjoyment. This is expressed especially in the design of water features. The medieval *fons salutis* became the centre of sensuous enjoyment in pastoral poetry (in Boccaccio's *Decameron* for example). It became a fountain representing the forces and pleasures of nature. The classical topos of the sleeping nymph in relation to a spring or grotto (nymphaeum) was associated with the Muses, the patrons of art and poetry. It was, after all, to a grotto dedicated to the Muses that Plato summoned his students for profound conversation.

The mythical garden of the Hesperides and the figure of Hercules were also important images, in which the Christian concept of paradise was coupled with classical culture. The transformation and architectural adaptation of similar classical literary quotations in the plan of the villa raised the enjoyment of nature to the desired intellectual and cultural level.

The rationalization of the concept of nature

Although in the Renaissance the relationship between art and science remained undivided, a profound change in the way in which nature was understood and represented was to take place in the fourteenth century. The medieval idea of art considered it to be a symbol of reality and metaphysics. The medieval garden referred, as did the Gothic cathedral, to both nature and the supernatural. For the Gothic architect the scientific basis of art was the science of geometry. Together with Pythagoras, Plato, and the neo-Platonists a long succession of theologians from St Augustine onwards was convinced of the thesis that 'all is number'. Divine numbers (such as 3, 4, 7, 12, 40), divine proportions (golden section) and divine forms (the equilateral triangle, the square, the circle) were, as a secret canon, partly derived from Holy Scripture, preserved by the guilds and employed by the masters in works of art.

The doctrine of nature corrupted by the Fall was gradually displaced, however, by the view that God's order is present in nature although concealed in an apparent chaos. This order could be exposed by keen observation. Leonardo da Vinci's minute investigations of natural shapes and phenomena are examples of this. 'I learn more from the anatomy of an ant or a blade of grass than from all the books written since the Creation', wrote Bernardo Telesio later in the first part of the sixteenth century.

In this way, according to the philosophy of Marsilio Ficino and his pupil Giovanni Pico della Mirandola, the two most important protagonists of Lorenzo the Magnificent's Florentine academy, terrestrial nature became a means of coming closer to God rather than an obstacle. Precisely because of his ability to gain insight into the patterns of nature, man is, here, placed in a central position. As art was still directly connected with science in the person of the *Uomo Universale*, the old platonic concept of art as imitation of nature was revived in fourteenth-century Italy: 'Natura artis magistra est'.

Although Cicero had already rejected the theory of literal artistic imitation, it was the neo-platonist Plotinus (*c.*205-270) especially who laid the foundations of a new abstract theory of art. What the artist 'sees' is a reality hidden under the outward visible appearance of the material world but ascertainable through human reason and intuition. By moulding this observation into comprehensive, visible shapes he makes explicit the harmony concealed in nature. Thus the artist designs images which are an interpretation of the principles of nature. In fifteenth-century Florence, the cradle of political, scientific and artistic experiment, the neo-platonist idea of the imitation of nature was stated mathematically. It was the architect-theorist L.B. Alberti (1404-72) who, in his *Della pittura e della statua*, and especially in his *De re aedificatoria*, formulated the mathematical interpretation of nature

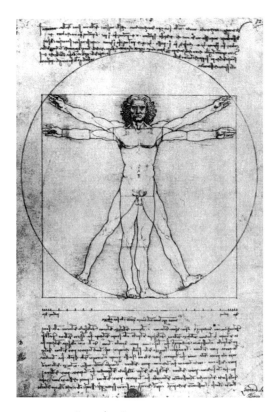

Introduction   2*a*

Introduction   2*b*

as an artistic concept. The study of proportion, based on the scientific measurement of the human figure (anthropometry), created a framework for a renaissance of classical orders and proportions (fig. 2*a*).

In the *De architectura* (the classical Roman source drawn on by Alberti) the proportions of an ideal human figure, with the navel as the centre of a defined circle and square, had already been given by Vitruvius. 'If nature has formed the entire body in such a way that the limbs are in proportion to the entire body, it would seem that the ancients reasonably determined that, when executing a building, they should also take into consideration the precise measurements of the parts in relation to each other and to the entire body [...] They derived the basic measurements, apparently essential for all buildings, from the limbs of the body, such as the palm, the foot and the yard.' For Vitruvius it was the human figure particularly that harboured the secret codes of natural order and beauty.

In the Renaissance this idea was justified by Holy Scripture, in which man is called 'the image of God'. As a reflection of the perfect Creator the human figure could now be interpreted in a wider sense, that is to say as an embodiment of the harmonies of the universe. As such he was a microcosmic image of the macrocosmos. Thus the architectural plan, which in its turn reflected *humanitas*, also obtained a cosmographic significance. It was a metrical diagram in which the hidden order of nature was made evident.

In Alberti's architectural theory three categories were distinguished for this purpose: number (*numerus*), dimension (*finitio*), and ordering (*collocatio*). Favoured numbers were 6 and 10, being respectively the ratio of the length and breadth and the ratio of the length and thickness of a human being. Ten was the sum of 1, 2, 3 and 4. Six was the same as $1+2+3$ as well as $1 \times 2 \times 3$. Series such as $2:4:6$, $2:3:6$, $2:4:8$, etc. were thus derived. In a graphic sense this preoccupation with small integers amounted to the search for square grids. Apart from Alberti contributions were made to the early architectural theory of the Renaissance by, among others, Filarete and Colonna. Filarete, too, preferred the square as a basis for plans and elevations. Colonna used the same source in order to achieve correct proportions for plans and elevations by means of square grids.

An important consequence for villa architecture was not only the concept that it should be possible to derive an ideal, proportional system, but also that, above all, the relationship between villa and landscape, or, in an even broader sense, between man and nature, could be resolved within this rational scheme of dimensions and proportions. As has already been mentioned in the introduction, it was important for the villa architect to represent natural landscape within the domain of the villa and, in addition, to deduce the hidden order from the chaos presented to him by nature. Within the confines of the garden, which formed the link between landscape and villa, the game could be played between the representation of nature and its regulation. Natural topography was defined geometrically in the plan of the villa.

In the Tuscan and Roman Renaissance villa this mathematical model is the new 'aesthetic', designed by the architect, which, within the domain of the villa, places the landscape under the control of human intellect. At the same time, this determined the position of the villa with regard to the surrounding landscape. In the model of the Veneto villa, as developed by Palladio a hundred years after Alberti, this aesthetic is placed in the centre of the classical Roman trio of 'useful, beautiful and correct'. In the plans of his Veneto villas, which are efficiently organized farms, the rational (Roman) division of the farmlands themselves is represented functionally and formally, thus establishing the villa and the landscape in one architectural order.

The objectification of space and horizon

The geometrical scheme of the Renaissance plan expresses the order revealed in nature by science as a 'divine model'. The point of view from
which the observer considers this plan is, however, still neutral: an internal
point of view has not yet been defined. This can only happen when the
geometrical plan is integrated into optical space. When the geometrical plan
is observed spatially its proportions become dependent on a subjective
point of view. It is the construction of a perspective that lays down this
position and systematically determines the observed proportions.

Space emerges as an independent condition and is made concrete by
scientific perspective. The discovery of perspective was closely related to
the discovery of the horizon. Alberti spoke of visible objects whose forms
were measured in the mind. Perspective was not an illusion or trick to
manipulate reality, but its hidden order – a mathematical structure which
provided space with coherence and gave a place to the objects in it. Perspective presupposes a vanishing point on the horizon, which thus becomes the
limit of the composition.

In medieval art the spectator was not involved in coincidences of optical
space. The ideas of the artist were subject to the evocation of a spiritual
truth. According to Aristoteles' philosophy place (*topos*) was an accessory
of the object. Space did exist, but not as an independent aesthetic entity.
On the other hand, Bernardino Telesio, in his *De rerum natura iuxta propria
principia* (1565), proposed that space and time could be independent of
matter and movement. He therefore made a distinction between *locus* (the
Greek *topos*) and *spatium*.

In Renaissance painting the symbolic-anecdotal relationship, or picture-
plane, evolved into a relationship in space. Foreground and background,
which were originally independent incidents of the picture-plane, were
placed in a spatial relationship by perspective experiments. The optical distinction between foreground and background, between the scene of action
and the landscape backcloth, was thus abolished; both were united in one
spatially continuous composition. Not only did the landscape, in which
the various actions were situated, form a spatial unity, there was also the
suggestion that it was accessible. The landscape was no longer a changeable
backcloth; it had become an integral part of the composition (fig. 2 *b*).

In sixteenth-century theatre design the question of a correct optical
relationship between painted background and three-dimensional stage
props also led to experiments with actual built space. The background,
however, still had the character of a painted surface, framed by columns,
arches and building projections. The whole of the stage was organized in
perspective from a viewpoint at the centre of the auditorium. Only from
this point, the seat of the monarch, was the perspective illusion of spatial
unity perfect.

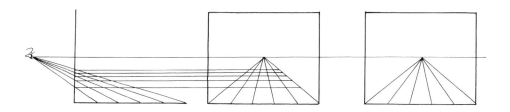

Introduction   3

Important theorists who by means of experimenting with perspective tried to rationalize subjective observation were Alberti (*Trattato della pittura*, 1435), Jean Pélerin, alias Viator, (1440-1524) (*De artificiali perspectiva*, 1505), and A. Dürer (1471-1528) (*Underweyssung der messung*, 1525). Leonardo da Vinci (1452-1519) experimented with it in his paintings and made practical perspective construction into a method, known as the *costruzione legittima*.

The experimental constructions of the first perspectivists proposed a new, speculative hypothesis. Whereas descriptive Euclidean geometry had until that moment stated that two parallel lines do not intersect, they experimented with a hypothetical intersection of such lines at infinity (the vanishing point).

Alberti assumed that a picture is nothing other than a particular section of the imaginary optical pyramid (formed by the rays of vision from the eye), depicted on a projection plane (fig. 3). To him the most important technical problem was the creation of a construction method which systematically correlated the observer's position with the size and the shape of the object depicted. Projected on to a picture plane the size depends on the observer's distance from this particular plane and from the object itself. The shape changes according to the direction of the main line of vision. In his shortened vision of the *costruzione legittima* Alberti, for the first time, created a rational method for the systematic construction (by means of a combination of the plan and the front and side elevations) of the proportions of perspective foreshortening and diminution. In addition he was able to make his construction to scale by drawing a screen in perspective with a dimensional unit of one *bracchio* (one third of the body's length). Perspective construction made seeing scientific and rationalized. The spectator was no longer concerned with metaphysics but with the actual, mathematical position of objects.

In the villa the perspective stage-management of natural space became an architectural exercise. When Petrarch (1304-75) gave his famous literary account of a completely new kind of spatial experience (1366) and of his 'stepping from time into space', the dramatic occasion took place on the summit of a mountain, Mount Ventoux near Avignon. Here an enormous distance from the spectacle of the surrounding world was achieved. The extreme remoteness had reduced conventional reference points to meaningless dots in the distance. When all reference points have disappeared it even becomes impossible to measure space. All movements in the panorama too are modified by the distance and reduced to nothing. Thus the notion of time, which can only be measured by movement, disappears. Petrarch 'placed himself outside reality'. Reflecting on our world, infinite space emerges as an unknown phenomenon, the uninterrupted vistas bring about a feeling of enclosure on a cosmic scale. Moreover, to Petrarch actual physical space was assimilated into the purely inner perspective of contemplation and poetry.

It is this experience of space which can be recognized in the villa and which was brought under control by means of architecture. The villa was always projected against the background of the landscape. This natural landscape was integrated into the panorama of the villa; it is the setting to which the villa, in the foreground, had to be linked perspectively. It was still impossible to design this background as a panoramic landscape of great spatial depth. It was, however, possible to place it in a perspectival relationship with the garden in the foreground. Framed by a loggia, arcade, or portico, or disconnected by foreground terraces, the panorama became a decorative and controllable part of the villa architecture. In such a segment of the panorama the horizon, framed by the architecture, could be presented as an orderly sensation of infinity. It was not the perimeter of the estate which was portrayed as the boundary of optical space, but the natural horizon, far beyond it.

The concept of stage-management

In the garden the organization, conversion and perfection of nature took place according to prescribed architectural rules, which brought about the *integrazione scenica* of the villa into the landscape. The plan of the villa can be regarded as a rational scheme superimposed on the landscape in which those parts of the landscape covered by the scheme are ordered and intensified. The situational properties are revealed by the projection of the geometrical scheme on to the natural topography. Thus at the Villa Medici (Fiesole) the position of the villa in relation to the contour lines of the landscape is emphasized by the oblique garden wall in the upper garden and by the verticality of the terraces in the sloping terrain. At the Villa Belpoggio in Frascati the *bosco* is related to the direction of the valley on to which the villa borders. The Villa Giulia in Rome is situated in such a way that its architectural axis coincides with the natural axis of the side valley of the Tiber in which the villa is situated. It is in the treatment of the edges of the garden particularly that the villa is defined in the landscape. At its eastern boundaries the geometrical plan of the Villa Doria Pamphili is intersected by a diagonal avenue of trees through a deep valley. At the Villa d'Este the boundary on the Tivoli side has been treated very differently to the one opposite which adjoins the panorama.

In the plan of the villa the dimensional system and its manipulation express the relationship between the villa and the landscape. In the elements of the garden, placed as objects in the grid, nature is ordered, the interaction with the landscape is established, and the representation within the overall composition of unordered nature is determined.

Apart from the manipulation of the geometrical matrix and the edges of the plan, the differences in interaction between villa and landscape are determined by number, grouping, and the specific architectural treatment of the elements in the garden. It is a matter of a codified context and a sequence of particular parts. Such a series of elements, or 'canon', which recurs in all plans, is formed, for example, by the sequence casino-parterre-*bosco*. Other canons are, for example, nymphaeum-grotto-cascade-reflecting pool, house-*giardino segreto*-terrace-panorama, and loggia-arcade-pergola.

The number of elements is limited if they are considered and categorized according to formal characteristics: a half-round wall, a screen, a gate, a reflecting surface, a column, a colonnade, and so forth. The separate elements only receive their different meanings through the organization of the garden.

The position of the house as an element in the plan is ambiguous. It is part of the architectural composition, but its siting in the villa complex also coincides with its symbolic significance. This is apparent, for example, in a comparison between the Villa Aldobrandini and the Villa Lante. At

Aldobrandini the villa is represented by the façade of the house, facing the valley, and the relationship with the landscape is directly determined by the incorporation of the hillside into the two intersected tympanums. The garden is situated between the slope and the house at the rear. At the Villa Lante the casino is divided into two equal pavilions and its position on both sides of the longitudinal axis of the garden is determined by the composition of the garden.

The significance of the garden as a link between villa and landscape did not remain constant, and in Palladio's villas, for example, a number of shifts occurred by which house and landscape became more directly involved with each other. Palladio's villas were situated in a vast, flat, fertile landscape, which did not encourage a direct reference to the Arcadian ideal of the *vita rustica*.

In Palladio's agricultural villas the garden forms a ceremonial introduction to the steps and the *piano nobile*, by which the status of the landowner is symbolized. The interaction between villa and landscape takes place using the means by which the landscape itself is organized.

There comes a moment in villa building, therefore, when one can ask whether the scenic staging is still controlled within the plan or whether its organization has been taken over by one of the elements of the plan. This is the case in the introduction of the axis, superimposed on to the landscape. At the Villa Crivelli, the Palladio villa and the Villa Cetinale, for example, this axis is made autonomous in such a way that the interaction with the landscape is determined by the incorporation of landscape fragments as 'ready-mades' in the arrangement. At Crivelli or at the Palladio villa this arrangement of the scenic elements outside the actual confines of the garden can be regarded as the organization of a coincidence within the hierarchical arrangement determined by the axis. This is not the case at the Villa Cetinale. Here the axis does not indicate random points, but parts of the landscape with pictorial qualities.

Further analysis of a number of villa gardens reveals that such elements, though they usually remain linked to the organizational axes, appear to 'escape' from the design matrix and to occupy strategic positions in the landscape; they cannot be directly explained by the formal scheme, but the positions of the elements are determined geographically and pictorially (in the Belpoggio and Cetinale villas for example). In the case of the Sacro Bosco at Bomarzo the stage-management of the elements along the route through the garden actually dominates its formal organization.

In the Renaissance villa the axis, even when it has become autonomous to a certain extent, remains one of the elements by which the plan is arranged. When special perspective effects have been used, such as the effect at the Villa Giulia or the perspective distortion of the cascade at the Villa Aldobrandini, they remain linked to the special development of one of the parts of the plan.

The point when the axis became more independent and detached from the plan signified the end of the development of villa architecture as such, and at the same time marked the inception of new regulating principles in landscape architecture related to another concept of nature and its spatial representation in the landscape. Up to the middle of the seventeenth century a number of developments can be discerned which lay the foundations of French landscape architecture and the development of landscape art as it evolved in England from the eighteenth century onwards. In the French Baroque garden, perspective was restricted to the central axis in order to dominate the plan all the way to the horizon. The *trompe-l'œil*, which is a small component of the plan in the Renaissance garden, became here an essential compositional device. The ingredients supplied by villa architecture to the development of English landscape art are, for example, to be found at Cetinale in the way in which the landscape elements are linked along the axis. When this axis is removed from the formal structure of the plan and when the route through the garden landscape connects the separate pictorially determined parts, the spatial concept of the English landscape garden is born.

LITERATURE

L.B. Alberti, *De re aedificatoria*. Florence 1485. Ed. Ticozzi, Milan, 1833.

R. Castell, *The villas of the ancients illustrated*. London 1728. Reprinted London & New York 1982.

F. Colonna (attributed to), *Hypnerotomachia Poliphili*. Venice 1499. London 1904.

T. Comito, *The Idea of the Garden in the Renaissance*. New Brunswick 1978.

H. Conrad-Martius, *Der Raum*. Munich 1958.

J. Gadol, *Leon Battista Alberti, Universal man of the early Renaissance*. Chicago 1969.

J. Gebser, *Ursprung und Gegenwart, Bd 1, Die Fundamente der aperspektivischen Welt*. Stuttgart 1949.

W.M. Ivins, *On the rationalization of sight, De Artificiali Perspectiva*. New York 1973.

P.O. Kristeller, *Eight Philosophers of the Italian Renaissance*. Stanford 1964.

E. MacDougall, 'Ars Hortulorum: Sixteenth Century Garden Iconography and Literary Theory in Italy', in

D.R. Coffin (ed.), *The Italian Garden*. Washington, DC, & Dumbarton Oaks 1972.

E. MacDougall, 'The Sleeping Nymph, Origins of a Humanist Fountain Type', *Art Bulletin* 57 (1975), pp.357-365.

G. Procacci [trans. A. Paul], *History of the Italian people*. N.p. 1978.

L. Puppi, 'The Villa Garden of the Veneto from the Fifteenth to the Eighteenth Century', in D.R. Coffin (ed.), *The Italian Garden*. Washington, DC, & Dumbarton Oaks 1972.

J. Ross, *Lives of the early Medici as told in their correspondence*. Boston 1911.

G. Schöne, *Die Entwicklung der Perspektivbühne von Serlio bis Galli-Bibiena, Theatergeschichtliche Forschungen* No. 43. Nendeln, Liechtenstein, 1977.

G. Smienk et al., *Architectuur en landschap*. Delft 1985.

O. Stein, *Die architecturtheoretiker der italienischen Renaissance*. Karlsruhe 1914.

Vitruvius, *The Ten Books on Architecture*. London 1960.

R. Wittkower, *Architectural Principles in the Age of Humanism*. London 1949.

Sesto

● 5

● 4
● 8

● 7

● 10

● 6

● 1

3 ●

Florence

2 ●

9 ●

1 Boboli
2 Bombici
3 Capponi
4 Castello
5 Corsi-Salviati
6 Gamberaia
7 Medici Fiesole
8 Petraia
9 Poggio Torselli
10 Pratolino

1 Tuscany

The introduction of the *integrazione scenica* 31

Boboli 36

Bombici 42

Castello 46

Cetinale 49

Gamberaia 54

Gori 59

Medici Fiesole 61

Petraia 71

Pratolino 75

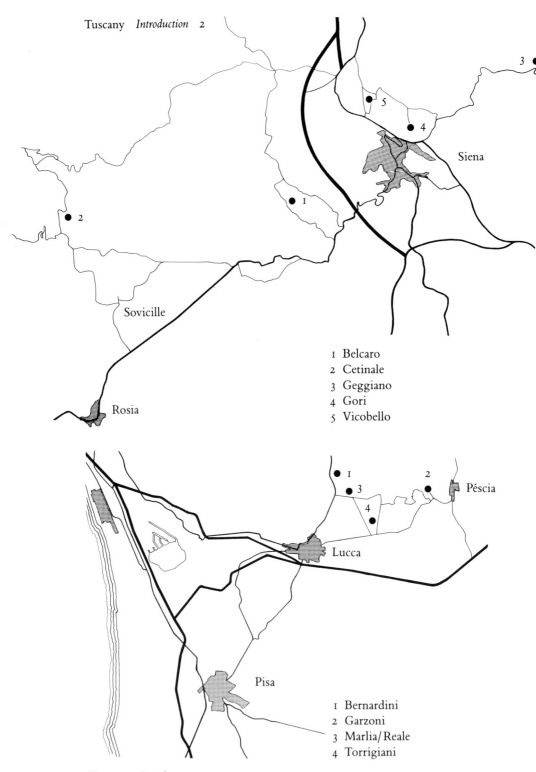

Siena

Sovicille

Rosia

1 Belcaro
2 Cetinale
3 Geggiano
4 Gori
5 Vicobello

Péscia

Lucca

Pisa

1 Bernardini
2 Garzoni
3 Marlia/Reale
4 Torrigiani

The introduction of the *integrazione scenica*

HISTORY   In Tuscany the *villeggiatura* was to be found around towns like Lucca, Pisa, Siena and Florence. Florence was the most important centre, which is why the Florentine *villeggiatura* and its impact on the Florentine landscape is discussed more thoroughly here.

In the fifteenth century numerous villas were built on the slopes of the hills surrounding the city of Florence by the many prosperous citizens. Villani says that the greater part of the nobility and the rich citizenry used to spend four months a year in the countryside. The city dwellers and the court followed a seasonal cycle, moving from town to countryside and from one villa to another. The villas built around Florence during the Renaissance suited the already existing system of the *case coloniche*, the modest residences in the countryside.

In the history of fifteenth-century Florence it was the Medici family in particular who were important in initiating the building of villas outside the city. Cosimo de Medici 'the Elder' (1389-1464) had the Villa Careggi, Villa Cafaggiolo and the Villa del Trebbio built by the architect Michelozzo. In the villas built by Michelozzo the transition from *castello* (castle) and farm to villa is visible. Michelozzo built the Villa Medici at Fiesole (1458-62) for Giovanni, Cosimo's son. This was one of the first villas in Tuscany in which the cultural ideal of country life had been separated from the traditional context of farm and *castello* and had evolved into an independent architectural shape. Lorenzo de Medici, who ruled from 1469 to 1492, commissioned Giuliano da San Gallo to build the agricultural Villa Poggio a Caiano and in 1477 he bought the Villa Castello.

When, in the sixteenth century, a new branch of the Medici family came into power, their possessions were expanded into an imposing territorial system of villas: Cosimo I (Villa Castello, the Boboli Gardens, Petraia, Poggio Imperiale), Francesco I (1541-87) (Villa Pratolino, Marignolle, Lapeggi) and Ferdinando I (1587-1607) (Villa Artimino, Montevettolini). The choice of new locations was determined by general economic, political and speculative considerations. Furthermore, the view of the town (the centre of their power) and the view of their other property played an important part (fig. 4). The villas were situated preferably in each other's field of vision. Ferdinando I placed his new Villa Artimino at Monte Albano in view not only of the ancient village of Artimino, but also of the other family villas (the villas Petraia, Castello, Careggi, Poggio a Caiano, Fiesole). In addition, in the grand hall of the Villa Artimino were the fourteen lunettes by the Flemish painter Giusto Utens (*d.* 1609), commissioned by Ferdinando I, which depicted almost the entire villa property of the Medici family. The villas which were not visible in reality could be seen, painted, in the interior. (The lunettes are now in the Museo di Firenze com'era.)

1 Villa Medici, Fiesole
2 Boboli Gardens
3 Villa Poggio Imperiale
4 Villa di Marignolle
5 Villa Artimino
6 Villa di Poggio a Caiano
7 Villa di Castello
8 Villa la Topaia
9 Villa Petraia
10 Villa di Careggi
11 Villa di Pratolino
12 Villa di Lapeggi
13 Villa Ambrogiana

THE LANDSCAPE, THE TOWN AND THE VILLAS   The landscape in which the city of Florence is situated is shaped by the valley of the Arno. The town is situated where the River Mugnone joins the Arno and the valley widens like a funnel towards the north-west. The northern and eastern slopes rise from the valley bottom with increasing steepness to more than 700 m. On the southern side of the valley the terrain is less accentuated. In antiquity Pliny the Younger had already described this natural space as a gigantic amphitheatre. The full extent of the panorama is 15 km. from east to west and 8 km. from north to south. From the villas, which were situated ideally at a height of 50 to 150 m. above the valley bottom, this space was observed from visually strategic positions (fig. 6). Thus the Florentine landscape was spanned by a network of lines of vision. In these views the town of Florence is an integral part of the panorama.

Yet the town also plays an active part in the architectural development of the natural space in which it is situated. This is particularly related to the town-planning work of Brunelleschi in Florence. The artist-architect Brunelleschi (1377-1446) regarded the town as a rational structure and as a spatially coherent system. This is most clearly expressed in his design for the dome of the S. Maria del Fiore Cathedral in Florence (1418-46). The dome shape is an expression of perspective equilibrium and continuity. From whichever side it is observed the dome is identical. Brunelleschi achieved with this dome not only a new coherence and spatial unity within the town plan, but also provided a reference point for the town from the landscape and the hills around it. This is indicated by the numerous toponyms in the Florence area, such as *L'apparita* and *L'apparenza*, which occur at places from which the city is revealed by the silhouette of the dome. Besides this the dome expressed the historical reality of a city with new cultural and political prestige, which controlled an extensive territory. Its 'shadow' had to 'cover' not only the Florentines but also the other inhabitants of Tuscany. It is the ideal shape with which to relate the town as a totality to the horizon of the surrounding hills, on which the natural dome of the sky seems to rest. In this sense Brunelleschi's dome transforms the natural landscape into an architecturally determined space (fig. 5).

This landscape, with its natural plasticity and scale, was incorporated architecturally with the villas situated in it. From the fifteenth-century Villa Medici in Fiesole this landscape and city panorama are represented as one undivided 'cosmic' space. The plan of the house, the façade and the garden terraces constitute a coherent dimensional system. In this system spatial elements such as the loggia, the portico and the stoa (pergola) were incorporated. In this way the panorama was connected with the villa in a controlled manner. The Villa Medici at Fiesole can be regarded as a prototype of the Italian Renaissance villa and is therefore considered in rather greater detail in this study than are other villas. In later villas, such as the Villa Gamberaia, and the Boboli Gardens, the view of the landscape was separated from the view of the city and both were given independent architectural treatment.

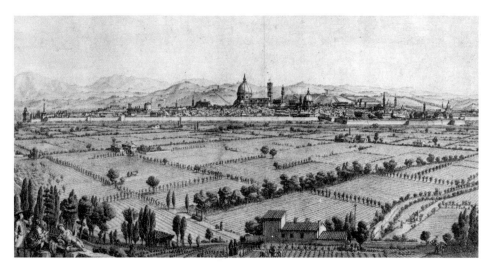

In the Boboli Gardens another refinement occurs. Various views of features of the city, such as the dome, the tower of the Palazzo della Signoria and the tower of the S. Spirito, could be seen from the garden. The villa had developed from a 'balcony' bordering free space into a central point in that space from which the various views could be distinguished and integrated.

Within the territory of sixteenth-century villas, views have been made autonomous in axes of vision which continue into the *bosco* (the Villa Castello, the Boboli Gardens, the Villa Gamberaia and the Villa Pratolino). In the Villa Cetinale (1680) at Siena the landscape outside the villa too is ultimately ordered by the linear avenue.

LITERATURE

G.C. Argan, *The Renaissance city.* New York 1969.

G. Fanelli, *Firenze, Architettura e Citta.* Florence 1973.

G. Fanelli, *Brunelleschi.* Florence 1977.

P.E. Foster, *A Study of Lorenzo de' Medici's Villa at Poggio a Caiano.* New York & London 1978.

M.L. Gothein, *A History of Garden Art.* New York 1979.

M. de Montaigne [trans. D.M. Frame], *Montaigne's Travel Journal.* San Francisco 1983.

Pliny the Younger [trans. W. Melmoth], *Letters.* Cambridge & London 1961.

H. Saalman, *Filippo Brunelleschi, the cupola of S.M. del Fiore.* N.p. 1980.

H. Tanzer, *The Villas of Pliny the Younger.* New York 1924.

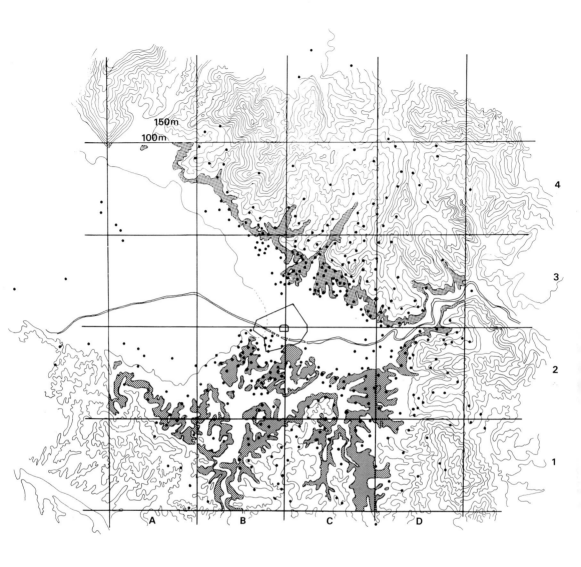

150m
100m

4

3

2

1

A   B   C   D

Boboli Gardens

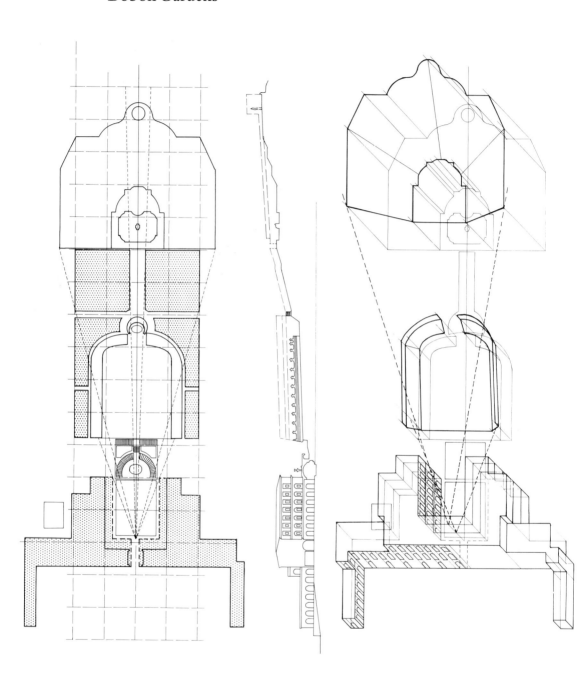

Tuscany   *Boboli Gardens*   2

Between 1450 and 1465 Lucca Pitti had a number of houses along the Via Romana in Florence demolished in order to build a palazzo with a piazza in front of it. It was designed by Brunelleschi. In 1550 Grand Duke Cosimo I de Medici's wife, Eleonora di Toledo, bought the palazzo. Behind it, on the slopes of the hill of Boboli, a garden was laid out after a design by Niccolò Tribolo, who, at the same time, was working on the Villa Castello. After Tribolo's death in 1550 Bartolomeo Ammannati began extending the palazzo and, in 1558, building the *cortile* and its grotto. In 1565 the Palazzo Pitti was connected to the ancient Palazzo della Signoria in the centre of the city by means of a covered, raised, walkway, which went over the Ponte Vecchio, along the Arno and through the Uffizi. The walkway was designed by Vasari on the occasion of the wedding of Francesco de Medici, Cosimo I's son.

The garden was adorned with statues during the celebrations. The *cortile* served as an open-air theatre. The larger stone amphitheatre, linking the garden to the *cortile*, is ascribed to Bernardo Buontalenti, who worked on the garden from 1583 till 1588. He also designed the *Grotto Grande* to the north-east of the palazzo. From 1620 to 1640 Giulio and Alfonso Parigi made further extensions to the palazzo. It was then that the *bosco* on the top of the hill at the end of the garden-axis was felled. A second, even larger amphitheatre was created consisting of grassed terraces (this theatre is not shown on the Utens lunette of 1599). It was used for important festivities. The niche with the Medici coat of arms at the termination of the garden axis was replaced by a statue of Abundance by Giambologna.

Alfonso Parigi also extended the garden westwards (fig. 5). Up until then the garden had been bounded to the west by the city wall of 1544. Parigi laid out the Viottolone, the long avenue which descends to the Porta

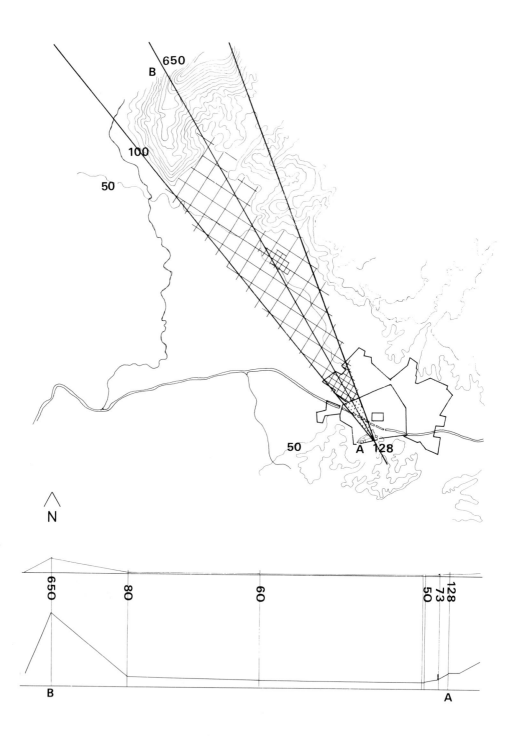

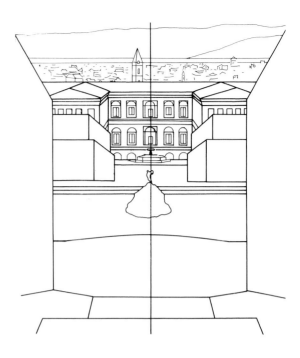

Romana (fig.6). Originally the avenue was overgrown like a tunnel, as many of the paths still are. It was later planted with cypresses. There were labyrinths along both sides. The *isolotto* (island), which was very similar to the one at the Villa Hadriana, was constructed at the lower end of the Viottolone. It consists of an oval pool with an island at its centre connected by two bridges to the Viottolone. On the island was the Oceanus fountain by Giambologna. Jets of water and lemon trees bordered the narrow mosaic paths around the fountain.

In the second half of the seventeenth century the Giardino del Cavaliere was laid out by the city wall which formed the southern boundary of the garden. This was a small *giardino segreto* near a casino of Cosimo III (1642–1713). In 1775 Zanobi del Rosso built the *Kaffeehaus* in the north-east part of the garden. The two non-aligned wings of the Palace, called the rondo, were built between 1746 and 1819. In 1860 the palazzo became the property of the Crown. In 1919 Victor Emmanuel III presented it to the Italian State.

The colossal dimensions of the Palazzo Pitti, made possible by the rock foundations, were kept under control by Brunelleschi by means of the square modular structure of the façade. This dimensional system was followed during the later extensions of the palazzo.

The building is symmetrical about the axis, which rises up the hill from the north-west to the south-east. On the axis are situated from below to above: the piazza on the Via Romana, the palazzo, the *cortile*, the Artichoke-fountain, the first (stone) theatre, the Neptune fountain and the second (green) amphitheatre. The piazza was used to introduce a sense of distance

39

from the Via Romana, and Brunelleschi's façade was placed against the background of the wooded hill. The *cortile*, which is cut out of the rock, is entered through the archway at the centre of the ground floor of the palazzo. The rock base remains visible to the garden side because of the grottoes of Moses, Hercules and Antaeus which have been cut into it. From here steps lead up to the garden. The garden on the hillside can be surveyed from the (former) loggia on the central axis on the *piano nobile*. The *cortile* and the first and second theatres are not only placed above each other, they also become successively larger, making them appear to be of the same size and giving the impression of a vertical plane facing the loggia (fig. 1). The first amphitheatre, with its elongated curved shape, seems visually to be a continuation of the palazzo's *piano nobile*. Its height is such that the rear façade of the palazzo functions as stage scenery and determines the view in the direction of the town. It is only along a diagonal line of vision that the sacred and political poles of the city of Florence become visible: Brunelleschi's dome and the campanile of the Palazzo della Signoria. From the large upper amphitheatre the palazzo is reduced to a neutral screen concealing the ancient city: only the campanile of S. Spirito protrudes above the palazzo roof (fig. 4). The Arno valley with its hills, however, becomes visible above this screen (fig. 3).

The sequence of spaces provided by the theatres, and which seems to cumulate at the top of the hill, is given a surprising sequel. The view back over the palazzo and the city shows the garden united to the natural arena of the Arno valley. This 'periscope' effect is a way of situating the urban palazzo as a villa in the landscape. The staging of Brunelleschi's dome from the first theatre and the landscape from the second had the additional effect of separating the experience of the landscape from that of the city. In contrast to the sequence of levels, spaces and dimensions on the axis of the palazzo, the Viottolone forms a continuous link with the Porta Romana and the Villa Poggio Imperiale outside.

BOBOLI GARDENS

Via Romana
Florence

Open: 9.00–sunset

LITERATURE

C. Bravero *et al.*, *Florence, guide to the City.* Turin 1979.
C. Caneva, *Boboli Gardens.* Florence 1982.
G. Fanelli, *Firenze, Architettura e Citta.* Florence 1973.
M. L. Gothein, *A History of Garden Art.* New York 1979.
G. Jellicoe & S. Jellicoe, *The Oxford Companion to Gardens.* Oxford & New York 1986.

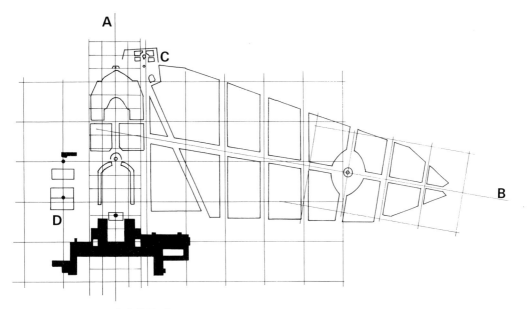

Tuscany   *Boboli Gardens*   5

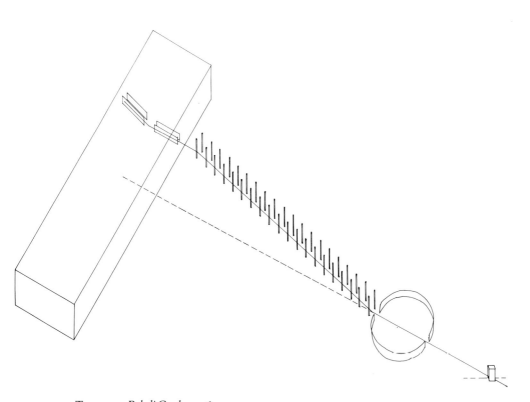

Tuscany   *Boboli Gardens*   6

Villa Bombici / I Collazzi

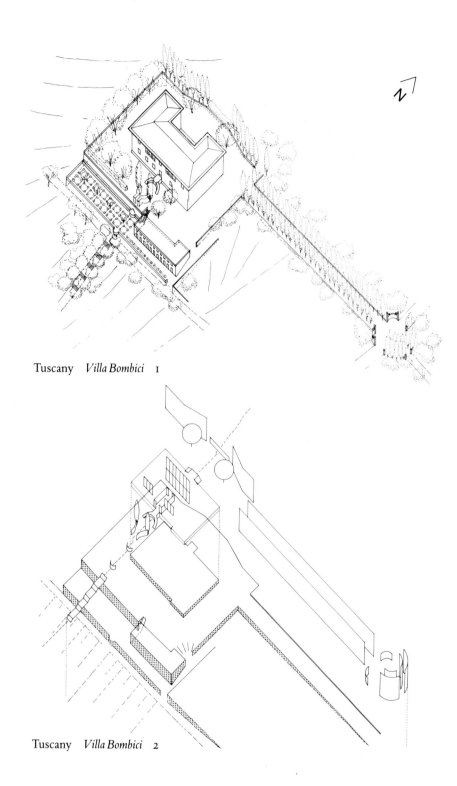

Tuscany   *Villa Bombici*   1

Tuscany   *Villa Bombici*   2

Tuscany   *Villa Bombici*   3

For a long time the design of this villa was ascribed to Michelangelo, who was a friend of the builder Agostino Dino. Nowadays it is supposed that Santi di Tito was the architect of this complex. In 1933 the villa was acquired by the Marchi family, who completed the unfinished east wing of the house to the original design. The villa is situated on the rectangular summit plateau on the ridge of a hill. From the imposing country house on this plateau two avenues lead into the landscape (fig. 1). One of them, monumentally lined with cypresses, forms the entrance to the villa. It connects an oval-shaped square, marking the intersection with the road, to a terrace on the north side of the house. This is given the character of a forecourt by the two projecting wings of the building. The other avenue on the south side of the villa is treated as a set of steps leading into the landscape.

The specific location on the top of the hill, which falls away on three sides, provoked a different treatment of each side (fig. 2). The east side offers hardly any view and is, with the exception of the link with the entrance road, subordinated spatially as well as formally. The other sides offer, each in their own particular way, a view of the surroundings. On the north side there are two screens of cypresses and two monumental deciduous trees at the point where the level between the plateau and the hillside changes. The landscape here forms a tableau vivant, stretched between the screens. It is on this side, on the forecourt, that the house is opened towards the landscape by means of an elegantly composed double loggia. On the west side there is a single row of deciduous trees and a hedge along the retaining wall. These, together with the façade, form a sort of canopied space, a kind of viewing pavilion in the landscape. On the south side the plateau is related in a very complex manner to the landscape. The terraces on the hillside are continued in the direction of the axis, which is fixed in the plan by a number of elements, such as a grotto, curved hedges, two cypresses and a semi-circular set of steps. Spatially contrasting areas are mirrored on either side of this axis. On the slope of the eastern side of the plateau, for example, a service building screens off the view of the panorama and redirects it in a southwesterly direction over the level parterre on the opposite side. In this way the panorama is separated from the axis so that its dramatic setting continually permeates the plan in an original and surprising manner. The Villa Bombici, though representing perhaps only a fragment of what was originally planned, thereby derives its significance as an architectural object in which the formal and pictorial conditions are defined in a way which is both distinct and ambiguous.

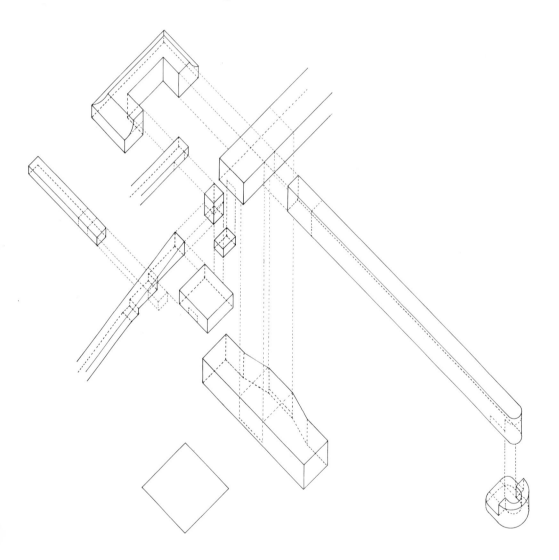

LITERATURE

Collazzi
South of Florence, along the old road to
    Volterra

Visitors by appointment only

H. Acton, *The Villas of Tuscany.* London
    1984.
G. Masson, *Italian Gardens.* London 1987.
J. C. Shepherd & G. A. Jellicoe, *Italian
    Gardens of the Renaissance.* London
    1986.

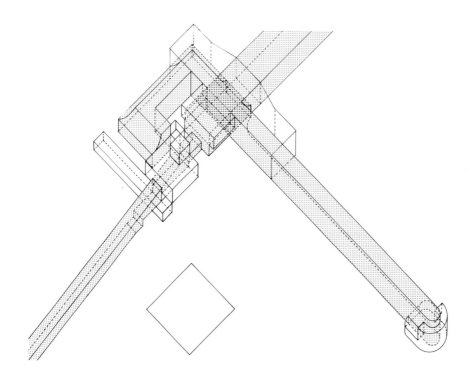

Villa Castello

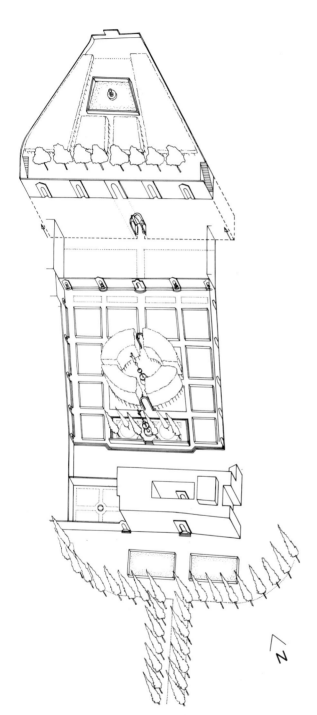

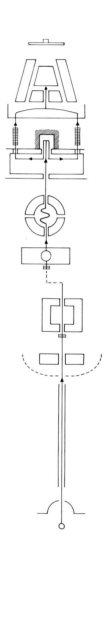

Tuscany *Villa Castello* 3

Villa Castello is one of the oldest Medici villas. From 1477 it had belonged
to Lorenzo di Pierfrancesco. In 1537 Grand Duke Cosimo I de Medici, who
had grown up in this villa, gave Niccolò Tribolo the task of extending and
decorating it. After Tribolo's death in 1550 the garden was completed by
Bartolomeo Ammannati and Bernardo Buontalenti. The garden, which
was already decorated with works of art before Tribolo's extensions, was
provided with a great number of new sculptures and artificial additions
inspired by nature. Apart from mythical and geographical references, these
garden elements were furnished with an iconographic programme (written
by Benedetto Varchi) in which, for the first time, the glorification of the
villa owner was a central motif.

   Villa Castello may be regarded as the first Mannerist villa in the Florence
area. In the design for this villa a series of autonomous spaces were placed
behind each other axially and linked by means of the route (fig. 2). The
lunette by Utens represents an idealized image of the villa; the house is
shown as standing at the centre of the main axis of the gardens, whereas, in
reality, it has been shifted sideways (fig. 1). In the painting the following
elements are placed in sequence: the access avenue, the front square with the
swan ponds, the house, the atrium, the *prato*, the tableau with the Hercules
and Antaeus fountain, the round labyrinthine space with, at its centre, the
fountain with the statue of Venus (representing Florence) wringing her
hair, the enclosed lime garden and the grotto with its figures of Orpheus
and exotic animals, and, finally, on the upper level, the viewing terrace, and,
in the centre of the *bosco*, the basin with the large bronze half-figure known
as January (and also as Appennino or Neptune). As the edge of the pool
follows the slope of the hill the water seems to lean backwards. On the
upper terrace one looks over the roof of the house and the village of

Castello, and here the panorama of the Arno valley is revealed, thus, in retrospect, adding the river valley to the axially organized series of spaces as its biggest and final element. Panorama is also integrated into the interior of the house, whose exterior is so enclosed. There, however, the view is evoked by means of painting; in one of the rooms all the walls are painted and present a series of 'windows' between fictitious columns, looking out on to an arcadian landscape.

In the sixteenth century Villa Castello had one of the most well-known gardens in Europe; Vasi, as well as the Frenchman Montaigne, devoted extensive descriptions to it. However, when a part of the garden was remodelled in the landscape style between 1739 and 1760, a number of essential elements were removed from the part which was arranged axially: the rear wall of the parterre was demolished, the labyrinth chopped down, and the statue of Venus removed to the nearby Villa Petraia (fig. 4). This largely destroyed the original spatial design of the villa. The spatial and botanical differentiation has almost entirely disappeared and, at present, the garden lacks almost any vertical accent.

VILLA CASTELLO

Castello

Open: 9.00-18.30
Closed Mondays
House not open to the public
Free access to garden

LITERATURE

D. Mignani, *Le ville medicee di Giusto Utens.* Florence 1982.

Tuscany   *Villa Castello*   4

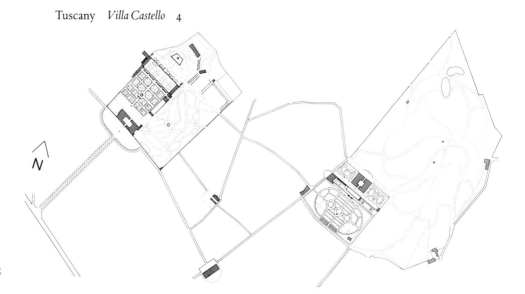

Villa Cetinale / Chigi

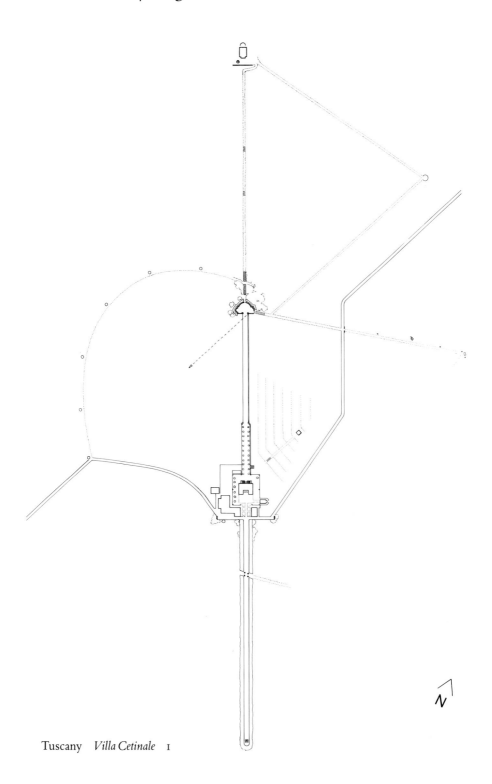

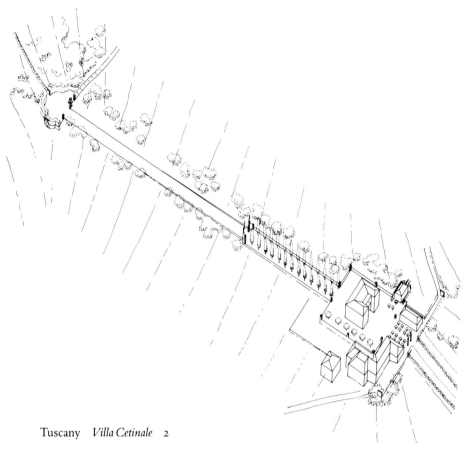

Tuscany *Villa Cetinale* 2

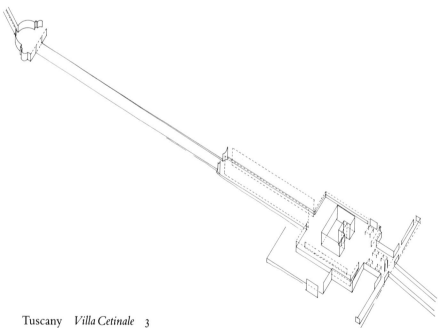

Tuscany *Villa Cetinale* 3

Tuscany *Villa Cetinale* 4

Villa Cetinale was built in about 1680 according to the design of Carlo Fontana as summer residence and agricultural headquarters for Cardinal Flavio Chigi, a nephew of Pope Alexander VII. The villa is sporadically mentioned in villa literature. It was built during a period in which all attention was concentrated on the axial plans being developed in France. This might be the reason why the independent significance of this design has been little considered in the history of the development of villa architecture. Fontana was, however, one of the most prominent villa architects of the mid seventeenth century. In the way in which apparently simple means are used to integrate the location into the plan, this villa represents one of his finest accomplishments.

The plan of the Villa Cetinale shows a number of similarities to those of the villas Bombici, Gori, Poggio Torcelli and La Pietra and, in a way, these villas form a separate typological category within Tuscan villa architecture. Remarkable in these plans is the introduction of linear elements (axes), with which a number of independent components not belonging to the villa scheme are nonetheless integrated into the geometrical plan. In contrast to Palladio's Veneto villas, in which the axis is used to make the building central in the landscape, the axis here is used to bring about a mutual relationship between the dispersed elements of the complex. In addition – and this is clearly an important step in the development of garden architecture into landscape architecture – the actual positioning of the disparate and autonomous components can be used actively and on different levels to involve the local topography in the plan.

At the Villa Cetinale the living quarters are intersected centrally by the main axis of the complex, which continues in two directions in the landscape (fig. 1). On the front side it is terminated by a statue of Hercules. On the other side the axis is formed by a closely-mown strip of grass, which for the first hundred metres from the house is edged by cypresses before being interrupted by an archway (fig. 2, 3). In this way the view from the house is visually enclosed. Finally, closely following the contour lines of the valley the axis leads to a nymphaeum. The nymphaeum is positioned at the point where the horizontally laid out lawn meets the slope of the hill and where the contour line of the base of the hill changes direction. Here, for the first time, the view over the landscape is activated. Two statues invite us to enjoy the panorama. One is looking at the other, which in turn looks away diagonally across the axis in the direction of the entrance road in the valley. With this the axiality of the system is put into perspective and brought into the context of the landscape's topography.

From this nymphaeum the axis continues as an almost inaccessible rock path, along which, with great difficulty, one can climb the steep mountain slope. Exhausted but purified, one finally reaches a plateau in front of a chapel at the summit (fig. 6); from here the entire villa can be seen. Here, too, the statue of Hercules reappears in the far distance, effecting the annexation of the intervening landscape. In the chapel itself one more staircase leads still further up. A Maltese cross forms part of the façade, and above this, in a round window (*oculus*), the panorama, with the villa as its centre, is once again repeated and framed in the circle of the cosmos (fig. 7). What is probably being indicated here is that knowledge of the ultimate relationship between the divine, as represented by the cosmos (horizon), and the created world can only be attained by way of penance (the path upwards) and purification (the chapel).

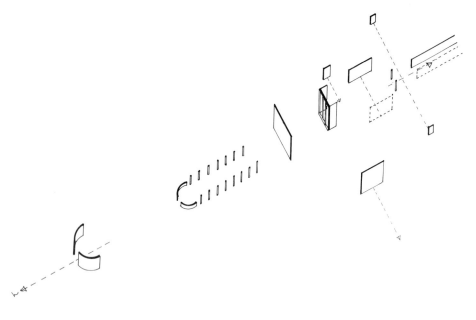

Tuscany *Villa Cetinale* 6   Tuscany *Villa Cetinale* 7

Relatively independent of the main structure of the villa and at the same time subordinate to it are two thematic gardens, situated on either side of the central axis and connected to the nymphaeum by a system of paths. On the lower western side a path with a number of chapels along it, in which the Stations of the Cross are represented, leads down the slope. On the higher eastern side a staircase in the slope at the beginning of the lawn provides an entrance to a terrace-like area that, at its highest point, forms the introduction to an enclosed sculpture garden situated in the wood and occupied by monsters and monks carved by the sculptor Bartolomeo Mazzuoli. This garden is in an advanced state of decay. The position of both thematic gardens cannot be explained in terms of the central axis model. They are related to the plan by means of their connection to the nymphaeum, which itself is situated where the base of the hill changes direction with respect to the main axis of the villa. In this way a number of elements at the Villa Cetinale are fixed for the purposes of the picturesque. The axis links these elements, providing the ingredients for a new development, the way of stage-managing the landscape which was later to become characteristic of English landscape architecture.

VILLA CETINALE/CHIGI

Cetinale

Visitors by appointment only
Owner: Lord Lambton

LITERATURE

H. Acton, *The Villas of Tuscany.* London 1984.
J.C. Shepherd & G.A. Jellicoe, *Italian Gardens of the Renaissance.* London 1986.

Villa Gamberaia

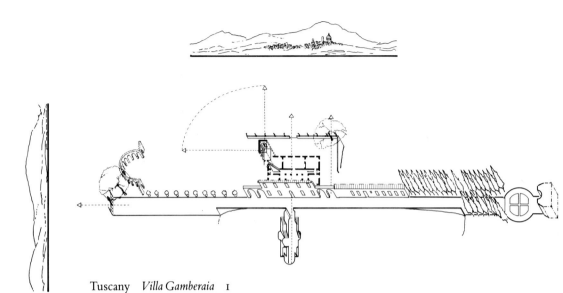

Tuscany *Villa Gamberaia* 1

Tuscany *Villa Gamberaia* 2

Tuscany *Villa Gamberaia* 3

Written sources do not reveal who designed this villa. An engraving of
1610 ascribes the creation to a certain Zanobi Lapi, whose heirs claimed
the property on his death in 1627. The villa came into the hands of the
Capponi in 1717; they enlarged the house, decorated the garden with fountains and statues, and laid out the bowling green with, at right angles to the
house, the grotto and the entrance to the orchard. In all probability the villa
was given its present shape during this period. Towards the end of the nineteenth century Princess Giovanna Ghyka came into possession of the villa
after a long period during which it had been neglected. She added the
reflecting pools in the parterre. The house, which was destroyed during the
Second World War, has been reconstructed in its original state by the present
owners, the Marchi family.

The location of the Villa Gamberaia is similar to that of the Villa Medici
at Fiesole, situated at a similar distance from Florence. Both villas are almost
invisible from their access road. The Villa Medici is separated from the
road by a high wall, and the Villa Gamberaia remains concealed from
the entrance road because of a difference in level; in the case of the latter the
road even runs beneath a part of the garden. There is also a similarity in the
modest setting of the two villas. The Villa Gamberaia, which occupies a
prominent position on top of a ridge of hills, is nevertheless tucked away
among the trees. In both villas the relationship with the landscape is revealed from within the villa in the way in which the panorama is unfolded
from the terraces.

The plan of the Villa Gamberaia was designed according to the *stanze*
concept. This means that it was built up from a number of autonomous and
separately designed parts, defined within the total composition (fig. 4, 5).
The various parts of the garden are devoted to one single motif, the strong-

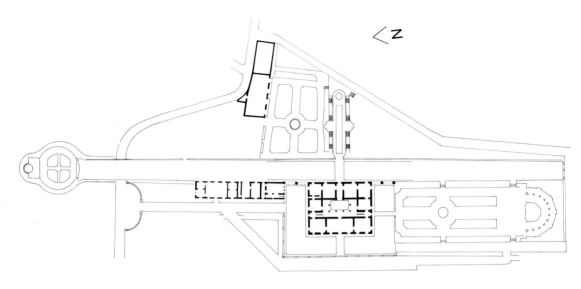

Tuscany   *Villa Gamberaia*   4

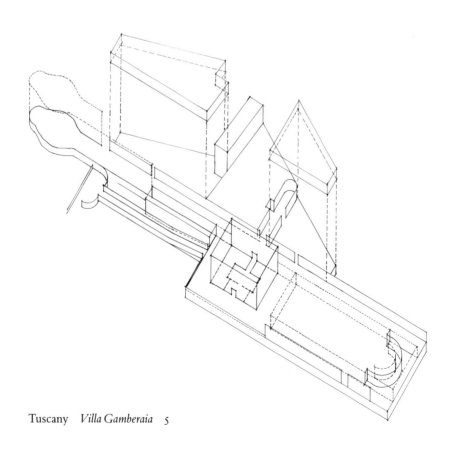

Tuscany   *Villa Gamberaia*   5

smelling lemon trees, the Amora *bosco*, and the perfectly cut topiary garden with its semicircular 'theatre' for example. The separate elements are unified by the long, central lawn – the bowling green – which, on one side, connects the villa to the earth by means of the grotto cut into the hill and, on the other, the statue of Diana on the brink of the ravine which directs the view to infinity.

There are several views from the villa. On the terrace at the top of the hedge-screened entrance avenue the villa opens itself, almost as if by surprise, to the panorama of Florence. The city can also be seen through the house itself from the grotto garden, which lies at right angles to the bowling green on the main axis of the building. The view of the panorama is repeated like a projected image in the archways on each side of the house which separate the terrace in front of and the topiary garden at the rear of the house from the bowling green, and is, thus, inserted into the series of themes which are connected by the long open central space. The house is an element of this series (fig. 1, 2).

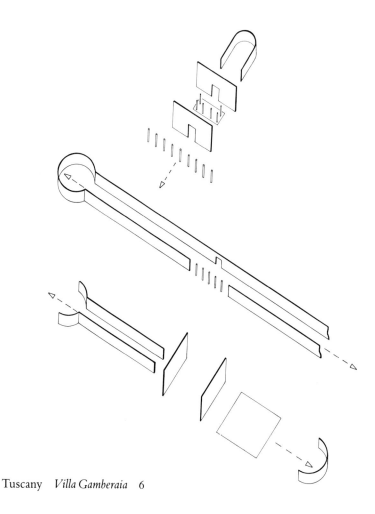

Tuscany *Villa Gamberaia* 6

From the side of the approach avenue the entrance to the house is not visible; nor is there direct access from the topiary garden. The entrance is directed to the bowling green. In this arrangement the patio of the house forms the counterpart of the enclosed space of the grotto garden. Whereas at the Villa Medici at Fiesole the spatial system of the villa is finally distilled in the house itself, at this villa it is the long rectangular open space between the hillside and the statue of Diana which constitutes the focus of the stage-management. According to this interpretation the patio may be conceived as an internal loggia which connects the two parts of the house on the axis from the grotto garden to the panorama (fig. 6).

Within the matrix of the composition the references to nature and landscape are determined in different ways. The topiary garden is used as an extract from nature. The secrets and patterns of nature are revealed in this geometrical garden and controlled by imitation. The trees and hedges are transformed into spheres, cones and statues. The reflecting pool mirrors nature and presents its image to man. The edge of this garden is enclosed by a high semicircular hedge in which archways have been cut, the central one revealing 'real' nature outside the domain of the villa. The loggia of the house is not situated at the centre of the façade but at a corner on the first floor. It is detached from the geometrical arrangement of the villa, and from here the view over the garden to the landscape and the town is organized into one single panorama (fig. 1).

VILLA GAMBERAIA

Via del Rossellino 72
Settignano

Open weekdays: summer 8.00-12.00,
   14.00-18.00;
winter 8.00-12.00, 13.00-17.00
Fee

LITERATURE

H. Acton, *Gamberaia*. Florence 1971.
H. Acton, *The Villas of Tuscany*. London 1984.
G. Masson, *Italian Gardens*. London 1987.
J.C. Shepherd & G.A. Jellicoe, *Italian Gardens of the Renaissance*. London 1986.

Villa Gori / Palazzina

The identity of the architect appointed by the Gori family at the beginning
of the seventeenth century to build this villa on a hill to the north of Siena
is unknown. The house and the small chapel next to it are placed directly
on the roadside. The entrance is not monumental and the entire design is
dominated by the clearly private atmosphere of a 'modest house and garden',
designed in a simple and clear composition.

    The north elevation on the street side is closed, whereas the south eleva-
tion is opened out towards the garden by the use of a loggia two floors high.
From the terrace two leafy corridors of holly oaks lead to two enclosed
garden rooms. The avenue following the ridge of the hill leads to a small
green theatre. Inside its oval shape is a single row of seats for spectators and
a stage with green wings, which, like the backdrop, were originally of
cypresses but which have now been replaced by laurel shrubs. A double
outer ring of holly oaks enabled the players to move unseen through the
theatre. Immediately behind the theatre rises an emphatically freestanding
cypress. In its solitariness, yet part of the geometrical plan, it provides a
symbol of free nature, in contrast to the clipped hedges of the theatre.

    Leading from the terrace near the house there is a second avenue of trees,
facing the loggia; at first this descends the gently southern slope before
rising slightly to the grove, which originally functioned as a small bird
snare or *ragnaia*. Blinded thrushes were tethered in its centre to lure other
birds, while the dense undergrowth provided cover for hunters.

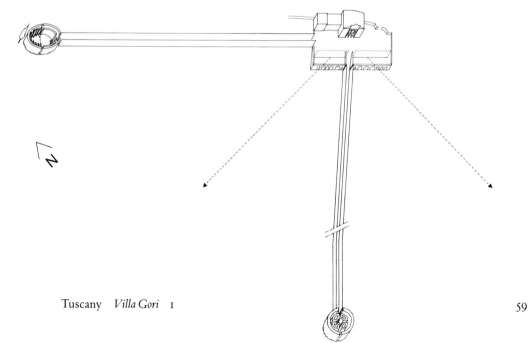

Tuscany *Villa Gori* 2

The dense overgrowth of both tunnels, and the theatre and hunting function, suggests a transformation of the traditional *bosco*. Though both tunnels penetrate relatively far into the landscape, a relationship between them and their surroundings is hardly created. The tunnels and the garden rooms are almost entirely enclosed spatially and are only connected to the main terrace, which, itself, is also enclosed on all sides.

Opposite the house, however, one can walk through a screen of cypress trees trimmed into arches. There, on either side of the axis and slightly raised with regard to the terrace, are two balconies. The all-pervading privacy of the orthogonally organized part of the design is shattered on these balconies; from one of them there is a diagonal view of the city of Siena on the opposite side of the valley, and from the other the surrounding green hills can be surveyed. The avenue of trees between both balconies functions as a screen, visually separating both of the elements from each other and guiding the viewer in one of the two directions (fig. 1). Once again the villa forms the setting from which the dialectic between culture and nature is revealed.

VILLA GORI/PALAZZINA

Strada del Paradiso
Siena

For admission apply to:
Signor G. Gianneschi
Strada di Ventena 28, Siena

LITERATURE

J. Chatfield, *A Tour of Italian Gardens*. New York 1988.
J. C. Shepherd & G. A. Jellicoe, *Italian Gardens of the Renaissance*. London 1986.

Villa Medici Fiesole

According to Vasari the Villa Medici at Fiesole was built between 1458 and 1462. It was designed by the architect Michelozzo Michelozzi for Giovanni, son of Cosimo de Medici 'the Elder' (1389-1464). A fresco in the S. Maria Novella in Florence by Domenico Ghirlandaio depicts the villa in what was possibly its original state. There the eastern loggia of the villa was shown as having four arches, and terraces also on the east side were entirely bounded by retaining walls. Agnolo Poliziano (1454-94) wrote a poem, *Rusticus*, about the villa and, in a letter to Marsilio Ficino, praised its location, the local climate and its view. In 1671 the Medici family sold the villa.

On the evidence of the few available sources, including some drawings by Zocchi of 1744 and by Buonaiuti of 1826, Bargellini and others stated that between these dates the villa had undergone some changes. The villa was at the time owned by Margaret, Lady Orford, (from 1772) and by Giulio Mozzi (from 1781). The part of the house to the north of the corridor would have been built during this period. This assumption is supported by the fact that the southernmost loggia-arch in the east façade was bricked up in order to restore the balance of the façade (fig. 1). Geymüller and Patzak also assumed that this arch had been bricked up. In another drawing by Zocchi of 1744, cited by Bargellini and her followers, the western loggia still has three arches, which makes it probable that the present fourth (northern) loggia-arch was added later. It is possible that during the same period stables and a coach house were built at the eastern entrance of the garden and connected to the Via Fiesolana by the construction of a *viale* (drive). The edges of the eastern terrace must have been reconstructed at the same time. Around 1850 William Blundell Spence became the owner of the villa and in 1860 he enlarged the *viale*. At the beginning of the twentieth century Lady Sybil Cutting-Scott-Lubbock bought the villa. She had the library on the *piano nobile* refurbished. In 1959 the villa was bought by Aldo Mazzini, whose widow is still in occupation.

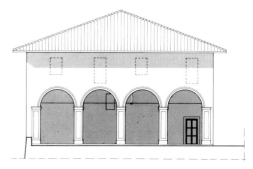

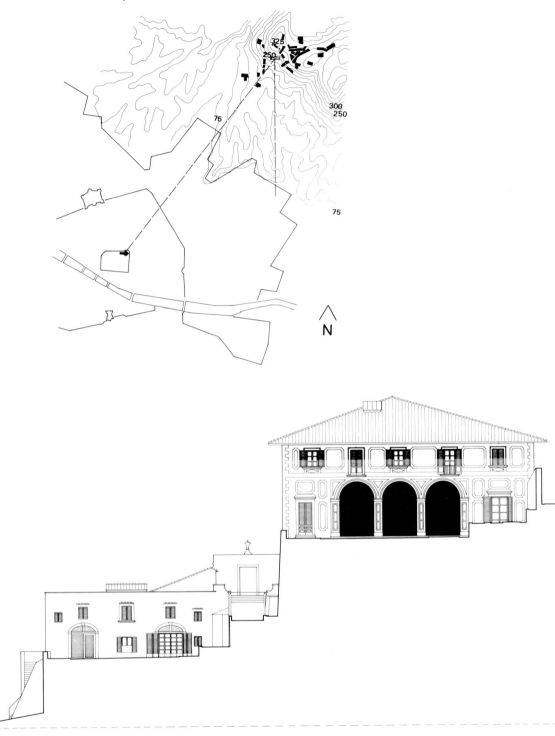

N

Tuscany   *Villa Medici Fiesole*   4

LOCATION   The villa is situated at a height of about 250 m. above the Arno valley, in which, about 5 km. further on, the old centre of Florence is situated. On the site of the villa the undulating foreground changes into a steeper, south-facing hilltop (325 m.), against which background the southern façade stands out forcefully on its foundation of terraces. A southern exposure of the garden is recommended by the theorist Pietro de Crescenzi. The slope protects the villa against the cold north-east winds in winter. In summer the sea wind can bring coolness from the west. The building is aligned to the points of the compass at an angle to the natural slope. This slope, therefore, closes the field of view to the east, whereas the building is oriented towards the Mugnone side-valley and, across that, towards the distant line of the Arno valley. In the transverse direction the scheme is laid out like a balcony overlooking the source of the Arno valley to the south, with the town of Florence as its western limit (fig. 2). The view is in accordance with what Alberti later recommended. Cosimo, however, was not particularly happy with it. He, more than his son, believed that the view was to be really part and parcel of his country property.

PLAN   The villa consists principally of three levels. The upper level is formed by the extensive north terrace, which is now reached along the *viale*. This level is joined to the *piano nobile* and the two loggias of the house. The lowest level consists of the south terrace, which today is bounded by coach houses on the east and west sides. The total difference in height between the north and south terraces varies from 11 to 12 m. and is supported by means of a massive retaining wall with a pergola running along it (fig. 3).

Inside the garden it is impossible to move from one terrace to another. Apart from a path outside that now meanders down along the *viale*, the two

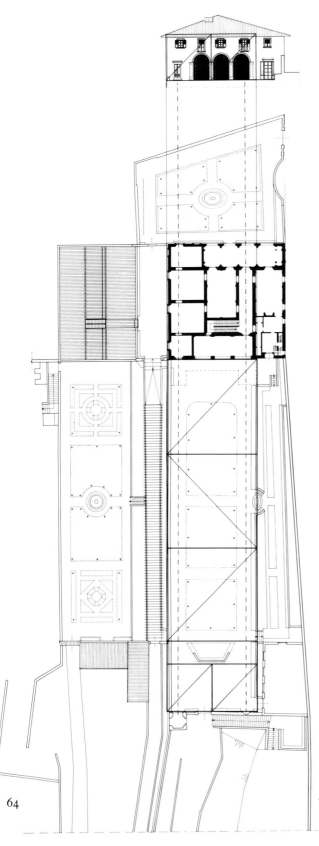

levels are only connected to each other inside the house. A long staircase consisting of a single flight drops one storey from the corridor to the level at which the garden rooms on the south façade are situated. The narrow terrace in front of this, the west terrace, and the rest of the basement, together form an intermediate level situated roughly halfway between the highest and lowest terraces. On this level there are large French windows in the south façade. In the west façade of the basement there are only small windows. It is striking that the ceremonial entrance to the villa in the west façade is not directly connected to the *piano nobile*. The north-east part of the basement is carved out of the rock and consists of storage space linked to the kitchen by means of a service staircase.

On the *piano nobile* is what is now the most commonly used entrance to the house, underneath the east loggia. A long off-centre corridor leads from there directly to the west loggia. The central position in the floor plan is occupied by the rectangular salon. North of the corridor are the dining room and the kitchen. The latter is connected by a service staircase to an intermediate floor above it and, subsequently, to the second floor of the villa. The façades of the *piano nobile* are determined primarily by the loggias. The north façade is closed, apart from a few high windows and a small service entrance. The second floor of the house consists mainly of bedrooms. Above the dining room and the kitchen, adjacent to the intermediary floor beneath, are separate living quarters for the servants. On this floor all the façades are defined by fairly small, identical windows. Several windows have been bricked up from the inside.

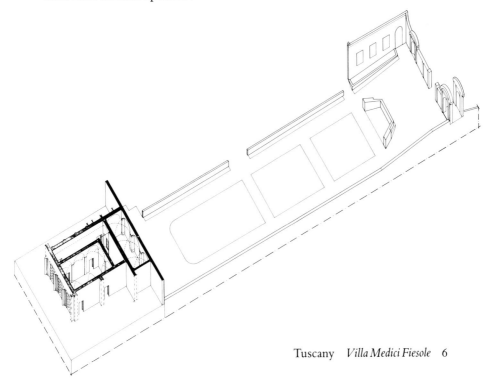

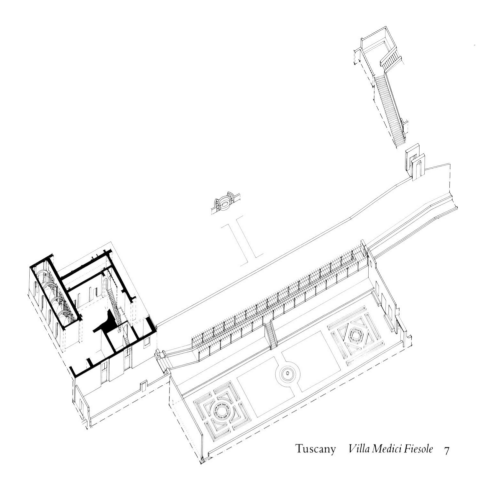

Tuscany   *Villa Medici Fiesole*   7

Generally speaking, the present state of the façade is remarkable for its lack of any system. In the existing west façade only the ceremonial entrance is symmetrical.

GEOMETRY   In the spring of 1986 the dimensions of the entire villa were surveyed and studied by G. Smienk and C.M. Steenbergen in order to permit a more detailed analysis of how the new way of thinking about nature, geometry and space was given form in the architectural plan. This survey enabled a hypothesis to be suggested concerning the precise manner in which the connection between house and landscape was realized. This resulted in a hypothetical geometrical model in which the villa can be explained as an architectural system. As a result of this the conclusions based on both historical research and the geometrical model can be cross-checked for consistency.

In the villa plan a certain dimension, which we shall call A, appears to occur regularly. A turns out to be approximately 4.9 m. The present plan of the whole *piano nobile* is 5A by 5$\frac{1}{3}$A. Excluding the area with the dining hall north of the corridor, which was added at a later date, the floor plan

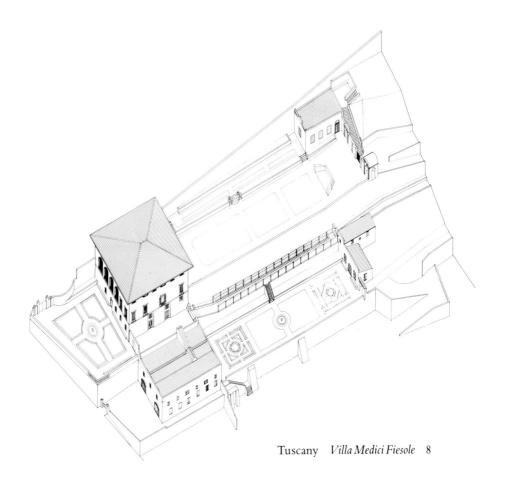

measures 5 A by 4 A. This rectangle can be interpreted as being composed of two squares, each 4 A by 4 A, with an overlap of 3 A. The overlap takes up precisely the central part of the house, while the loggias with a depth of A are not included. Likewise, if a certain strip on the north side of the villa is omitted the plan of the north and south terraces together measures 9 A by 14 A, from the back wall of the east loggia to the back of the half-round wall and hedge on the top terrace. This rectangle, too, can be read as consisting of two squares, each of 9 A by 9 A, now with an overlap of 4 A. The north-south axis, which formally connects the two terraces with each other, is situated centrally and symmetrically within this overlap.

A, which functions in the house as a margin which accommodates the depth of the loggias, therefore appears to have a similar role in the garden. The geometrical systems of the house and of the garden overlap each other by this dimension A (the depth of the east loggia). Furthermore, A can be recognized as the margin of the half-round hedge at the end of the upper terrace. A is also the depth of the pergola along the retaining wall between the north and south terraces. Even the main dimensions of the east façade (wall height of 2 A and width of 4 A) seem to fit into the geometrical system if its northern part is omitted (fig. 5).

It is clear that some parts of the present villa plan do not conform to the hypothetical geometrical system of squares. This is especially the case with the strip on the north side of the villa. Bargellini and her followers had already assumed, on the basis of their historical research, that this northern part of the house had been added in the eighteenth century. This is confirmed by the geometrical interpretation of the villa. It now seems safe to suppose that at the same time the changes were made in the eighteenth century the entire garden edge was also shifted northwards. With this a zone of varying width was created which enabled the irregularities of the hillside to be accommodated. The levelling operations associated with the construction of the *viale* also led to modifications to the edge of the east terrace. Excepting the north-south axis the patterning of the upper terrace does not comply with the geometrical system and is probably also of a later date.

In short, the original ground-floor plan of the villa can be seen as a system of squares: two small ones in the house and two larger ones in the garden. Further refinement of the analysis shows that the large squares in the garden appear to be constructed from the basic square (module) found in the casino (4 A by 4 A). In the overlaps of the squares are situated central-plan elements: the salon and the north-south axis. The transitional elements are incorporated in the margin, whose width is A: the west retaining wall, the two loggias, the winter and the summer houses on the upper terrace and the pergola.

The hypothetical geometrical system can be regarded as a dimensional scheme in which the connection between the plan of the house, the garden and the landscape could be controlled mathematically. It is a means of rationalizing this connection. In the following section it will become clear that the elements defined by the geometry of the plan also play a leading role in the spatial *integrazione scenica* of the villa.

'INTEGRAZIONE SCENICA'   The parts of the villa which in the previous geometrical model were distinguished as essential elements must now be placed in their spatial context. In what manner do they form a coherent architectural system, and how is the particular location of the villa, with regard to the panorama, determined?

The house is the representative centre of the villa. In the salon, which has no windows in the outer façade, the *villeggiatura* is represented by paintings. The feeling of enclosure is not really overcome, however, by the landscape painted on the walls. There is still no connection between the natural perspective of the salon and the perspective of the framed paintings. The salon is directly connected to the loggias by a corridor. Because of the low situation of the west terrace the panorama from the west loggia has no foreground. The panorama itself is deep and lacks architectural features to lend scale to the space. On the west side this causes the meeting of the villa and the natural space to appear as a confrontation.

At the other end of the corridor is the east loggia. This is moved south-

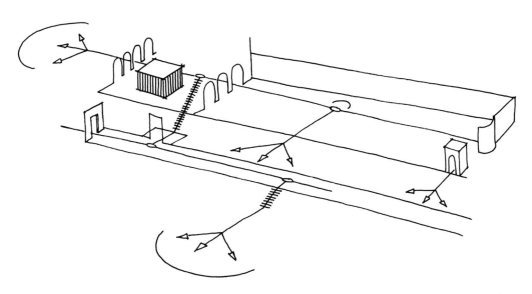

Tuscany *Villa Medici Fiesole* 9

ward, downhill from the west loggia. The east loggia looks on to the north terrace, which, sloping up away from the loggia, presents itself as an enclosed garden (fig. 6). It is the *giardino segreto*, which meets the *bosco* on the natural hillside at the *viale*. In the present layout the east-west direction of the terrace is accentuated by the symmetrical location of a niche and belvedere at the rear of the *giardino segreto*. These correspond, respectively, to the corridor and the door in the bricked-up loggia-arch of the house. On the rear wall of the belvedere is a painting which represents the reality behind it. It is possible that this device was intended to suggest the view from the garden while at the same time obstructing the actual view from the *viale* in the garden. In the middle of the north terrace the east-west direction is pierced by a transverse axis of symmetry, which begins at a natural spring (fig. 7). It is an incidental reference to the south panorama, which, from here, appears as just an indefinite space without any scale.

To return to the corridor in the house the downward-leading steps and the garden rooms form the first links in the connection with the south terrace. However, the most important spatial link is the pergola, situated high up along the massive retaining wall, between the north and the south terraces. Visually enclosed by ramps at each end, it is a shady porch facing the southern panorama. Apart from the framing effect of the columns, the view is given depth by the carpet-like foreground on the south terrace. On the terrace, vases and topiary provide the panorama with a readable scale and subdivision. Brunelleschi's dome in Florence is, after all, clearly visible from here. This gives the natural space of the panorama an architectural definition. It may be said that the spatial system of the villa consists of three levels: the salon, the *giardino segreto* and the panorama. Inside the house itself these three (scale) levels are connected by the corridor, the two loggias, the staircase and the garden room. The panorama is the new spatial type which had to be integrated into villa architecture. The elongated terrace and the lateral porch (stoa) are the classical means which were used to control this natural space. In the Villa Medici this lateral structure is only incidentally intersected by axial elements. This serves to direct the view, which is not yet fixed, by, for example, interventions in the panorama itself.

SIGNIFICANCE   The Villa Medici at Fiesole was one of the first villas in Tuscany in which the cultural ideal of country life was separated from the traditional context of farm and *castello* and evolved into an independent architectural form. In the house this is shown most clearly in the way in which Michelozzo made use of the loggia, a traditional element in Tuscan farm building, as a separate element added to the exterior of the house.

A second aspect which distinguishes the Villa Medici as an independent architectural type is the scale and the shape of the terrace structure (fig. 8). This must have involved the usual technical and financial problems which arose in dealing with the steep, poorly accessible slope. The ground is also entirely unsuitable for agriculture. This all suggests that the choice of location must have been determined primarily by social, visual and climactic factors. The terraced construction of the villa was possibly inspired by Pliny the Younger's description of his terraced villa. When visiting the villa one is struck by the fact that these two elements, the loggias and the terraces, still occupy key positions in the architectural effect of the villa's interaction with the landscape. The eighteenth-century modifications discussed earlier do not seem to be of overriding importance. They do not essentially affect the original *integrazione scenica* of the villa, but in some respects actually reinforce it. The villa remains one of the first and clearest examples of the new way of thinking about nature, geometry and space in the quattrocento (fig. 9).

VILLA MEDICI FIESOLE

Via Fiesolana
Fiesole

Visitors by appointment only
Owner: signora Anna Mazzini

LITERATURE

C. Bargellini & P. de la Ruffinière du Prey, 'Sources for a reconstruction of the Villa Medici, Fiesole', *Burlington Magazine* CXI (799) (1969).

E. Battisti, '*Natura Artificiosa* to *Natura*

Artificialis', in D. R. Coffin (ed.), *The Italian Garden*. Washington, DC, & Dumbarton Oaks 1972.

E. Borsook, *The Companion Guide to Florence*. London 1973.

R. Castell, *The villas of the ancients illustrated*. London 1728. Reprinted London & New York 1982.

G. Fanelli, *Firenze, Architettura e Citta*. Florence 1973.

B. Patzak, *Die Renaissance und Barockvilla in Italien*. Leipzig 1913.

C. Stegman & H. Geymüller, *Die Architectur der Renaissance in Toscana*, vol. 2. Munich 1885-93.

Villa Petraia

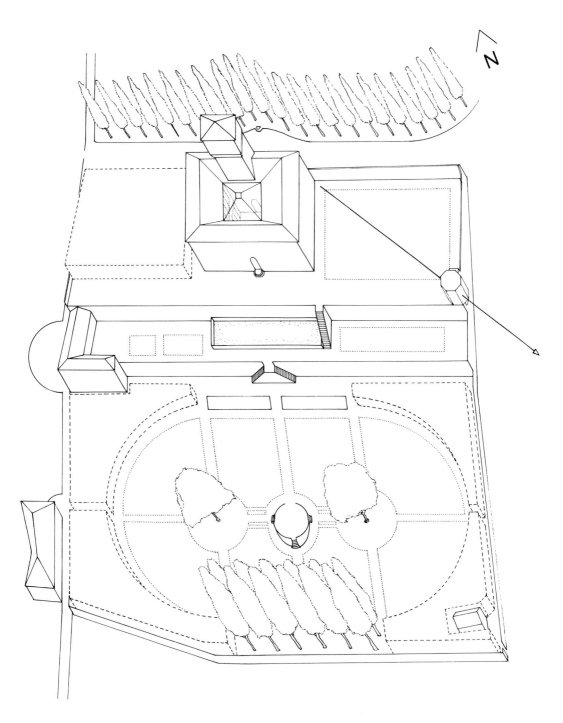

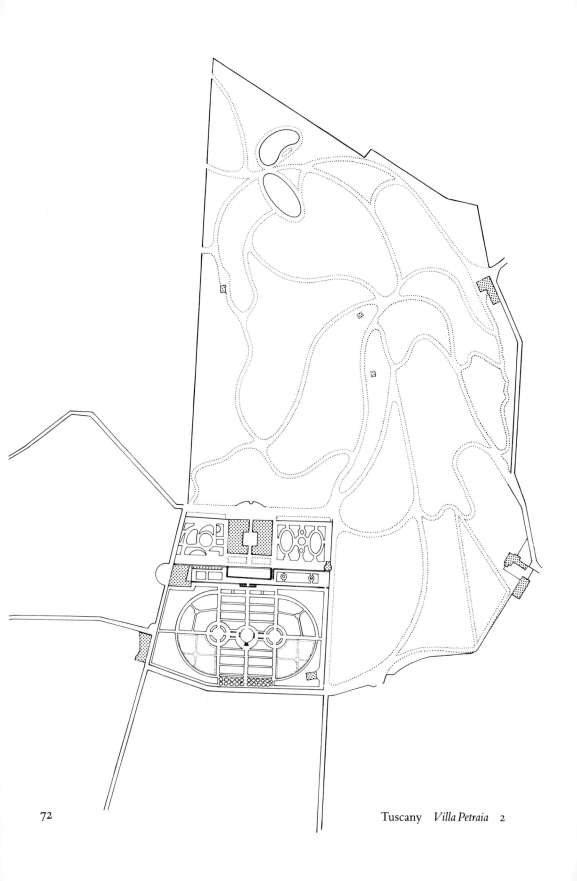

Tuscany *Villa Petraia* 2

Tuscany *Villa Petraia* 3

On the site of this villa originally stood a castle which, in the fourteenth century, had belonged to the family Brunelleschi. In about 1532 it came into the possession of the Medici family when Alessandro de Medici confiscated it from the Strozzi. In 1568 Grand Duke Cosimo I de Medici, who lived in the Villa Castello situated nearby (Tuscany, Villa Castello, fig. 4), gave it to his son Ferdinando. Between 1575 and 1590 Ferdinando transformed the castle and its grounds into a villa. The design, in which the central tower of the building was preserved and was provided with a belvedere, is ascribed to Bernardo Buontalenti. The atrium of the almost square building was painted by Volterrano with scenes from the career of the Grand Duke Cosimo I. During the nineteenth century the courtyard was provided with a glass roof so that it could be used as a ballroom, and the paintings were restored.

The garden, probably designed by Tribolo, is situated on a steeply sloping hillside and divided into three terraces, which, in contrast to those at the Villa Castello, are situated in front of and below the building; here one did not look at the garden, but over it (fig. 1). The lowest and also the largest of the terraces follows the slope of the hill and contains a flower garden. Around 1805 a horizontal arrangement with a fountain was introduced in the centre of this parterre. On the next terrace there is a fishpond and the hedges were once clipped in the shapes of animals. This terrace is connected to the first one by a double set of steps in line with the axis of the building. The highest terrace, on which the building is situated, can only be reached from the garden by means of eccentrically placed steps to the east of the fishpond.

The existing situation does not correspond with Utens' lunette, which shows a strict symmetry. However, the picture was probably made before

73

the garden had been completed; one of the two eccentric set of steps, the pergolas, and the gate at the bottom of the central main axis were never executed. In the executed design movement flows naturally towards the east. On the upper terrace is a level plane that directs the view diagonally over the panorama of the Arno valley towards Florence; the diagonal view of the town is accentuated because the one down the central axis is, to a large extent, obstructed by a screen of tall vegetation at the bottom of the flower garden. Moreover, the equivalent of this plane on the other side of the building is so thickly overgrown that a similar view towards the west is less pronounced. During the nineteenth century the uniqueness of the view from the east terrace was confirmed by the construction of a belvedere, partly cantilevered over the outer wall at the edge of the terrace. By emphasizing the view of the town in this way the axial layout is given an asymmetrical effect.

In 1631-32 the villa was enlarged to its present shape by Giulio Parigi; next to the parterre garden a landscape park was laid out higher up the hillside (fig. 2), and from here a further view of the river valley is offered. At the highest part of the park is, among other features, a pond in which the surface of the water appears to be convex.

VILLA PETRAIA

Castello

Garden: summer 9.00-18.00
winter 9.00-17.00
House: 9.00-13.00
Closed Mondays
Fee

LITERATURE

G. Jellicoe & S. Jellicoe, *The Oxford Companion to Gardens.* Oxford & New York 1986.
D. Mignani, *Le ville medicee di Giusto Utens.* Florence 1982.
G. C. Sciolla, *Ville Medicee.* Novara 1982.

Villa Pratolino / Parco Demidoff

In 1568 Francesco I de Medici (1541-87) bought the first part of the land for the Villa Pratolino and almost annually continued to expand the estate with new purchases until 1586. In 1569 he entrusted the versatile and talented Bernardo Buontalenti with the building of a villa with an extensive *parco*. The execution of this villa probably took place in two phases. During the first (1569-*c.*1579) the Parco Vecchio and the palace of Francesco and his wife Bianca Capello were built, as can be seen in the lunette by the Flemish painter Giusto Utens (fig.1). Most of the Parco Nuovo was laid out from 1579-81. Here the *genius loci* was represented in the form of a personification of the hills in which the villa was located, the gigantic Appennino, executed by Giambologna (Giovanni da Bologna). Among those invited to work on the great number of grottoes and fountains were, in addition to Giambologna, three other favourite Florentine artists: Bartolomeo Ammannati, Valerio Cioli and Vincenzo Danti. The design of the palazzo seems to have been inspired by the Medici villa at Poggio a Caiano (built by Giuliano da Sangallo for Lorenzo de Medici in 1480-85).

At the end of the seventeenth century Prince Ferdinando (Cosimo III's son) had a theatre built in the garden. After Ferdinando's death in 1713 the complex was seriously neglected. Almost all the freestanding sculptures were removed. A number of them can still be seen in the Boboli Gardens: the Perseus fountain, the Aesculapius fountain, the Farmer fountain, the Pegasus fountain and the original Jupiter fountain by Bandinelli.

Tuscany *Villa Pratolino* 1

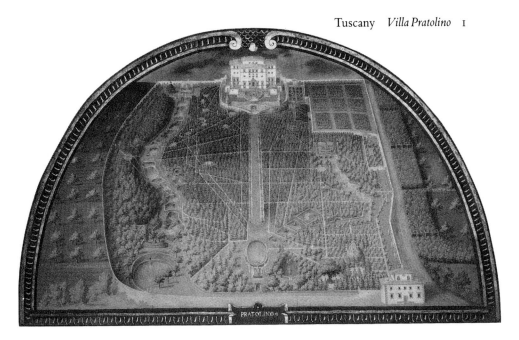

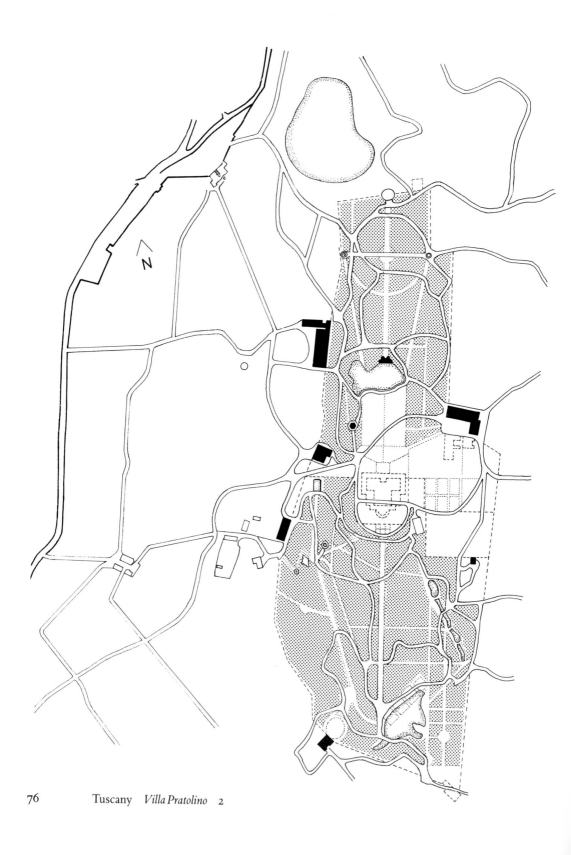

Tuscany   *Villa Pratolino*   3

Deterioration occurred to such an extent through the years that in 1819, two years after the garden had been transformed into the English style (by G. Fichs, fig. 2), the palazzo was demolished. In 1872 Prince Paul Demidoff bought the estate and moved into the former *paggeria* (villa of the page boys). He restored several of the remaining structures. Only a few fragments of the original plan remain. One of these is the colossal Appennino, which was restored in 1986-87. During earlier restorations in 1877 the Appennino's hands and feet were replaced: they are now at the 'villa of the page boys', the Villa Demidoff. Nowadays the best impression of the villa can be obtained from the drawings by Zocchi, S. della Bella and B. S. Sgrilli (*Descrizione di Pratolino*, 1742) and from its description by Montaigne, who kept a diary of his stay in 1580. From its beginnings the villa attracted international attention; before its completion it was already a curiosity and was easy to reach from the busy road between Bologna and Florence.

The villa is situated in one of the southern foothills of the Apennines. From the villa a panorama unfolds to the south as far as Fiesole. According to Montaigne, Francesco 1 chose these bare arid mountainous grounds deliberately to demonstrate his mastery over nature. Buontalenti compared the landscape around the villa to a natural amphitheatre. This theatre shape was repeated twice on a smaller scale in the design of the villa: in the *prato*, with its termination in the semicircular pond with the Appennino, and again, on a higher level, in the maze. This can be compared with the series of theatres placed behind each other in the Boboli Gardens, on which Buontalenti worked from 1583-88. Theatre literally occupied a central position in these spaces: in the arena (*prato*) statues were placed at the edge, as if waiting in the wings of a stage, and the second space was dominated by the theatre of errors in the labyrinth. The theme of theatre, the drama of imitation, was central to the entire design. Even in the house there was a small theatre, as in the Medici villa in Poggio a Caiano.

Harmony with nature was suggested by a great number of landscape scenes. Mimicry was in this villa not so much on the level of symbolic representation of 'nature', but more on that of literal imitation of naturally occurring scenes. At Pratolino automata were extensively used. These machines not only enabled natural scenes to be reproduced, so that a perfect imitation seemed to have been achieved, they also created a fantasy world which surpassed and excelled natural creation. The manufactured figures seemed to be subject no longer to the laws of nature but to human manipulation. With the help of science and artists the owner of the villa, the Medici prince, thus changed from being a demiurge (demigod) into a thaumaturgist (maker and factor of wondrous works). Apparently without effort a three-dimensional tangible dream world was evoked. Since the sophisticated hydraulic machinery remained carefully hidden, its super-

LIST OF ATTRACTIONS

1 palazzo
2 *prato*, area with statues around its perimeter
3 Appennino with pond
4 'villa of the page boys'/the Villa Demidoff
5 cloakroom, skittle alley, fives court and jousting area
6 hexagonal chapel (Capella Reale): 1580, Buontalenti
7 kennels
8 farm (Fattoria Nuova) and stables: 1579-80, Buontalenti
9 guest quarters, lodgings (Vecchia Posta)
10 timber store, pheasant pen; converted to Viletta in 1687 and in 1874 to hunting lodge
11 mill
12 gardener's house
13 Jupiter fountain (replaced by a nineteenth-century figure)
14 boundary posts
15 laurel maze
16 ice cellar
17 grotto with she-bear fountain
18 Aesculapius fountain
19 Perseus fountain
20 turrets, one with sundial and one with weather vane
21 fishpond with mask
22 farmer's fountain
23 frog fountain
24 Cupid's grotto
25 cock's fountain
26 flower garden (*giardino segreto*)
27 large aviary; cage with various types of birds, iron grasshoppers and a fountain
28 orchard
29 fountain by Ammannati
30 series of water basins and fishponds
31 marmots' casino
32 three fish-breeding ponds
33 Mount Parnassus with Pegasus, the nine Muses and a water organ
34 a hundred-year-old summer oak with viewing platform
35 pond with statue of washerwoman
36 the limestone fountain
37 the avenue with water jets (Zampilli) roughly 300 m. long
38 miller's fountain (*del mugnone*)
39 Neptune's lake (Tritione)
40 swan lake

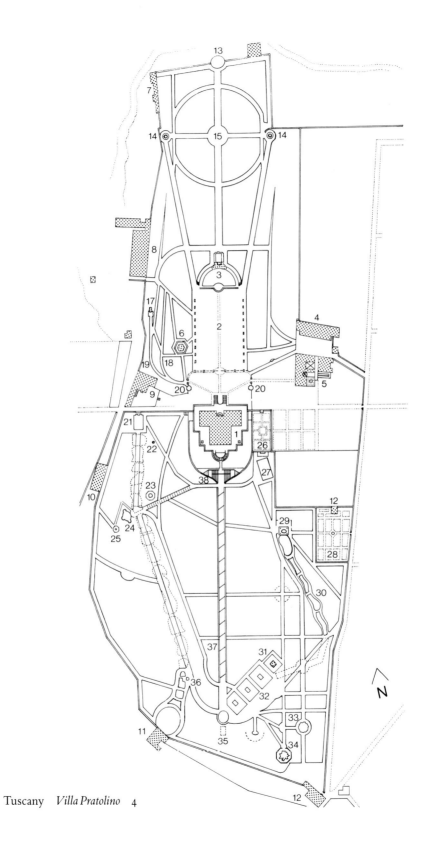

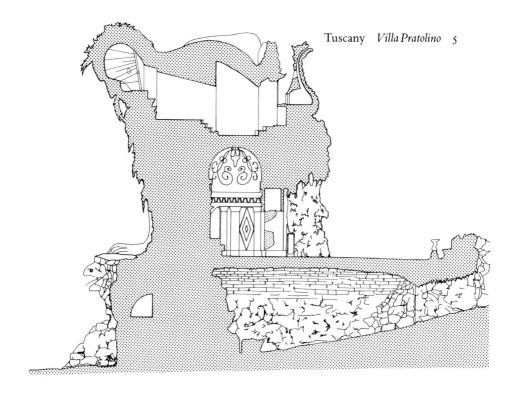

natural character was confirmed, for 'wonderful and amazing are all those things whose causes are not known, being concealed while we live in this world' (Fagiolo). In front of the fascinating robots the spectator would stand, open-mouthed and as if turned to stone, gazing at the moving sculptures, causing a reversal of roles and demonstrating the might of the machines. If these automata did not deprive their human *alter ego* of his breath (and 'devitalize' him for a moment), they would certainly cause an identity crisis. There was, for example, the statue of the god Pan, who, when approached, got up and began to play the flute while numerous animals bent their heads to drink. In the basement of the palazzo there were ten thematic grottoes. At the lowest level were the grottoes del Dio Pan, della Fama (of fame), dei Satiri (of satyrs) and la Grotte Grande (the large grotto). In the layer above were the grottoes della Stufa (of fire), della Samaritana, della Galatea (of decency), del Tritone (of Neptune), della Spugna Bianca (of white pumice) and del Diluvio (of deluge, flood). If one were to take a seat on an inviting bench in the latter this would cause the entire cave to be filled knee-deep with water within a few seconds. Shocked visitors making their escape would get a further soaking from the gargoyles outside the grotto.

The Parco Vecchio and Parco Nuovo were intentionally separated from each other by a wall: in order to go from one to the other one was forced to go past these grottoes. Appennino too, pressing his hand on the head of a monster from which water spurted into the pond, was not only designed to impress (*stupire*) through his outward appearance, but also had, inside, a number of grotto-like spaces (fig. 5), richly decorated with frescos and water effects. The little dragon on his back was added in the second half of the seventeenth century by G. B. Foggini. If a fire is lit in the interior of the giant the smoke escapes through the dragon's nostrils. The colossus, placed in the axis of the palazzo, functioned as a casino.

Along the broad central avenue on the south side of the house small jets of water spurted from one side to the other, causing a fine mist in which a rainbow might appear to surround the palazzo with a multi-coloured halo. Many of the devices created music and other sounds at various locations in the garden: the water organ on Mount Parnassus produced an artificial alternative to the natural gurgling of fishpond cascades. The design was, according to Montaigne, an assault on all of the five senses.

In the exuberance of this villa design Mannerism, in all its aspects, came to fruition; sensuality, movement, ambiguity, surprise and imagination all played leading roles here. The Villa Pratolino can be compared with the large Mannerist villas which had mainly been developed in the Roman Campagna, such as the Villa Farnese, Villa d'Este, Villa Lante and the garden at Bomarzo. The combination of an axial and a labyrinthine arrangement within one concept is, however, more developed than at the Villa Lante, where these two facets were placed next to and separate from each other. At Pratolino they formed a dualistically interwoven unity (fig. 4).

Movement was an essential condition in this design, and not only for the machines; just like the water in the cascades and the fountains, the visitor had to move from one attraction to the next. Compared with other Mannerist villa designs, however, movement along the central main axis became less important and was, more or less, equal to the other paths: it is only a linear incident (event) in the total route. There was, therefore, no entrance gate in the wall below the wide *viale*; the entrance to the villa was at the side, beside the palazzo. The main function of the axial structure was to create a large, well-ordered space, directing the view from the steps of the villa over the bounds of the estate towards Florence in the distance.

VILLA PRATOLINO/
PARCO DEMIDOFF

Via Bolognese
Pratolino

Open Fridays, Saturdays, and public
    holidays: May-September 9.00-17.00
Fee

LITERATURE

M. Fagiolo & A. Rinaldi, 'Artifex et/aut natura', *Lotus International* (1981).
G. Jellicoe & S. Jellicoe, *The Oxford Companion to Gardens*. Oxford & New York 1986.
D. Mignani, *Le ville medicee di Giusto Utens*, Florence 1982.
A. Vezzosi, *Villa Demidoff, parco di Pratolino*. Florence 1986.
L. Zangheri, *Pratolino, il giardino delle meraviglie*, 2 vols. Florence 1979.

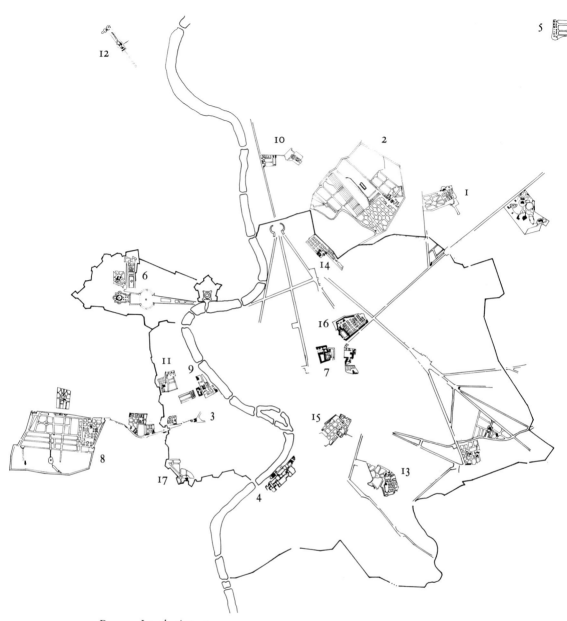

Rome *Introduction* 1

1 Albani
2 Borghese (see also chapter 3)
3 Bosco Parrasio
4 Cavalieri di Malta
5 Chigi (see also chapter 3)
6 Cortile del Belvedere
7 Colonna
8 Doria Pamphili (see also chapter 3)
9 Farnesina
10 Giulia (see also chapter 3)
11 Lante
12 Madama
13 Mattei
14 Medici
15 Orti Farnesiani
16 Quirinale
17 Sciarra

2 Rome

The mastery of the urban landscape   85

Bosco Parrasio   90

Colonna   94

Cortile del Belvedere   97

Farnesina   103

Medici   106

Orti Farnesiani   111

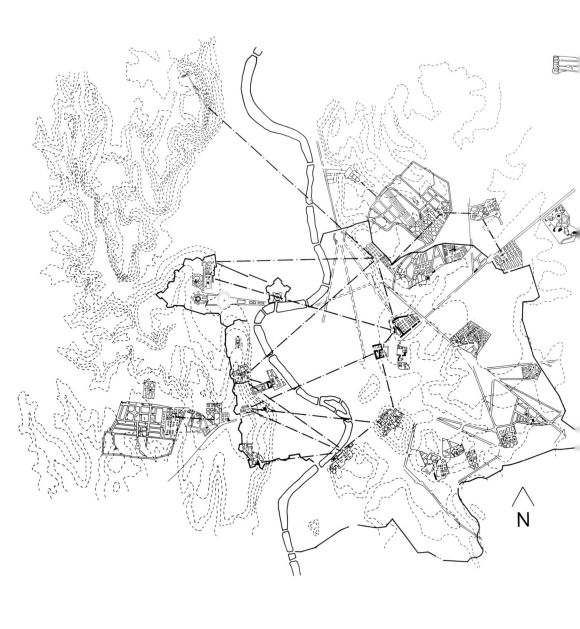

N

The mastery of the urban landscape

The Roman *villeggiatura* of the fifteenth and sixteenth century was greatly influenced by the pursuit of the church for the predominance of Renaissance culture. Popes and cardinals acted as protectors and patrons of humanists and artists; they were convinced that the leadership of culture was the responsibility of the church. Two periods can be distinguished in the prelates' endeavours to turn Rome into the leading city of world culture. The first began during the reign of Nicholas v (1447-55) but was dramatically interrupted by the sack of Rome (*sacco di Roma*) in 1527. The second period started with the Council of Trent (1545-63) and lasted for a hundred years. During both periods the papal *villeggiatura* was, more than ever before, absorbed by cultural life. In the Middle Ages, too, the popes had fled from the oppressive heat of the city during the summer. Their country seats were in the hill towns of the Roman Campagna. It was only during the Renaissance that villas were built in Rome itself, giving the city an important cultural and representative significance. Between about 1485 and the sack of Rome important villas were built near the Vatican, on the west bank of the Tiber. During the period after the Council of Trent villas were built in the hilly eastern area of the city. This took place within the framework of the urban schemes of Gregory XIII (1573-85) and Sixtus V (1586-90) in particular. They granted licences to build and provided water supplies, with the intention of systematically developing the eastern part of the city. Finally, towards the end of the sixteenth and at the beginning of the seventeenth century competing cardinals were building increasingly larger villas on the outskirts of the city. The largest of them all were the Villa Borghese and the Villa Doria Pamphili, situated just outside the city wall.

In Rome the topographical conditions faced by the *villeggiatura* were determined by the structure of the Tiber valley. On its western side the north-south line of the main Tiber valley is bounded by the steep slopes of the Janiculum, which sends out a strategic finger of land to the north, jutting into the Tiber valley: Monte S. Egidio, on which the stronghold of the Vatican lies. Beyond the deep side valley north of this promontory the river continues its way past the steep hills of the Monte Mario. The difference in height between the Tiber valley and the western hills is roughly fifty metres. On the east bank the relief is less pronounced, the differences in level being on average about twenty-five metres. There is therefore no steep slope here, only hills gently rolling down to the river. Here are the proverbial seven hills on which the ancient city was built. The geographical origin of Rome was the Palatine Hill above the Forum Romanum, where, at a sharp bend in the Tiber, an island facilitated the fording of the river. The successive hills lie more or less orthogonally along the winding main Tiber valley. The topography of the old city, defined by the Aurelian wall, consists principally of the low-lying asymmetrical Tiber valley, which widens into a bowl-shaped valley at the city, and the hills which surround this valley like an amphitheatre.

In imperial Rome there was already an important difference between the settlement of the valleys and the hills. In the valleys, rich in water, lived a population originating from all points of the compass and housed in tenement blocks, while the arid, wooded and inaccessible hills were sprinkled with gardens and country residences. When the Emperor Constantine (312-327 AD) moved his capital to Constantinople, decay and depopulation set in in Rome. Despite the efforts of the popes, Rome at the end of the Middle Ages was still a chaotic town. Among the ruins of the imperial city were several densely populated areas, concentrated in the bend of the Tiber valley opposite the Vatican fortress. 'The hilly district was wild and deserted; there were flocks of animals grazing everywhere and there were many *vignas* (vineyards) and vegetable gardens' (Platina, cited in Levedan). It was these overgrown ruins of the ancient city which, at the beginning of the Renaissance, formed the stage properties of the gigantic amphitheatre, evoked by the topography of the Tiber valley. In Rome the ruins were often visually connected with the villa and also bodily incorporated into the plan of the garden.

Three elements of the ancient city show a structural relationship with the situations of the villas. The first of these are the consular roads, the great ancient Roman arterial roads. In the hilly district it was especially along the Via Pia and Via Appia that numerous villas were constructed. In the north the Via Flaminia and, in the west, the Via Aurelia also connected a series of villas. The second element is the Aurelian wall. In the Middle Ages the area enclosed by these fortifications had become too big for the decayed city and numerous villas were built in a wide green belt inside as well as outside the wall. In this way the wall was quite often breached and integrated in the villa plans (Villa Medici, Villa Belvedere). Finally, the water supply was an important factor in the siting of the villas. The deserted hilly area only became inhabitable after old aqueducts had been repaired and new ones built by the popes (including the Aqua Vergine by Sixtus IV, the Aqua Felice by Sixtus V, and the Aqua Paolo by Paul V). Aqueducts were an indispensable source of water for the villas (the Aqua Vergine for the Villa Medici, the Aqua Felice for the Villa Montalto for example).

One of the first villas to be built along the Tiber valley was the Villa Belvedere. This villa was built by Pope Innocent VIII in 1485 just outside the Vatican, where the strategic north wall of the stronghold dominated the Tiber valley. The Villa Belvedere radically broke with the closed character of the medieval Vatican fortress. In the north wall of the villa an open loggia has an unrestricted view of the *prati* (meadows) along the Tiber, the city, Monte Mario and the Sabine Hills. Most pilgrims and processions from the north on their way to the Vatican could be seen from far away and also as they passed below the villa. The closed rear wall of the loggia was decorated with a landscape panorama. Vasari mentions that in this painted panorama the city of Rome was depicted as well as Milan, Genoa, Florence and Naples. The painting shows much more than can be seen in the real panorama. As the city of Rome could not be seen from the north-facing loggia this 'defect' was remedied by its representation on the rear wall. Thus the art of painting made it possible to include the entire conceivable space in the panorama.

At the beginning of the sixteenth century other villas were built on prominent viewpoints on the western slopes of the Tiber. The Villa Sciarra and the Villa Lante (1518) were built on the Janiculum, and the Villa Madama (1517) was built outside the town on Monte Mario. The Villa Farnesina on the other hand was located on the Tiber. The Villa Barberini (which no longer exists) on the Janiculum near the Vatican, Villa Corsini and the Villa Bosco Parrasio belong to the period after the Council of Trent.

The plan of the Villa Lante was based on a topographical association with the classical villa of Julius Martial on the Janiculum. 'Hinc Totam Licet Aestimare Romam' was inscribed above the loggia: 'from here you can see all of Rome'. This inscription is taken from an epigram by the Roman poet Martial about Julius' classical villa: '[...] From here the seven hills can be seen and the whole of Rome set against the Alban and Tusculan Hills can be appraised [...]'. In order to make this view possible a loggia was built over the full width of the east façade of the villa.

From the Villa Farnesina (1505), situated down in the Tiber valley at the foot of the Janiculum, there was no panorama. This was, however, compensated for by the skill of the architect and painter Peruzzi (1481-1536). In the so-called Sala delle Prospettive (1515) the walls of the hall were transformed into illusionary open loggias. The natural perspective of the real space was continued into a constructed perspective painted on the walls. In this way the villa was lifted up to an imaginary height by the art of painting and the lack of a panorama was corrected.

The representative layout of villas to the east of the Tiber was established during the period of the Counter-Reformation. The Villa Medici (1564), the Villa Quirinale (1574), the Orti Farnesiani (1570) and Villa dei Cavalieri di Malta are all situated on hills along the Tiber. Towards the end of the sixteenth and at the beginning of the seventeenth century the Villa Ludovisi, the Villa Montalto (neither of which now exists), the Villa Colonna and the Villa Mattei were built.

The Villa Medici is situated on Monte Pincio. Even since classical times this hill had been called Collis Hortulorum (Hill of the Gardens), because it was covered by the luxurious gardens of prominent Romans such as the Acilii, Domitii, Lucullus, and Pompey. The villa is situated on a terrace between the massive city wall, which shuts off the landscape behind it, and the fairly steep slope of the Monte Pincio. From there the low-lying parts of the city near the Porta del Populo, the Tiber valley and the hills on the opposite side can be seen. Ammannati, who had been involved in the building of the villa, was impressed by the view. Important for the inter-action between the villa in its landscape and the city is also the so-called Mons Parnassus. This artificial hill is situated on the remains of an antique nymphaeum in the former garden of the Acilii, and stands out above the trees on the terrace. A spiral route, with a changing view of landscape and city, led to the top, past water trickling far below. Thus was unrolled the *non plus ultra* of the panorama of Rome.

The Villa Quirinale, on the hill of the same name, was already well-known at the time that Cardinal Carafa's modest villa still stood, not only for its view over the city, but also for the free access given to the citizens of the town. From the beginning of the Renaissance it was customary in Italy for people who owned works of art and gardens to give free access to the public. The so-called *Lex Hortorum*, already voluntarily applied in Rome, implied that the gardens were freely accessible to friends and the general public, and even that they had been created for their pleasure. Gardens were also the favoured settings for theological disputes, processions and ser-mons. When Cardinal Carafa's villa came into the hands of Cardinal d'Este the garden was laid out by Girolamo da Carpi, Cuzzio Maccarone (foun-tains) and Pirro Ligorio (antique statues) on a geometrical plan at right angles to the Via Pia. A belvedere on the northern slope of the garden gave a view of Monte Pincio and the Villa Medici. A high-level terrace on the north-west corner of the complex looks towards the real panorama of the city, with the Vatican on the horizon. The intervisibility over the low city, between the Villa Quirinale and the Vatican, was given formal status when, in 1584, the villa was converted into a fortified papal palace. In that same year the central and dominant position of the villa was underlined by the building of a tower over the most central salon of the villa. This '... should not only dominate the seven hills, but should also be visible from the far distance, even from the sea' (Pastor, cited in Coffin).

The Villa dei Cavalieri di Malta dominated the entire western flank of the Aventine. This hill, which narrows the Tiber valley in the south, is the last in the series of visually strategic locations in the hilly eastern area. The panorama over Rome which unfolds here is especially well-known because of the so-called 'keyhole-perspective' by Piranesi. This is the view of St Peter's through the keyhole of the gate of the Piazza dei Cavalieri di Malta.

From this it would appear that in the western as well as the eastern areas of the town the visually strategic locations were occupied by villas. In the bowl shape (2 or 3 km. in diameter) formed by geomorphological forces the town is the stage for the villas nestled on the balconies of this gigantic open-air theatre. The occupants of the villas could look down on the eccle-siastical and political centre of the world.

Raised above the low-lying city the villas were in each other's field of vision (fig. 2). As such, they were an affirmation of the ecclesiastical and social hierarchy. Just as in Florence, the villas balanced on the edge of free space. They make the space perceivable without creating it themselves. In Rome, however, the scale of the theatre form, created by 'natural forces', was different. In Florence the panorama measured about 15 km. from east to west and 8 km. from north to south. In Rome it was 2.5 km. from east to west and 3 km. from north to south. The vertical as well as the horizontal differences were less. In Florence the villas were situated higher (about 150 to 200 m. above the valley) than in Rome (about 50 m.). The most important difference, however, was that in Rome the entire panorama had been urbanized. Towards the end of the sixteenth century control of this urban space was confirmed by the building of the 119 m. high dome of St Peter's (1558-89). Just like Brunelleschi's dome in Florence, it was a central point of reference in the panorama. It gives the natural space of the town landscape a precise definition.

At the same time, the views changed character. The area of the villa grounds increased after 1550. This demanded adequate internal organization, which was solved by the axial organization of the villa plan. The panorama of the town, however, was not yet included in this arrangement (see, for example, the Villa Medici and the Villa Quirinale). Towards the end of the sixteenth century the view from the terraces was channelled by view axes (as in the Villa Doria Pamphili, for example). The origin of this development can be seen at the Cortile del Belvedere (1504), in which Bramante created an axial link between the Vatican and the Villa Belvedere. In the late seventeenth century intervisibility between villas continued to play a role, as can be seen in an etching of the Villa Doria Pamphili by Piranesi in which he also depicted the view from the villa to the Villa Abamelek (eighteenth century) and the Villa Corsini on the Via Aurelia. The Villa Medici, too, was mentioned in connection with views from the nearby villas Mandosi, Borghese and Giustiniani. Through the axial framing of views the villas were more forcefully connected with each other, like a powerful chain.

LITERATURE

I. Belli Barsali, *Ville di Roma*. Milan 1983.

D. R. Coffin, *The Villa in the Life of Renaissance Rome*. Princeton 1979.

P. Foster, 'Raphael on the Villa Madama: The Text of a Lost Letter', *Römisches Jahrbuch für Kunstgeschichte* 11 (1967-68), pp. 307-312.

M. L. Gothein, *A History of Garden Art*. New York 1979.

Johannes, Cardinal de Jong, *Handboek der Kerkgeschiedenis*, vol. 3. Utrecht & Antwerp 1948.

P. Levedan et al., *L'Urbanisme à l'époque moderne*, XVI-XVIII *siècles*. Geneva 1982.

C. Scheiberling, *Het leven van de H. Philippus Nerius*. 's-Hertogenbosch 1874.

A. Schiavo, *Villa Doria Pamphili*. Milan 1942.

Bosco Parrasio/Il Paradiso

There are various opinions as to the exact date of the villa's construction. Isa Belli Barsali places it in the second part of the eighteenth century, whereas Jellicoe suggests 1725 as the date of its construction, basing his argument on the date of Antonio Caneraia's design for the Accademia degli Arcadi. This academy, established in 1690 as a splinter group of the academy created by Queen Christina of Sweden, became the most famous of the Italian literary societies. After their expulsion from the Farnese gardens on the Palatine, where they had held their meetings, the members decided to build a meeting place of their own, and their first meeting took place in the new Villa del Bosco Parrasio on 9 September 1726. In 1850 the casino was transformed into its present shape by the Roman architect Giovanni Azzuri, who was responsible for the round hall, executed in a classical style and crowned with a dome, and the curved façade facing the amphitheatre.

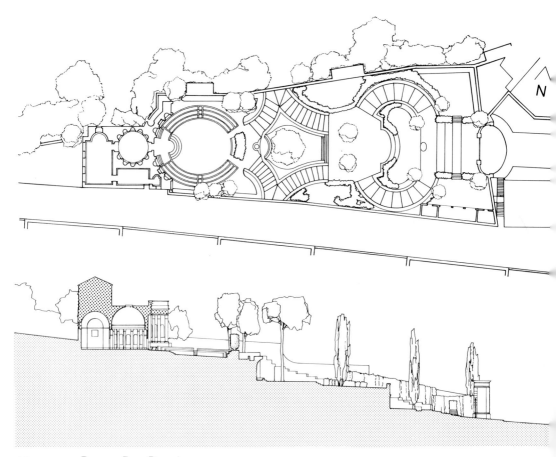

Rome *Bosco Parrasio* 2

Within an enclosed irregular quadrilateral, the garden is laid out in three terraces, interconnected by steps on the steep slope of the Janiculum (fig. 1). The arrangement is strictly symmetrical around a central axis, which stretches between the main entrance and the entrance to the round hall of the casino facing the garden. The movement is directed upwards and is stopped at the amphitheatre, the seat of lofty discussion. There is an alternation of rest and movement. The resting points are between the steps on the terraces and are directed backwards to the entrance; hectic urban life is gradually left behind and makes way for the contemplation of the panoramic view. Rest and movement are united in the upper terrace, the amphitheatre, where intellect is fed by the fusion of urban culture and the Arcadian ideal (see p. 92–93).

BOSCO PARRASIO/IL PARADISO

Arcadian Academy
Via di S. Pancrazio
Rome

Visitors by appointment only

LITERATURE

I. Belli Barsali, *Ville di Roma*. Milan 1983.
G. Jellicoe & S. Jellicoe, *The Oxford Companion to Gardens*. Oxford & New York 1986.
G. Masson, *Italian Gardens*. London 1987.
J. C. Shepherd & G. A. Jellicoe, *Italian Gardens of the Renaissance*. London 1986.

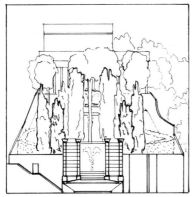

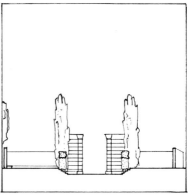

1A The eye is caught by the abundant greenery which veils the casino. Only the roof is visible.

1B The entrance gate points towards Rome, reflecting the return to urban life. In the *giardini segreti* one can escape from the busy city.

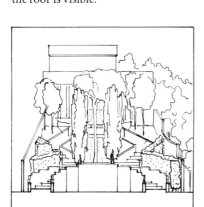

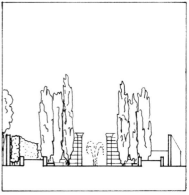

2A Once inside, the steps catch the eye. The *giardini segreti* are hidden and will be passed on the way up.

2B It is pleasant to linger in the hollow of the steps. Sitting, one enjoys the greenery and the water; standing, the view back to Rome.

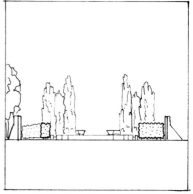

3A On the next level the garden becomes more intimate and more introverted; it is tempting to stop here for a moment.

3B Leaning over the balustrade or descending the steps, the panorama of Rome and its landscape can be seen.

4A The second set of steps leads to the theatre, which now reveals itself.

4B Here the view over Rome is directed primarily to the side. The passage to the next terrace is still closed off by plants and water.

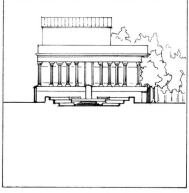

5A Only when entering the theatre does the entrance to the casino become visible.

5B The theatre has an intimate atmosphere. The bustle of Rome is shut out. Nothing can disturb the concentration on the forthcoming debate.

Villa Colonna

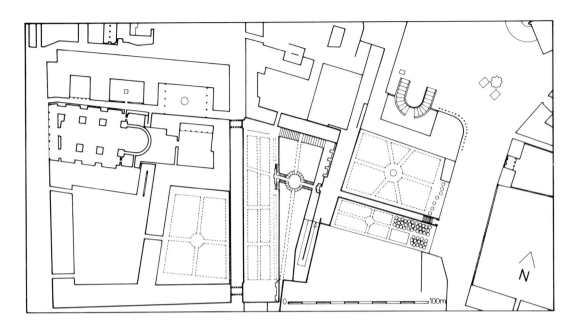

Rome *Villa Colonna* 1

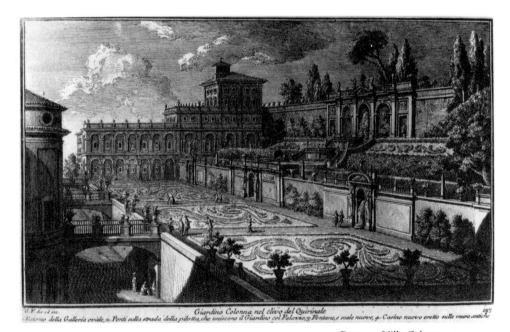

Giardino Colonna nel clivo del Quirinale

94

Rome *Villa Colonna* 2

Rome *Villa Colonna* 3

The Palazzo Colonna, situated at the foot of the Quirinal, is one of the largest and most luxurious palazzi in Rome and was built by Martinus v in the first half of the fifteenth century. In 1730 many new buildings were added and the church of S.s. Apostoli was integrated into the complex. In 1564, when Pope Pius IV gave the palazzo and the site on the other side of the road to his cousin Carlo Borromeo, there were only the ruins of the Temple of the Sun (casa antica di Nerone) and a few medieval buildings built on the overgrown hillside.

In 1517 an entrance gate was constructed at the top of the hill, near the Piazza di Monte Cavallo (the double set of steps below the entrance was added when the Via XXIV Maggio subsided as a result of levelling work on the Roman road network in 1870). It was only under Filippo Colonna I, head of the family after 1611, that a garden was laid out on the hill and connected to the palace by two bridges, one at each end of the garden (fig. 1). In about 1713 the garden was developed further by Filippo Colonna II. It was he who erected the statue of his ancestor Marco Antonio Colonna.

In 1730 the palace was considerably extended. The brick wall, which screened off one of the courtyards of the palace from the Via della Pilotta, was replaced by a new wing. This was also connected to the garden by two new bridges. The engraving by Vasi (1761) shows the completed complex (fig. 2). The casino at the north side of the garden, built in two different periods, was demolished in 1923 to make way for the Universita Gregoriana. The garden is, for the greater part, still intact.

The layout of the garden is based on terraces. Because the lowest terrace is connected to the palace by bridges, this area has an almost Venetian character; the Via della Pilotta works as an imaginary canal parallel to the lowest terrace (fig. 4). A real water axis cuts through the successive terraces. A

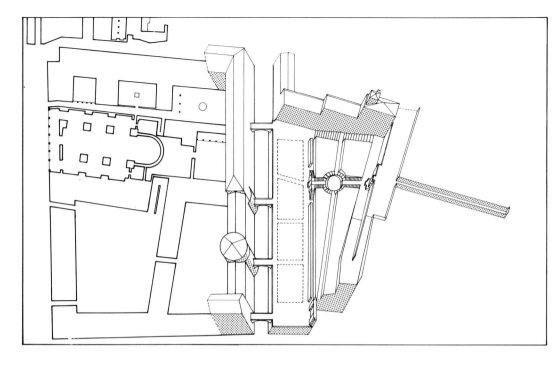

double set of steps on both sides of a cascade leads straight up to the penultimate terrace, where the source of the water axis rises from a monumental nymphaeum. From there a path climbs sideways up to the highest level. Above the nymphaeum is a viewing platform. From here it is possible to look back not only over the garden but also over the palazzo and the whole of Rome. The path from the upper entrance also joins the platform (the path runs between two other gardens). The angle at which this path joins the terraced garden is taken up by the cascade and directs the view towards St Peter's. The garden, placed like a vertical tableau opposite the palazzo, connects the lower building to the panorama of the town landscape (like a periscope).

VILLA COLONNA

Via della Pilotta
Rome

Gallery open Saturdays: 9.00–13.00

Closed August
Garden usually closed to visitors
Request for admission: Palazzo Colonna, Piazza S. s. Apostoli, Rome
Fee

LITERATURE

I. Belli Barsali, *Ville di Roma*. Milan
    1983.
A. Blunt, *Guide to baroque Rome*. London
    & New York 1982.
D. R. Coffin, *The Villa in the Life of Renaissance Rome*. Princeton 1979.
A. Peneira, *American Express Pocket Guide to Rome*. London 1983.

Cortile del Belvedere

The Cortile del Belvedere was part of the cultural programme undertaken by the popes, from Nicholas v onwards. Giuliano della Rovere (*Il Terribile*) especially, as Pope Julius ii (1503-13), wished to make Rome the centre of civilization. In particular he took it upon himself to restore the ecclesiastical state which, under his predecessor, Alexander Borgia vi, had been on the verge of collapse. This aim was furthered by, among other things, a building programme intended as the *renovatio imperii*, the revival of imperial Rome, and which was to have a great impact. The Vatican was the starting point of the *instauratio Romae*. The old Basilica of Constantine and the papal palace next to it were to be transformed into a complex that could compete with other imperial seats, such as Constantinople. In order to achieve this, Donate Bramante was appointed architect.

The Cortile del Belvedere was Bramante's most important commission in connection with the extensions to the papal palace. In 1505 a start was made on the northern extension and the link to Innocent viii's Villa Belvedere (fig. 2a). Bramante's plan consisted of an elongated, enclosed courtyard between the palace and the villa. It is possible that this idea was derived

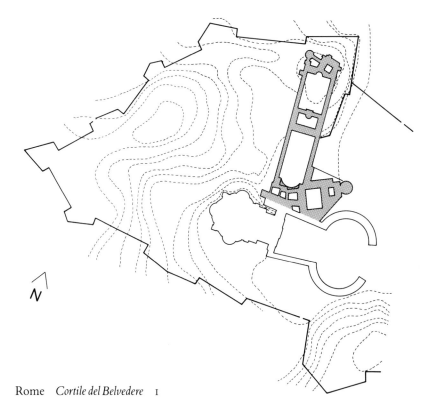

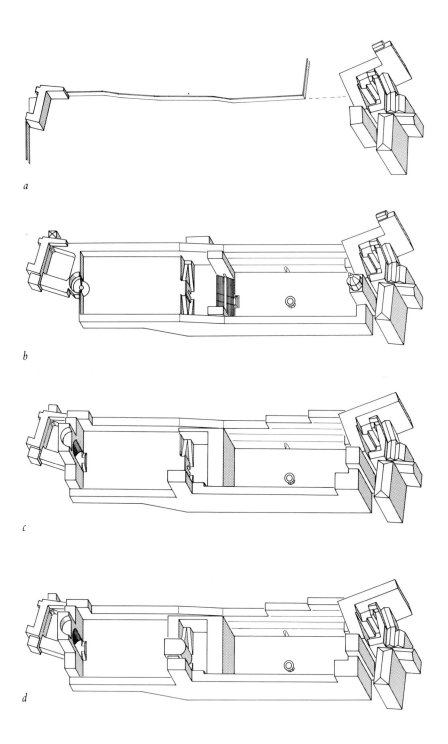

a

b

c

d

Rome *Cortile del Belvedere* 3

from ancient villas (such as the Domus Aurea) and from fragments of imperial Rome (such as the Vatican naumachia of the first century). Internally the
courtyard was divided into three terraces (fig. 2*b*). The lowest served as a
hippodrome or open-air theatre; the middle had seating terraces, a nymphaeum and steps; and the highest was arranged as a garden with parterres
and trees. On their long sides the terraces were flanked by *ambulationes* (corridors) with crypto-*portici* (galleries). In Bramante's plan the latter consisted
of superimposed orders (Doric, Ionic and Corinthian) in the lowest courtyard and one single order in the top courtyard. Two small projecting towers
were placed beside the seating on the central terrace. The east wall, which
coincides with the city wall, was the first part to be completed. The entrance
from the Porta Julia was in the centre of the section bordering the lower
courtyard. The north end of the *cortile* consisted of a round concave-convex
set of steps adjoining an exedra, which originally had only one storey. To the
north, as a last link between the *cortile* and the Villa Belvedere, was an anti-
quarium in the shape of an open, square sculpture gallery. After 1505, when
Bramante concentrated all his attention on the new plans for St Peter's, the
construction of the *cortile* was entrusted to other architects, among whom
were Antonio da Sangallo and Baldassare Peruzzi. Under Julius III (1550-
55) the exedra in the rear wall was raised by one storey, as were parts of the
east gallery (fig. 2*c*). At the same time, the concave-convex set of steps by
Bramante was replaced by a straight one. Under Pius IV (1559-65) Pirro
Ligorio converted the exedra into a niche, crowned by a semicircular shaped
loggia. He was also responsible for the earlier design of the west gallery of
the *cortile*. Pius V (1566-72) had all the antique pagan sculptures moved from
the Belvedere and transported to cities such as Florence. Gregory XIII
(1572-85) had the Torre dei Venti built roughly in the centre of the west
wing.

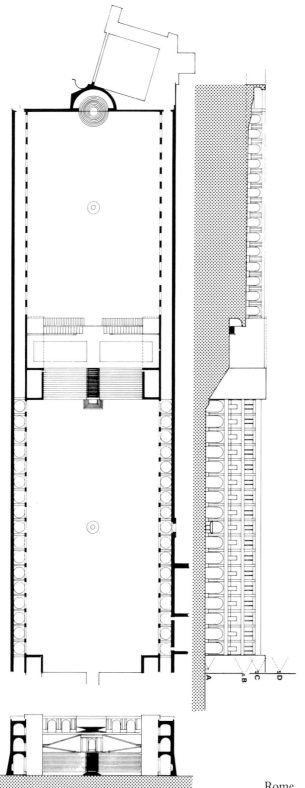

Rome   *Cortile del Belvedere*   4

Sixtus v (1585-90) who, together with his architect Domenico Fontana, made a breakthrough in the hilly part of Rome by the construction of axial streets, created an obstruction in the axial structure of the *cortile*. He built the Biblioteca Sistina, cutting straight through the *cortile* at the point where the seating terraces were. This destroyed the original spatial concept. Under Pius vii (1800-23) the Braccio Nuovo was also built straight across the *cortile*, this time where the steps and the nymphaeum were situated. In its present state, then, Bramante's *cortile* has disintegrated into a series of separate courtyards (fig. 2 d).

The overall size of the original Cortile del Belvedere was about 100 by 300 m. (fig. 4). Seen from the ground floor, the *cortile superiore* and the exedra were hidden from view. The visitor, entering the complex through the gate and looking north, saw a vertical accumulation of galleries, steps and a nymphaeum (fig. 5a). The total plan could only be seen from the papal rooms (fig. 5b, 5c) situated above (the Borgia apartments and Stanze of Raphael). The best viewpoint was the window of the Stanza della Segnatura, the private study of Julius ii (fig. 5d). Seen from there, all the elements of Bramante's plan coalesced into one central perspective scene. The floor of the *cortile superiore* slants up in a northerly direction more than the architrave of the sidewalls. This shortened the columns of the adjacent galleries in the direction of the garden, causing an illusory increase in the depth of the space, just as in Mannerist and Baroque stage constructions. Viewed from the papal rooms, the horizon was, as it were, pulled forward and placed within the area of the *cortile*. This optical lengthening is reinforced by the treatment of the walls of the *cortile*. The junction of the sidewalls of the *cortile superiore* was concealed by two small towers, placed, like the side wings of a stage, level with the middle terrace. The exedra, whose depth is difficult to

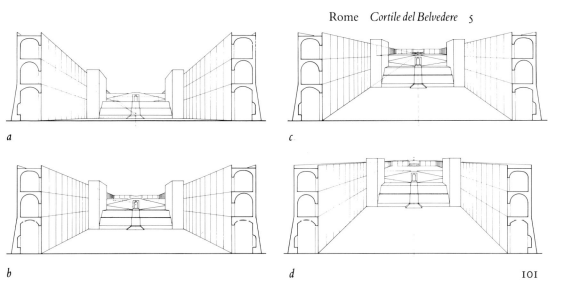

a

b

c

d

judge because of its semicircular shape, is wider than the opening in the back wall, making this junction also invisible. The optical lengthening is also reinforced by the treatment of the orders. The openings in the porticoes of the *cortile inferiore* are separated by a single pilaster, whereas in the *cortile superiore* there are two, making the opening smaller.

Due to this perspective distortion, space, in Bramante's design, was manipulated by architectural means as if in a painting. Like an illustration framed by the Stanza della Segnatura window, this scene became a part of the mural decoration of the room.

The *giardino segreto* on the upper terrace only became visible by moving in an axial direction through the plan. The raising of the exedra at a later date changed this. Moreover, Ligorio's loggia built above the exedra introduced a view in the opposite direction over the Vatican to St Peter's, which was then under construction. The Torri dei Venti, built even later on the west wing, offered Gregory XIII a view over the town to Villa Buoncompagni (family property of the Pope) and the Quirinale (the papal summer palace), both on the east bank of the Tiber.

CORTILE DEL BELVEDERE

Viale Vaticano
Rome

Part of the Vatican Museum
Open: 9.00-14.00
Closed Sundays, except last of the month
Fee

LITERATURE

J. S. Ackerman, 'The Belvedere as a Classical Villa', *Journal of the Warburg and Courtauld Institutes* 16 (1951), pp. 78-79.
J. S. Ackerman, *The Cortile del Belvedere.* Vatican City 1954.
A. Bruschi, *Bramante architetto.* Bari 1969.
A. Bruschi, *Bramante.* London 1977.
D. R. de Campos, *I palazzi Vaticani.* Bologna 1967.
J. C. Shepherd & G. A. Jellicoe, *Italian Gardens of the Renaissance.* London 1986.

Villa Farnesina

The client for this villa was Agostino Chigi of Siena, one of the richest men in Europe at that time. He was the son of the banker Mariano Chigi, who in the last decade of the fifteenth century had had a villa – Villa Chigi – built at Le Volte Alte near Sovicille to the south-east of Siena by his fellow Sienese, Baldassare Peruzzi (1481-1536). This first villa by Peruzzi was completed in 1505. From the moment Agostino held a position in his father's business in Rome he quickly rose to become a banker to several successive popes. His wealth gave him such status that in 1506 Pope Julius II made him and his heirs members of his own family.

In 1505 Agostino bought a plot of land along the Tiber at the foot of the Janiculum and invited Peruzzi to design a villa there. Work started in 1508; in 1510 Peruzzi started the decorations and in 1511 its first phase was completed. Within only five years of completion Peruzzi was asked to make drastic alterations to the interior. A room on the first floor was, not without structural problems, enlarged and provided with an extensive programme of decorations (Sala delle Prospettive).

The completion of the interior decoration, including the painting of the bedroom by Sodoma and of the entrance loggia by Raphael and his assis-

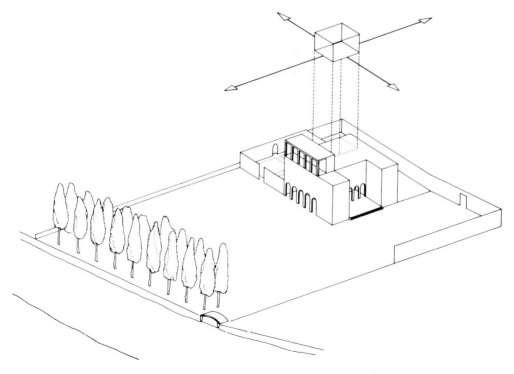

tants, took until 1519 – one year before Agostini Chigi died. The villa was later bought by Cardinal Alessandro Farnese, who also owned the plot of land to the south-east of the villa. Both sites were combined to form the 'Villa Farnesina'. More than half the garden was destroyed when the Tiber was embanked at the end of the nineteenth century.

The Villa Farnesina occupies a special position among the Roman villas, situated as it is at the foot of the Janiculum, on the floor of the Tiber valley. Peruzzi used the same scheme as the basis for this building as he had used for the Chigi villa at Le Volte Alte, which was situated on a hilltop. The absence of a real panorama in the Roman villa, however, was compensated for by a painted view in the Sala delle Prospettive. The closed walls of the hall are transformed into illusionary open loggias. The perspective of the real space is continued in a constructed perspective painted on the walls. Beyond the painted balustrade of the loggias the artificial panorama shows rustic scenes on the rural western side of the villa and views of Rome on the side of the villa facing the city. The Torre delle Milizie can be recognized to the right of the chimney, and, on the opposite wall, a view over the area around Porta Settiniana includes a view of the villa itself. By means of the paintings the villa was raised to an imaginary height, and the lack of a panorama was thus corrected (fig. 1).

The architect of the villa, Peruzzi, was originally a painter; he had mastered the art of perspective and was also involved in the design of stage scenery. His architecture often showed a relationship to the other disciplines. Villa Farnesina is a example of this: it was richly decorated with frescos on the outside as well as the inside. Between the side wings of the u-shaped building and in front of the entrance loggia there was formerly a

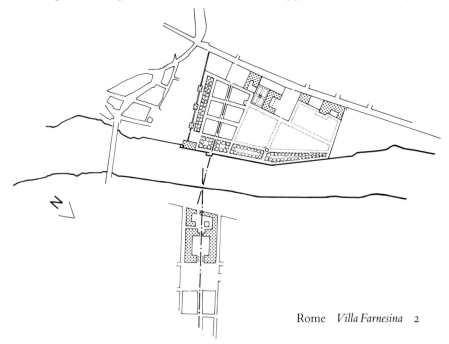

Rome *Villa Farnesina* 2

Rome   *Villa Farnesina*   3

platform several steps high, intended for open-air stage performances in the forecourt. The frescos on the outside façade formed a background for this, evoking strong associations with the classical *scaenae frons*.

The symmetrical design of the house was modified under the influence of situative factors; only on the north-east side was there a loggia opening from the ground floor on to the garden (the Sala Galatea, painted by Peruzzi and Raphael) and, on the same side, a belvedere loggia was placed on the roof. This belvedere, originally five bays wide, was reduced to three in 1861-63 in order to restore the symmetry of the building.

Little is known of the original layout of the garden. There was a dining loggia on the bank of the river and Raphael built guest quarters along the street side; these elements were demolished, however, in the seventeenth and nineteenth centuries. After the villa had passed into Farnese's hands, Michelangelo made an ambitious proposal to connect the Palazzo Farnese on the other side of the Tiber with the Villa Farnesina by means of a bridge. This would have established one line of, successively, public square, palazzo, two inner courtyards, bridge and garden, creating thus a Mannerist axial system, with the Villa Farnesina functioning as a casino for the palace (fig. 2).

VILLA FARNESINA

Via della Lungara 230
Rome

Open: 9.00-13.00
Closed Sundays
Fee

LITERATURE

I. Belli Barsali, *Ville di Roma*. Milan 1983.
D. R. Coffin, *The Villa in the Life of Renaissance Rome*. Princeton 1979.

Villa Medici

The villa is situated on Monte Pincio, an area much in demand for building villas since antiquity and which had, therefore, come to be known as the Collis Hortulorum (Hill of the Gardens). The site, on which the famous Gardens of Lucullus and Nero's tomb were situated, is bounded by the city wall on the east side and on the west side overlooks the low, flat Campus Martius, which extends to the Tiber. The development of the Medici villa has a long history. In all probability it was Cardinal Giovanni Michiel who, at the end of the fifteenth century, constructed the first building, in the form of a Roman country house (*casa coloniche*), with a patio and, on one side, a tower (depicted on a fresco in one of the garden pavilions). Subsequent owners, the Creszenzi, sold it in 1564 to Giulio and Giovanni Ricci, cousins of Cardinal Giovanni Ricci of Montepulciano. The garden was extended to the north by the addition of a part of the Sta. Maria del Populo monastery domain and to the south by one of the Buffalini vineyards, in which the remains of the nymphaeum of the Acilian gardens (Horti Aciliorum) were situated. A new approach road was built alongside this section from the Via di Porta Pinciana, and on the Campomarzio side an existing approach was enlarged. By 1572 the house and the garden, both designed by Lippi, whose work was continued by his son Annibale, were almost finished.

Two years after the death of Cardinal Ricci in 1574 the villa was sold to Cardinal Fernando de Medici. On the advice of Bartolomeo Ammannati he added a new *portico* (hall), a new tower (connected by a viewing balcony to the existing tower), a new interior arrangement with an *appartamento nobile*, and a second set of steps. A new garden façade with deep niches and a gallery wing at right angles to the house were also added in order to house part of the cardinal's extensive art collection. The most important addition to the garden was a *bosco*, which was crowned by an artificial mountain – the so-called Mons Parnassus – built on top of the remains of the antique nymphaeum (fig. 2, 3). This new building phase was completed soon after 1580. It is not known which architects were involved in the remodelling of the house, though on stylistic grounds della Porta has been suggested. In spite of some alterations to the planting of the garden the basic outlines of the sixteenth-century plan have scarcely changed at all.

The design of the villa is, for the greater part, determined by its situation: the balance on the border between town and countryside provides the main theme of the villa. This dualism can also be recognized in the story of its development: how within the town walls a modest rural structure developed into an extensive urban villa. In the paintings by Zucchi in one of the small pavilions at the eastern end of the garden which served as Cardinal de Medici's studio, the history of the villa is depicted in three scenes: 'past', 'present' and an imaginary 'future'. In the first scene the rural origin of the

Rome *Villa Medici* 1

vigna Michiel is portrayed (and, in the painting, almost revived as an ideal). Its urban counterpart is depicted in the scene of the future. A monumental unexecuted forecourt can be seen in it, linking the villa to the town (fig. 3). Moreover, the façade on the town side gives no hint of a villa: being on one of the most prominent sites in the city, seen from and seeing over all, the building assumed in its city façade the 'representative' character of an urban palace. Even the steps did not present an inviting transition to the garden (an external detour being the preferred access). In the third picture the villa is shown, apart from a few details, as it had looked in about 1580. This painting shows the garden side with its lower, more differentiated and open façade. It was in this state, at the end of the sixteenth century, that the villa could be seen in its most complete form.

The garden is divided from north to south into three main zones, in which urban and rural elements are increasingly counterposed (fig. 4*a*). The northern zone, with its squares edged by rows of trees, is bounded by the Aurelian Wall to the east and by the wall with the main garden entrance to the west. Both walls have openings. A central path connects the entrance gate (opening on to the town) with the Cleopatra pavilion, through which there are views over the hills in the direction where the Villa Borghese would, at a later date, be built.

In the central zone is the house with its piazza and parterre. The axiality of this section was originally emphasized by two symmetrically placed granite baths taken from the Baths of Titus. This enclosed part of the garden was screened off on all sides. At first the landscape could only be viewed from the house over the Aurelian Wall and, on the other side, over the city. However, just between the north and the middle sections of the gardens there was a path connecting the two walls. At the end of this path, on the

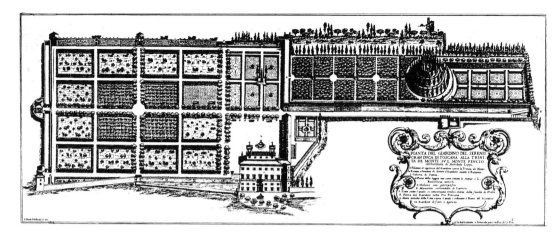

eastern side, part of the old city wall was breached for the benefit of the view and, on the western side, there was even a set of four windows, with nearby benches placed to enable the view of the city to be more easily enjoyed. From the time that these walls were almost entirely demolished the spatial experience has changed completely; a visual axis to St Peter's came into existence (fig. 4*b*) diagonally over the central zone (as drawn by Piranesi).

The third zone consists of a raised terrace, capped by a *bosco*. Both the town and the landscape are always in view from the sidepaths on this high narrow strip of garden. Mons Parnassus could be climbed past water gushing from the Pegasus fountain to beyond the tree tops where, on the summit, the *non plus ultra* of the panorama in all directions was unfolded. Moreover, the strap work of the little dome and its gilded weather vane could be seen from all over the city.

The garden is also divided into three zones from west to east (fig. 4*c*). The middle zone is a path that cuts completely through the garden from north to south. On either side of the path the garden is treated differently. On the house side are the more enclosed spaces: the *giardino segreto*, reached from the gallery wing, the piazza at the back of the house, and the two northern quadrants with their pergola covered paths. On the other side the two quadrants with open paths and the parterre form, together with the *bosco*, a continuous, spatially integrated zone. With the removal of the covered walks, however, the difference between the eastern and western parts disappeared to a great extent.

Fountains were planned at the three intersections of the main axes of the different garden sections. The Medici cardinal placed a decorative element at the end of almost every path. At the edges of the garden sculpture niches and pavilions were placed in and on all the walls. A narrow strip along the Aurelian Wall was made into a zone of amusement with the menagerie built

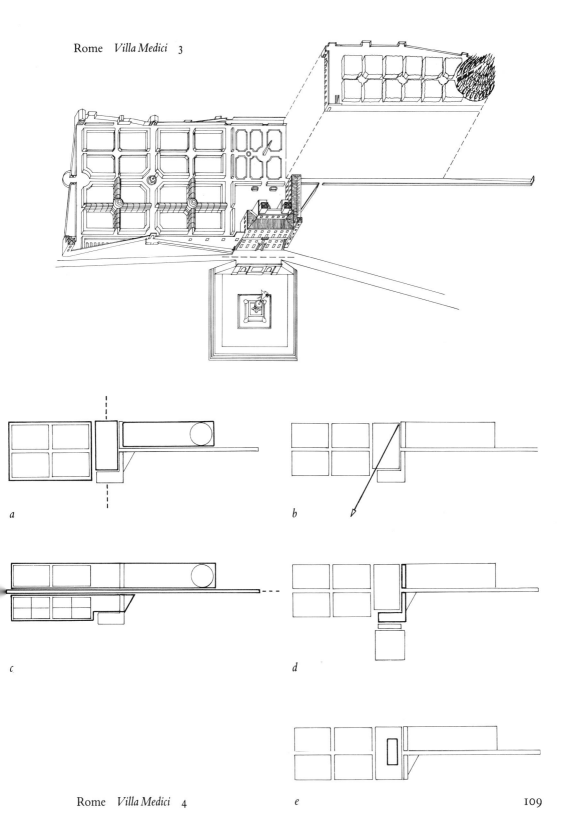

by Ferdinando de Medici. Between the inner and outer walls, in a number of rooms, were lions, bears, leopards and peacocks. The grotto designed by Ammannati is situated in the same zone, in the continuation of the gallery.

Except in respect of its size, the Villa Medici did not conform to the large Mannerist villa designs being constructed at that period, mainly in the area of Rome, which had an axial structure and a strong dynamism, often reinforced by various spectacular water elements. The intended axial plan of the villa on the Pincio, in which the building was to have been erected above a monumental forecourt (fig. 4d), was never realized (the cardinal had already purchased the ground, but the execution of the expensive plan fell through when he left Rome to become Grand Duke of Tuscany in 1587). Eventually it was the north-south axial stress, which had originally been secondary, that came to dominate the design. As the house was not situated on this axis (fig. 4e) but beside it, a situation arose in which house and garden were only loosely related to each other. In contrast with many villas in the Roman Campagna there was here no elaborate iconographic programme. This was probably in order to avoid disturbing the aura surrounding the objects exhibited in the villa. Only the Parnassus myth was shown as a symbol of the villa (with its owner as patron of the Muses). The Mons Parnassus stands out above the trees on the terraces. A spiral route, with a changing view of landscape and city, led to the top, past water trickling far below. Thus was unrolled the *non plus ultra* of the panorama of Rome.

The villa gained a wide reputation. The elevation with the two connected belvedere towers was copied frequently in and around Rome, at, for example, the Villa Borghese (1608), which also has sculpture niches, the Villa Patrizi (1717), the Villa Albani (1760), and even at the nearby Trinita dei Monti church, at the top of the Spanish steps.

VILLA MEDICI

Accademia di Francia
Via Trinità dei Monti 1
Rome

Open Wednesdays: 9.00-11.00
Or apply to: Uffico Intendenza di Villa
  Medici
Telephone: 6789030
Fee

LITERATURE

G.M. Andres, *The Villa Medici in Rome*,
  2 vols. New York & London 1976.
D.R. Coffin, *The Villa in the Life of Renaissance Rome*. Princeton 1979.

Orti Farnesiani

The Orti Farnesiani were situated on the Palatine, the hill sometimes called the cradle of Roman civilization. At its foot, on the south side, was the Lupercal, the cave in which Romulus and Remus were supposed to have been nursed by the she-wolf. The place at which, according to legend, they were washed ashore was close to its entrance. A little higher on the hill, at the reputed spot of 'Romulus' hut', excavations have revealed definite traces of huts dating from the Iron Age (ninth century BC). There would have been an agrarian settlement on the hill, the abode of the first Romans.

Towards the beginning of the Christian era the aristocratic and rich Romans lived here in a kind of residential area. The widely spaced complex of palaces and temples on the north side of the hill contrasted with the busy Forum Romanum below. On the southern side the games in the Circus Maximus could be followed as if from a higher gallery of the stands. The spot on which the Orti Farnesiani were later laid out was occupied mainly by the Domus Tiberiana and, nearer the edge, the Domus Flavia and the Palace of Caligula.

In the early Middle Ages the palaces on the Palatine were abandoned and during the Renaissance the ruins of ancient buildings were often used as quarries for building material (Palazzo Venezia, the Cancelleria and Palazzo Farnese were, for example, mainly built from the stones of the Colosseum). At the beginning of the sixteenth century the Palatine was a labyrinth of ancient ruins interspersed with vineyards, where people would dig for ancient sculptures and frescos, and the Forum had deteriorated into a place where cows grazed: the Campo Vaccino. For Charles V's triumphal

Rome *Orti Farnesiani* I

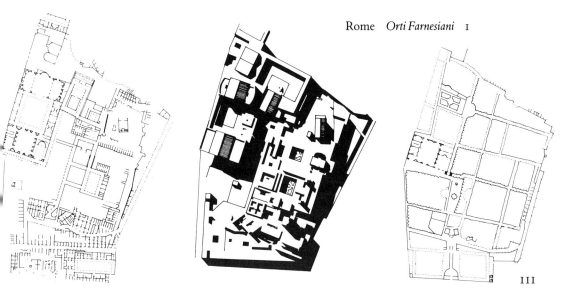

entry in 1536 the Palatine was used as a natural grandstand. From 1539 to 1579 ground on the Palatine was bought by the two brothers Alessandro and Ranuccio Farnese, who were both extremely interested in the study of the Antique. Cardinal Alessandro (1520-89) had his official residence in the Cancelleria and owned several country houses in the Roman Campagna, at Capodimonte, and Gradoli; after 1557 he commissioned Vignola to design the Villa Farnese at Caprarola. He left the *vigna* on the Palatine for his younger brother Ranuccio (1530-65). Ranuccio's permanent residence in Rome was the Palazzo Farnese and a modest villa at Frascati served him as a country seat (the Villa Vecchia, which was later to be converted by Vignola).

The gardens on the Palatine were referred to by the word *Horti*, which indicated that they were town gardens as opposed to the *villa surbana*. On his brother's early death in 1565 they passed once again into the hands of Cardinal Alessandro. Under him the northern fringes of the garden were transformed into a new architectural complex. The large wall on the side of the Campo Vaccino has often been ascribed to Vignola. As the design of the Orti Farnesiani was only completed after 1576, Vignola, who died in 1573, cannot be considered to have been its sole architect. The main architect of the scheme was probably Giacomo del Duca (1520-1601), who from 1565 worked for the Farnese princes but returned to his native Sicily in 1588.

After Cardinal Alessandro Farnese's death in 1589 work probably ceased

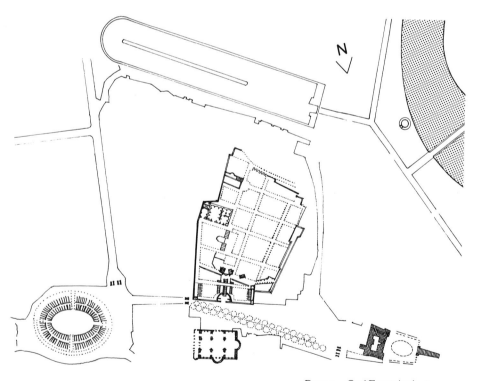

for some years and the complex was only completed at the beginning of the seventeenth century when the two aviaries by Girolamo Rainaldi (1570-1655) were added for Cardinal Odoardo Farnese, who resided in Rome from 1593. From that moment the garden developed into a famous botanical centre. The Accademia degli Arcadi was established in the gardens in 1693 and remained there until 1725, when it moved to the Bosco Parrasio on the Janiculum. After this the condition of the gardens deteriorated. The Filippini family and the Bourbons removed much of the marble and most of the sculpture collection to Naples. This collection in its turn had partly been taken from Hadrian's Villa at Tivoli, where Cardinal Alessandro Farnese had been governor. In about 1860 Napoleon III initiated the archaeological excavations which would by 1882 ruin most of the complex. In 1957 the entrance gate was reconstructed, out of context, in the Via S. Gregorio.

The design of the Orti Farnesiani was mainly determined by the pattern of the underlying ancient plots (fig.1). On top of the hill these have an orthogonal structure, which is related to the direction of the Circus Maximus (fig.2). On the low Campo Vaccino an east-west structure, clearly visible in the alignment of the Colosseum, predominated. The extent of the sixteenth-century design was for the greater part confined to the northern side of the Palatine. The part on top of the hill was almost untouched; it remained a garden of ruins, determined by the old plot pattern. The two parts were formally separated; their main axes did not interconnect (fig.4). The two different directions met at a triangular piece of ground half-way down the hillside. This wedge-shaped area, which was already present in the substructure of the Palace of Caligula, was incorporated as one of the terraces of the Farnese garden. The enormous ancient walls with their arched structure were clad in marble. A retaining wall was constructed at the

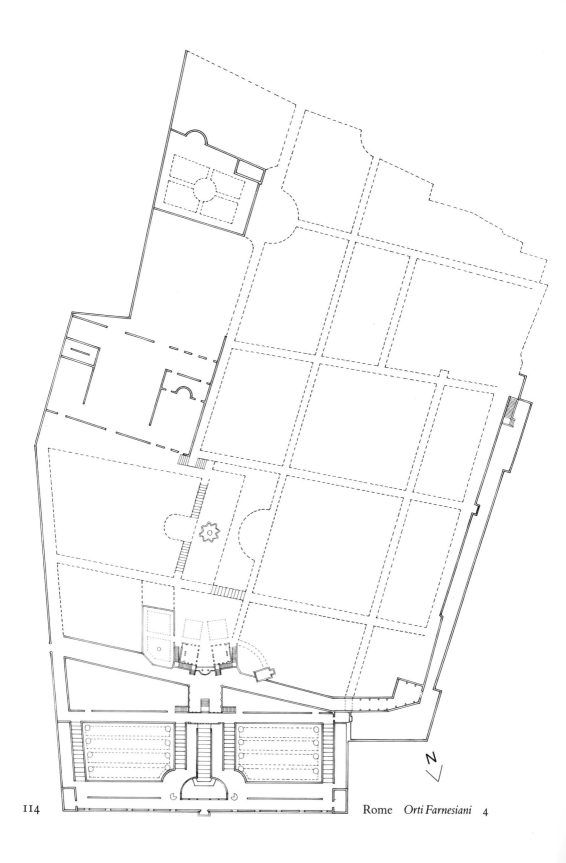

Rome *Orti Farnesiani* 4

bottom of the hill roughly along the full width of the garden, which it separated from the Campo Vaccino. This wall was crowned with two corner pavilions, and in its centre was the main entrance to the garden, a double entrance gate with, on its upper part, two large female herms and the inscription 'Horti Palatini Farnesiorum'. The nature of the inscription indicated that it was not a villa in the usual sense that was being referred to, but rather a *hortus*, a garden. In this design there was no physical building in the form of a house; there was no residential function, and the gardens were designed purely for recreation. They offered no more than the diversions of pleasure-making, the surprising architectural route and the attractions linked to this.

Immediately inside the entrance gate, in the 'semicircular' courtyard (*teatro*), the two aviaries which formed the architectural climax of the hill could just be seen. These cages, which formerly housed brightly-coloured birds, were a visual stimulus, impelling movement (fig. 5). While the way to these aviaries appeared to be by way of a ramp (*cordonata*), however, one unexpectedly found oneself in a cool, dark grotto with a fountain. This could only be left at the sides by small sets of steps; movement along the central axis was interrupted for a moment. Back on the axis again one climbed up to a higher level. On a bright square with a fountain a surprising new scene was unfolded: the aviaries appeared to be part of a more extensive and more complex architectural tableau which, until then, had been hidden from the view in the perspective. To reach the highest level one had to leave the axis once again and climb up one of the small sets of steps on either side of the birdcages. Turning around, one had a view of the aviaries presented in the same manner as at the beginning of the route. By this *déjà vu* the revelation of a moment ago was called into doubt.

On the viewing balcony between the aviaries the axiality of the plan was surpassed by the width of the panorama, which was reinforced by setting the aviaries at a slight angle to each other (the oblique position of the two aviaries seems to be derived directly from a drawing of Varro's Aviary by Pirro Ligorio). The architecture of ancient Rome in the Forum was not only transcended figuratively, but Rome and the Campagna as far as the Alban hills could be observed literally over the Basilica of Maxentius, situated monumentally on the main axis. The design transformed the hill into a formal viewing gallery with the town as the spectacle.

It was not until this balcony either that, for the first time, the total architectural system could be appreciated, including a hidden garden (*giardino segreto*) which, until then, had remained almost hidden from view, due to its being built above the ceremonial approach route (the approach route was partly through a sort of trench in the garden, fig. 6, 7). Descending again, one reached the *giardino segreto* automatically: because of the subtly designed system of steps one never took the same route back. The steps next to the aviaries provided a visual introduction to the ramps which followed. In the drawings by Letarouilly, which are generally speaking very precise, the figures in his drawings confirm the assumed direction of movements. Small windows in the wall along the Campo Vaccino made it possible to look outside the *giardino segreto*. The wall benches, however, were directed inward and reinforced the garden's closed character (fig. 7). This hidden garden could only be left by means of two small spiral sets of steps, which emerged near the entrance gate in the semicircular *teatro*. These were placed behind two niches so that they would remain unnoticed when entering the garden.

Although there is no documentary evidence which provides clear proof of the authorship of the Orti Farnesiani, there is some justification in ascribing the design to Giacomo del Duca. It shows great similarity to two other villa designs on which he worked as an architect: the Villa Lante at Bagnaia (1560-87) and the Casino Farnese at Caprarola (1584-86). At the Villa Lante the theme of separate building volumes on either side of a central axis was employed in a series, at the end of which, on top of the slope near the grotto, there also used to be two symmetrically placed aviaries. The similarity to the Casino Farnese goes much further. Apart from the elements used and the formal language, there is also a resemblance at the level of architectural grammar. In both designs the elements are assembled in a similar manner. The surprising way in which perspective scenes are linked along the route, as well as the tension created between route and axiality, are more or less identical in both plans. Just as in the Caprarola system the symmetry at the Orti Farnesiani is also broken by the view of a situational element over the diagonal of one of the squares; to this end an extra square was added to the east of the aviaries. Over the diagonal a clear view of the Colosseum is presented; the circle in the centre of the paved area, which, in perspective, is an oval, even repeats the shape of the Colosseum. Moreover, there is a painting in the lowest loggia of the Casino at Caprarola which shows a hybrid between the designs of the Casino and Orti Farnesiani.

The low enclosed *teatro* of the Orti Farnesiani also shows a certain resemblance to the sunken nymphaeum of the Villa Giulia. In this villa, too, there were two small concealed spiral staircases and two symmetrical birdcages. It is not known for certain whether there was any actual collaboration between the two architects, Vignola and del Duca. Both were in the service of the Farnese family during the period 1565-73, and both worked on a number of the same projects.

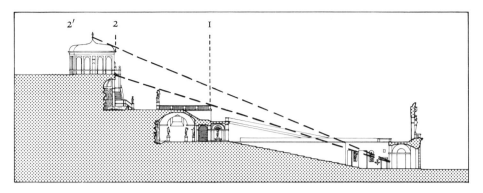

Rome *Orti Farnesiani* 5

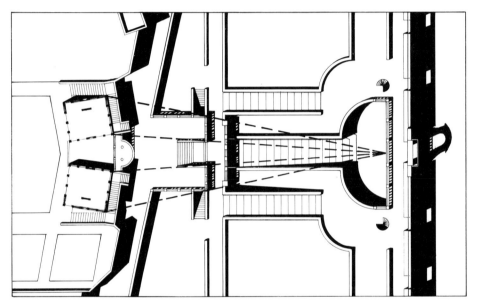

Rome *Orti Farnesiani* 6

Rome *Orti Farnesiani* 7

Via del Fori Imperiali/Via di S. Gregorio
Forum Romanum
Rome

Open: June-September 9.00-19.00;
   October-May 9.00-17.00
Closed Tuesdays
Fee

LITERATURE

I. Belli Barsali, *Ville di Roma*. Milan
   1983.
A. Berendsen, *Kunstschatten van Rome*.
   Zeist 1961.
P. Bigot, *Rome Antique au IV Siècle*.
   Paris 1942.
A. Blunt, *Guide to baroque Rome*. London
   & New York 1982.
H. Giess, 'Studien zur Farnese-Villa am
   Palatin', *Römisches Jahrbuch für Kunstge-*
   schichte 13 (1971), pp. 179-230.
G. Masson, *Italian Gardens*. London 1987.

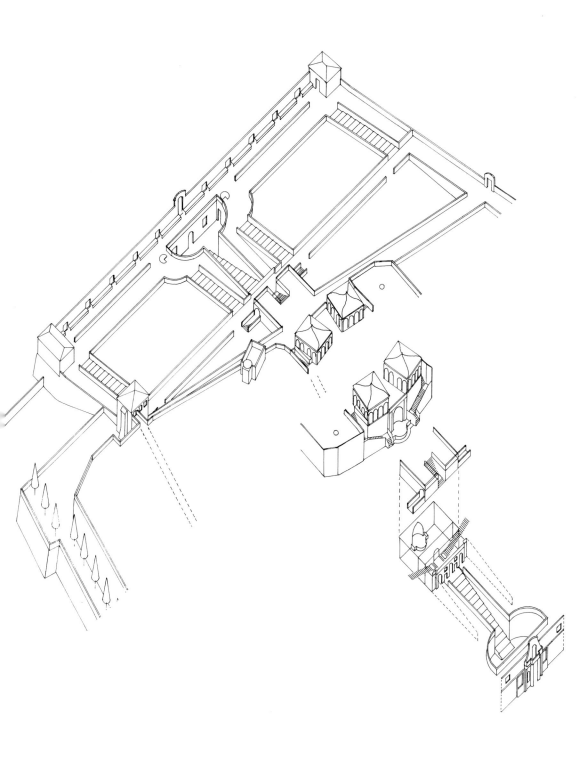

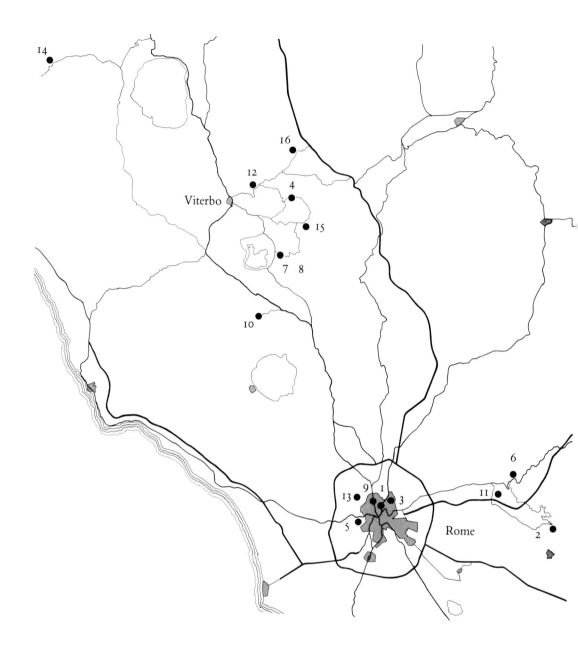

Roman Campagna *Introduction* 1

1 Borghese
2 Catena
3 Chigi
4 Chigi-Albani
5 Doria Pamphili
6 d'Este
7 Villa Farnese

8 Casino Farnese
9 Giulia
10 Giustiniani
11 Hadriani
12 Lante
13 Madama
14 Orsini
15 Ruspoli
16 Sacro Bosco di Bomarzo

3 The Roman Campagna

Mannerism: ambiguity as impulse to movement   122

Borghese   127

Catena   130

Chigi   133

Chigi-Albani   135

Doria Pamphili   140

d'Este   146

Villa Farnese   153

Casino Farnese   159

Giulia   163

Giustiniani   170

Lante   177

Orsini   183

Sacro Bosco di Bomarzo   187

Mannerism: ambiguity as impulse to movement

The fifteenth and sixteenth-century *villeggiatura* in the Roman Campagna was mainly concentrated in two areas. A great number of villas are situated in the neighbourhood of Lago Albano, south-east of Rome, and another conspicuous group of villas is found in the neighbourhood of Lago di Vico, near Viterbo, north-west of Rome. There were two distinct motives which determined the choice of these locations.

The first group of villas is situated in direct proximity to the ruins of classical Roman villas. From the beginning of the Christian era this rural area had formed a favourite location for the *villeggiatura* of the affluent nobility. Between 118 and 138 AD the emperor Hadrian built his Villa Hadriana about 25 km. to the east of Rome. The remains of this gigantic villa complex at Tivoli were to inspire many Renaissance architects. In the sixteenth century this villa was almost matched in grandeur by the Villa d'Este, built in 1550 in the immediate vicinity by the Cardinal of Ferrara. During the same period the small town of Frascati, close to the remains of classical Tusculum in the Alban Hills, became the most fashionable location for the summer residences of the ecclesiastical hierarchy.

The location of the second group of villas, near Viterbo, was determined by earlier medieval history. During the Middle Ages ecclesiastical dignitaries escaped the internal conflicts in Rome by taking refuge in the Roman Campagna. In many cases a complete removal of entire residences to a safer region took place; Viterbo, for example, functioned as the centre of papal power from 1266 to 1281. Moreover, during the thirteenth century the phenomenon of papal summer residences grew. A number of towns, including Viterbo, Orvieto and Anagni, became the regular abode of travelling prelates. This was determined by the religious calendar and the weather: during the summer months popes and cardinals avoided the oppressive heat of the city by retreating to their summer residences. As far as the accommodation itself was concerned, the existing facilities, local monasteries, episcopal palaces and castles, were mostly adequate.

It was only in the second half of the fifteenth century, at the beginning of the Renaissance, that political stability in the Roman countryside allowed a greater degree of openness towards the landscape. Many of the country residences wee decorated, extended and, in many cases, provided with extensive gardens, and thus transformed into villas. Because of a change in the local political situation at the beginning of the sixteenth century, however, especially around the time of the sack of Rome in 1527 by the Emperor Charles v, numerous buildings with a fortified character were again erected in the Roman Campagna. It was the Tuscan architects Peruzzi and A. da Sangallo who were particularly involved in the construction of these fortified country residences in the centre of Italy.

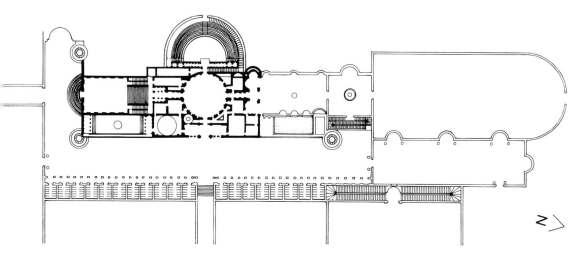

Roman Campagna *Introduction* 2

At the beginning of the sixteenth century an important change in villa architecture took place; a new approach was born which was to have much influence, especially on villa designs in the northern part of the Campagna: Mannerism. The basic principles of Mannerist villa architecture can be traced to the design of the Cortile del Belvedere, designed by Bramante and built within the walls of the Vatican in 1504. The axial construction, the linking of a series of autonomous inner and outer spaces, and the internal manipulation of perspective, which were characteristic of the Cortile del Belvedere, were further developed in subsequent Mannerist villa architecture. The first villa design to which these principles were applied and in which house and garden were treated simultaneously was the Villa Madama (1516-27), designed by Raphael and Giulio Romano (fig. 2). While still under completion the villa was almost completely destroyed by fire during the sack of Rome in 1527 and the second half of the villa was never finished.

Because of the insecurity in this period, villa building in the Roman Campagna ceased almost entirely during the following years and Mannerist villa architecture developed only in the north of Italy. In Mantua, Giulio Romano, one of the architects who had fled to take advantage of the more stable political and geographical climate away from Rome, built the Palazzo del Tè and its gardens (1525-35). The elaborately painted iconographic programme in the palace, with themes from classical mythology and geographical references, became one of the characteristics of Mannerist villa architecture, for which the Palazzo del Tè would serve as an example. Such a programme was first used in a garden in the design of the Medici villa at Castello, near Florence, in 1538.

Yet it was in and around Rome, however, that in the second half of the sixteenth century a more mature form of Mannerism developed. Its most important representatives were the archaeologist-architect Pirro Ligorio (1491-1580), the Bologna educated architect, perspective designer, and theorist Jacomo Barozzi da Vignola (1507-73), and the architect Giacomo del Duca (1520-1601). An individual contribution was made by the noblemen Niccolò and Vicino Orsini. The most important clients at that time were the Farnese and Orsini families, who owned the greater part of the north of the Roman Campagna. The design which heralded the new period was that of the Villa Giulia (1550-55), which lay just outside the walls of Rome and which Vignola and Ammannati built for Pope Julius II. The main elements of this villa were arranged geometrically in a linear series of screens and views.

As with the Villa Giulia, most of the Mannerist villa designs which followed were characterized by a marked axiality. Forecourt, building, courtyard, garden, landscape and horizon are placed along one line. They remain, however, autonomous elements; they can never be seen simultaneously. The route is introduced as the structuring principle and it is only by movement along this route that the axially-linked spaces are related to each other. The route thus becomes a vital condition for understanding the architectural system. Although movement is ordered along the main axis, in the architecture of Vignola and del Duca it is necessary to diverge from the axis in order to reach the next space. In this way a field of tension has been created between axiality and route. The architectural space is disclosed as if in a climatic sequence. Even the illusionistic paintings of the interior often reinforced this spatial sequence, thereby integrating interior and exterior. This principle is perfectly developed in the villa and the Casino Farnese at Caprarola and the Orti Farnesiani in Rome. The subtlety here lies in the control and precision with which perspectively constructed scenes, comparable with those designed by Serlio for the stage for example, are set up in a series behind each other in the landscape. The meaning of the natural panorama is put into perspective: the view of the surroundings is framed and integrated as an incident along the route.

In Mannerist villa designs it was not only the aspect of axiality which evolved into an independent and essential part of the garden, but also the *bosco*, which served as a representation of wild untamed nature and which, in its labyrinthine organization, provided a contrast to the linearity of previous designs. The *bosco* increased in size and significance in relation to the garden. In many cases a piece of natural landscape of considerable size, frequently a former hunting ground (*barco*), was integrated into the design in a slightly formalized form. The resulting *barchetto* was a wooded garden park incorporating specific functions. One of these functions was that of the casino, a small building for the purposes of recreation, in the middle of the 'natural' landscape and used for open-air banquets and so forth. The earliest examples are Pius IV's casino (1560) by Ligorio, next to the Cortile del Belvedere in Rome, and the Casino Farnese at Caprarola by del Duca (1586).

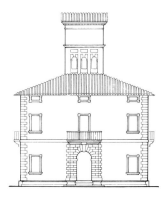

Roman Campagna *Introduction* 3

In addition, Vignola literally integrated the *villeggiatura* with 'rural life' by introducing the *casotto alla rustica*, a new type of building derived from a local vernacular type of farm; he intended this to serve as a country residence or a hunting lodge. Examples are the Villa Vecchia (1568) at Frascati, the Casino Gambara (1568) of the Villa Lante, and the hunting lodge south of Caprarola (1569) (fig. 3). The *casotto alla rustica* was often imitated.

Two designs in which the *bosco* occupies a special place are the gardens by Vicino and Niccolò Orsini, at Bomarzo (1548-80) and Pitigliano (*c.*1557-80) respectively. The relationship between the natural and the artificial is the central theme in both of these designs. The sculptures at Bomarzo compete with nature, but they are also part of it because they are carved from the colossal lumps of stone that where available on the site. This is also true of the benches and seats at the Villa Orsini at Pitigliano. It is only the route that organizes these objects. The system is labyrinthine, a straightforward reading is impossible. The objects and inscriptions (as bearers of meanings) are continuously interactive. Nor are the boundaries fixed; one can imagine the *bosco* expanding: several fragments near the previous entrance of the Sacro Bosco still seem unfinished.

In Bomarzo and Pitigliano the point of departure of the *genius loci* is clearly noticeable, but the link with the town and the palazzo in it is minimal. The Sacro Bosco at Bomarzo, at the foot of the hill, is still directed towards the village. The architecturally treated ravine wall near Pitigliano turns right away from the urban context towards the natural landscape beyond the precipice.

It is not certain whether the *boschi* of Bomarzo and Pitigliano were linked to a geometrical (Renaissance) garden which possibly already existed, or whether they were independent. This remains, for the time being, a mystery. The attention paid to the *bosco* at these villas was comparable to that at the Villa Lante (1560-98). The situation at the Villa Lante, designed by the architects Vignola and del Duca, is different because here the *barchetto* is an equal element next to the geometrical terrace garden and both were designed at

125

the same time. Unity has been achieved using two contrasting elements which reinforce the character of each other.

Whereas at the Villa Lante the axial and labyrinthine were placed next to each other, in the design of the Medici villa at Pratolino near Florence (1569-81) Buontalenti superimposed both formal principles upon each other and united them within a new concept. This gave rise to the spatial duality which was characteristic of Baroque villa designs. In the axial section one large surveyable space replaces the series of autonomous spaces. This leads to a direct relationship with the horizon and infinity, which in the villas of the seventeenth and eighteenth centuries was finally incorporated into the villa grounds. Movement through autonomous spaces, linked together by means of a route, was transferred to the *bosco*, which during the Baroque period developed into an area for amusement and cultural events. Instead of a place which mimicked nature, it became an entertainment park in which culture was expressed through theatre and opera (as, for example, at the Villa Pisani (1735) at Stra in the Veneto, and at the Villa Doria Pamphili (1645) in Rome).

The Villa d'Este and Villa Catena were built to the east of Rome in around 1560. They tried to outdo the designs of the Villa Farnese and Bomarzo; the one in 'splendour' and the other in 'whimsicality'. As the name Catena (chain) suggests, an effort was also made to create, together with the villas at Frascati, a concentration of villas to counterbalance the one in Viterbo.

In conclusion, it can be stated that in Mannerism the logical vision of perspective disappeared; Mannerism stood for the era of ambiguity. Several spatial values were created, as in the cinema, in which space, portrayed by projection, obeys laws other than the space in which the spectator stands. It was the era of movement, which tried to reveal 'reality', because behind every reality another one was hidden. More emphasis was laid on a subjective, directly sensual, perception of architecture rather than on the objective, cognitive experience which belonged to the Renaissance concept.

LITERATURE

H. Bredekamp, *Vicino Orsini und der heilige Wald von Bomarzo*, 2 vols. Worms 1985.

D.R. Coffin, *The Villa in the Life of Renaissance Rome*. Princeton 1979.

C. Constant, 'Mannerist Rome', *A.D. Profiles 20* 49 (1979), pp. 19-22.

G. Jellicoe & S. Jellicoe, *The Oxford Companion to Gardens*. Oxford & New York 1986.

Villa Borghese

The Borghese family already owned the land on which the Borghese villa was to be built and had been using it as a vineyard. Around 1600 some bordering land was added to the property and in 1608 Cardinal Scipio Caffarelli Borghese began the construction of the villa. With an estate covering several square kilometres it was one of the first large villa estates in Rome in which the plan of the house played no more than a minor role (fig. 1).

The architect of the casino was Flaminio Ponzio and, after his death in 1613, Jan van Santen, known as Giovanni Vasanzio. The casino was primarily intended as an exhibition space for the cardinal's huge collection of classical sculpture. The decoration was carried out using, among other things, variously coloured marbles, chosen to highlight the splendour of the art collection. Its outer aspects were also extensively ornamented. The four façades were entirely covered with sculptures. The fact that the villa was to have a public character, even at the beginning, is reflected in the inscription which is carved in marble in the garden: 'Whoever you are, enter

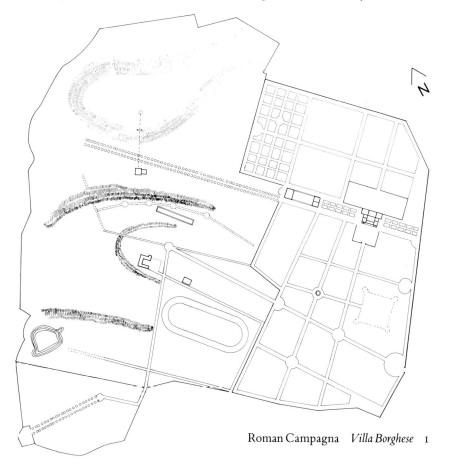

here when you desire. Here are you free to go where you will, to ask what you wish. This is the place of honest pleasures made for those other than the owner. But do not abuse civilized rules if you do not want to be sent away.'

On the map drawn by Simon Felice Delino around 1670 it is specified that the whole estate was divided into a number of separate walled sections (probably three). To the south of the casino extensive terraces were built around a forecourt. On either side of the casino there are two side gardens, designed by Girolamo Rainaldi in 1617-19. In the western garden he placed an aviary, and a second, which came to be called the Palazzo della Meridiana, was added later. The name of Luigi Vanvitelli has also been linked to the design of the aviaries. On the other side a small open-air theatre has been built. In the grounds of the villa there is a menagerie connected to the *barco*, the hunting grounds which were accommodated within the walls.

The area of the complex was so large that a number of villas are contained within it, one of which, the Villa Graziani, was probably used as the cardinal's residence. The land, with the exception of the *barco*, was divided by criss-crossing avenues in which every available corner and turn contained statues, fountains and grottoes. The grounds also included an ice house at the eastern end of one of the avenues. The gardens are given dendrological interest by the unusual use of tree species which were little used at that time, like the holly oak, which has been placed next to cypress and pine trees.

The plans were fundamentally altered by Prince Marcantonio IV after he inherited the villa in 1763. The hippodrome, known as the Piazza di Sienna, dates from this time, as does the English garden which Jacob Moore built in the south-west corner. From 1825 to 1828 still more expansions and striking changes were made, as a result of which a substantial part of the villa was transformed into the so-called 'English style'. Many of the balustrades, pictures and fountains were purchased by Viscount Astor and shipped to Cliveden. A plan to redistribute the property and use it for building development was aborted in 1885 when the mayor of Rome appealed in favour of the villa retaining its original function. Since 1902 the villa has been owned by the state and, along with the Pincio gardens, is a public park.

Although the villa was originally placed within a very extensive estate, its interaction with its surroundings has been restricted to the immediate environment of the casino. The decoration of the façades serves to link the side gardens, the forecourt and rear courtyard with the interior. These elements were related to the geometric system that determined the construction of the casino. They can be regarded independently of the plan and seen as a separate group.

It is also clear that the traditional elements of the Renaissance villa, including the *giardino segreto*, have been developed in these components. If the remainder of the estate is viewed as a landscape, we shall find no reference in the rest of its implementation to a panoramic stage-management by which the entire complex might be brought under the control of perspectivist construction. There is more reason to talk of the combining of sepa-

Roman Campagna   *Villa Borghese*   2

rate parts, including the placing of the *barco* and the adjoining menagerie within the villa's surrounding wall, forming a representation of nature which is neither formalized any further, nor incorporated into any panoramic organization. The stage-management in relation to the city landscape was minimally signalled by a small structure, the Casino di Raffaello, placed in the encircling wall. The main entrance to the villa was not treated in any special way. It was shifted to a less conspicuous position on the south of the domain, close to the Porta Pinciana, the nearest entrance to the city. The garden between the entrance and the main building is divided by a series of avenues bordered with pine trees running north-south and east-west, forming a chessboard pattern in which the avenue leading to the main building is only found by accident.

Because of the way in which interpretations of nature and of villa layout are brought together, the Villa Borghese no longer adheres consistently to formal definitions of the traditional villa. It is more an attempt at an early definition of park landscape; it was subsequently for this that the villa concept was abandoned, even though a more coherent concept had not yet been developed for the control of such a substantial landscape project.

VILLA BORGHESE

Pincio
Rome

Art gallery and museum
Gardens open between 7.00 and sunset

LITERATURE

I. Belli Barsali, *Ville di Roma*. Milan 1983.
G. Jellicoe & S. Jellicoe, *The Oxford Companion to Gardens*. Oxford & New York 1986.
G. Masson, *Italian Gardens*. London 1987.

Villa Catena

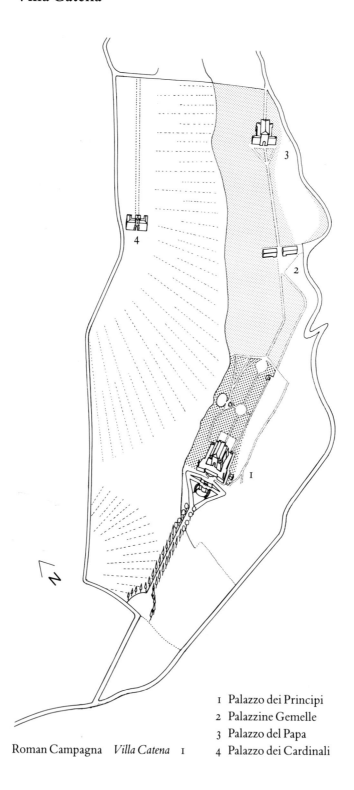

Roman Campagna   *Villa Catena*   1

1 Palazzo dei Principi
2 Palazzine Gemelle
3 Palazzo del Papa
4 Palazzo dei Cardinali

Roman Campagna   *Villa Catena*   2

This villa, situated on the slopes of Monte S. Maria, near the hill of Fausti-niano, was built in the sixteenth century for Torquato Conti (1519-72), a general in the papal army and Duke of Poli. The Conti family had ruled Poli since the end of the twelfth century. The layout of the garden was begun in 1563. When, and by whom, the Palazzo dei Principi was designed and built is unknown, but it is obvious that it originates from the same period as the first garden plan. Work on the garden was continued by Lotario Conti in the first years of the seventeenth century. An important change which took place under Giuseppe Lotario almost a century later, in 1721-23, was the construction of a number of new buildings and the extension of the bound-ary around the grounds. The reason for this impressive development lay in the fact that, in 1721, Michelangelo, Giuseppe Lotario's brother, became Pope Innocent XIII. Due to his desire to use the villa in Poli as his country seat, work was carried out at a rapid tempo. The Palazzo del Papa, also known as the Casino Torlonia, was built especially for his visits, and the two *palazzine gemelle* and the Palazzo dei Cardinali (Villa dei Padri di S. Antonio) were constructed to accommodate his entourage. In 1815, when the Conti line in Poli died out, the complex passed to the Torlonia family, and after the Second World War it became the property of Dino de Laurentiis.

The architects of the Villa Catena are unknown, but one of the people who certainly influenced the design was Annibale Caro, humanist and secretary to the Farnese. Caro, with his comprehensive knowledge of icon-ographic programmes, was from the beginning directly involved in the design of the garden. Another was Vicino Orsini, ruler of Bomarzo. Vicino Orsini and Torquato Conti were good friends. Furthermore, they were brothers-in-law, being married respectively to Giulia and Violante Farnese. They also spent several years in the same prison after being captured during one of Cardinal Farnese's campaigns in Germany (1552-57). While Vicino had started his Sacro Bosco at Bomarzo just before this campaign, Torquato began the layout of his villa at Poli some years after his return. The Vicino garden, however, continuously served as a reference for its design; it was Torquato's intention to surpass the important villa designs in the Viterbo area, such as those for the Villa Farnese at Caprarola and especially the *bosco* at Bomarzo, with all its whims and fancies. In a letter of 1563 Annibale Caro explained to Torquato that the usual motifs would probably be insufficient to achieve this. He was not completely satisfied with the proposed gardens, hunting grounds, woods and parkland, with their springs, fountains, waterfalls, a lake, a water bridge, hunting grounds, park, rabbit hutches and dovecotes. He suggested the addition of a windmill, a rocky island in the middle of the lake (an idea inspired by the Italian poet Silvio Antoniano) and a water organ. The fact that the final design was a success can be inferred from the fact that in 1569 Cardinal Alessandro Farnese invited Torquato to advise him on the layout of his *barco* south of Caprarola.

Together with Annibale Caro, who from 1563 had owned his own modest *villetta* in Frascati, the idea was developed of building a 'pearl necklace of villas' all the way to Rome, with the villa at Poli as the first link. The name of the villa at Poli, Catena (chain), expresses this idea. With the extensions of around 1720 this name was given an extra meaning. The Palazzo dei Principi, the two split symmetrical *palazzine gemelle*, and the Palazzo del Papa form a chain of architectural elements within the grounds of the villa set against the hill (fig. 1). The axial structure of this series is not absolutely linear, but adjusts itself to a bend in the ridge. The direction of the Palazzo dei Principi, at the bottom of the range, seems to be determined by the view over the axis, between the hills, to Rome (which can be seen on the horizon in clear weather). The Palazzo del Papa is, by means of a slight twist with respect to the linking axis inside the villa, directed towards the hill of Tusculum in the remote distance, the hill on which Frascati, with its papal villas, is situated.

Together with the villas at Frascati and the nearby Villa d'Este the concept of a 'chain of villas' to the east of Rome was realized, a chain which rivalled the concentration of villas in the region of Viterbo.

VILLA CATENA

Poli

LITERATURE

I. Belli Barsali & M.G. Branchetti, *Ville della Campagna Romana*. Milan 1975.

H. Bredekamp, *Vicino Orsini und der heilige Wald von Bomarzo*, 2 vols. Worms 1985.

D.R. Coffin, *The Villa in the Life of Renaissance Rome*. Princeton 1979.

Villa Chigi

This villa involved the remodelling and extension of an already existing building which formed part of a vineyard bought by Cardinal Flavio Chigi in 1763. Work proceeded from 1763 to 1766 under Pietro Camparese. The interior of the casino was richly decorated with murals. The most remarkable room was the hermitage, which was painted with sylvan tableaux, executed in *trompe-l'œil*, covering even the windows and doors. The paintings on the first floor were by F. Nubale, G. Rubin and Monaldi, while those on the ground floor were mainly by Filippo Cataldi.

The villa plan consists of two terraces on different levels (fig. 1). The casino and a geometrically laid out garden are situated on the upper terrace, while the lower terrace remained for the most part pasture. Both terraces are linked by an axis which, leading through the casino, also indicates the entrance to the villa. The axis divides the ground floor of the building into two separate parts, one on each side of the entrance passage. The ground floor and *piano nobile* are connected by two flights of steps to one side of this passage (fig. 3). The landing leads to the mezzanine in the short section of the building. The split levels, which are determined by the way in which the rooms are connected to the staircase, are not expressed in the façades.

The asymmetrically positioned archway in the west façade is counter-

Roman Campagna   *Villa Chigi*   1

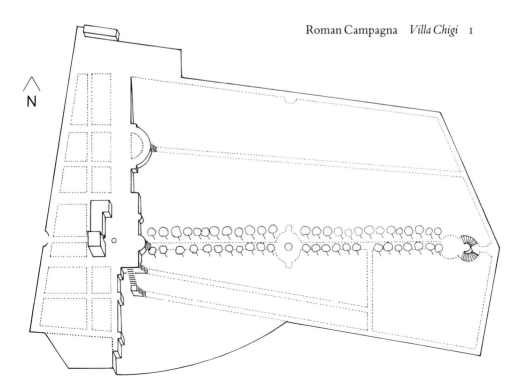

N

Roman Campagna *Villa Chigi* 2

balanced by a painted one, creating an illusionistic symmetry and at places where they should have been inconvenient for the interior – but necessary for the harmonic composition of the façade – windows have also been painted. An almost absolute separation was thus created between the interior of the casino, where an imaginary setting is staged by the frescos, and the actual location in the urban landscape outside. Only the passage and staircase are intermediary between the two concepts of space. The axis does more than order the separate elements; it also indicates the moments where illusion and reality confront each other. The pastoral landscape, introduced by the lower terrace, functions within this framework as a point where this confrontation is connected to the actual town plan by the axis.

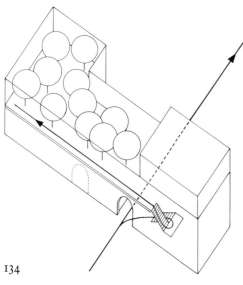

VILLA CHIGI

Via di Villa Chigi
Rome

Uninhabited, currently in a state of
disrepair

LITERATURE

I. Belli Barsali, *Ville di Roma*. Milan 1983.

Roman Campagna *Villa Chigi* 3

Villa Chigi-Albani

Towards the end of the thirteenth century Soriano functioned as a country seat for ecclesiastical dignitaries. Popes Nicolas III and Nicolas V fled there from Rome in 1278 and 1450 respectively to escape the political situation and the plague. They chose Soriano because of its favourable situation in the Cimini hills, which provided peace and fresh air. In 1561 Cristoforo Madruzzo, Cardinal of Trent and a university friend of Cardinal Alessandro Farnese, who was building a villa in nearby Caprarola, bought two houses in the Viterbo region: one at Gallese and the other at Soriano.

Immediately after the purchase Cardinal Madruzzo began building the villa at Soriano. It was an elongated single-storey building with a nymphaeum (the Fontana Papacqua) at one end and a loggia with a beautiful view, equalling that from the Villa Farnese at Caprarola, at the other. The original design is ascribed to Vignola by, among others, Penazzi (*c.*1700) and Ferruzzi (*c.*1900), though Benedetti (1972) suggests that Giacomo del Duca could have been responsible for the design. After Cardinal Madruzzo's death in 1578 building was continued by Cardinal Altemps, who completed the palazzo and the several gardens in around 1585-90. At the beginning of the eighteenth century the complex, then in the possession of the Albani family, took on its present shape (fig.1) when a second floor was added, strictly adhering to the style of the original design.

The villa is situated on an extremely steep slope in the Cimini mountains. At the heart of these mountains lies Monte Cimino, an extinct volcano. The slope of the terrain is integrated into the design by means of a great number of terraces (fig.2, 3). The round tower on top functions as the centre of the villa design: it orders the several terraces and building units and thus is an imaginary pivot around which everything turns (fig.5). The house and

Roman Campagna *Villa Chigi-Albani* 1

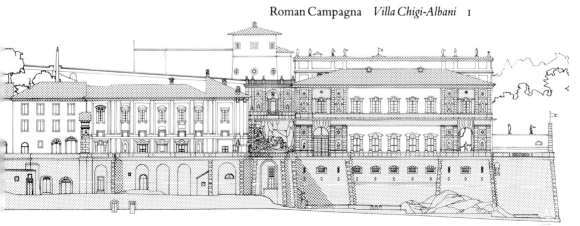

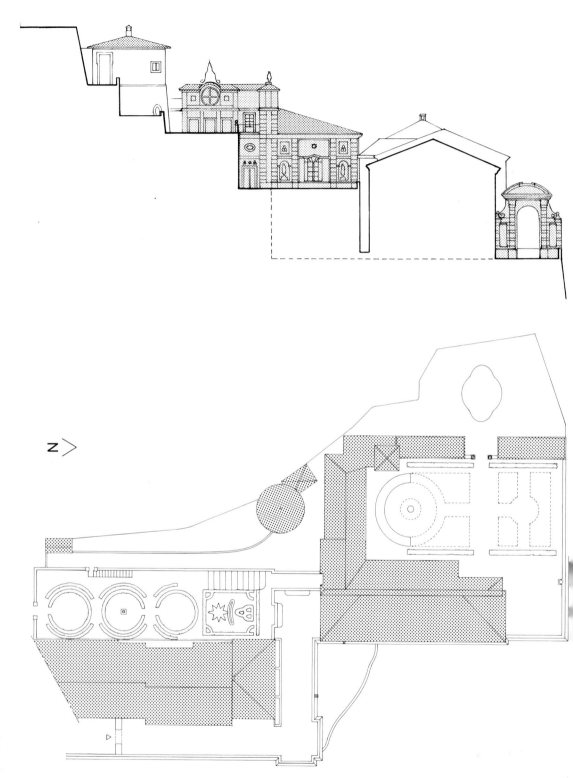

N

Roman Campagna   *Villa Chigi-Albani*   2, 3

Roman Campagna   *Villa Chigi-Albani*   4

the garden are very strongly interrelated. Each part of the garden is formally connected with a specific part of the façade. The orthogonal structure of the design is broken by the diagonal direction of the panorama of the low-lying plain (fig. 6). This direction was reinforced by the large chamfered pond at the base of the villa. The panorama is also incorporated into the system diagonally across the square area on the north side of the villa.

At the nymphaeum of the villa rises the Papacqua fountain (dedicated to the *genius loci*). The rock itself has been sculpted. Two contrasting scenes, situated at right angles to each other, were carved out of the rock. On one side the rock was transformed into a landscape with trees and various forest and field animals (the realm of Pan): a small flock of goats, an owl, a tortoise, fish and a snake. The most striking figures, however, are those of the female satyr, Amaltheia (Jupiter's wet nurse), lying beside the water, a smaller male satyr, and, on the left, the half-figure of Pan himself, with a wine sack on his head. Rising above the whole composition sits a piping shepherd.

This scene can be interpreted as the classical myth in which a shepherd from Syracuse discovered the second set of pipes made by Pan and played them so beautifully that the whole of nature, including all the nymphs and fauns, listened enraptured. Thus Papacqua was compared with the Sicilian well Arethusa.

On the other side, at right angles to this arcadian idyll, a biblical tableau related to water was placed: Moses striking the rock, from which, miraculously, water sprang. This scene was, in contrast to the arcadian one, framed in an architectural setting. On both sides of the niche with the main tableau were four smaller ones containing the four seasons: male and female figures with children, putti and cornucopias – horns of plenty. Placing obviously contrasting main tableaux opposite one another expresses the ambiguous position held by the church leaders of the time. After all, to what extent can a religious function be combined with the pleasures of country life?

A number of aspects of the Papacqua fountain suggest the presence of the Sicilian architect Giacomo del Duca. Firstly, the reference in the arcadian scene to the Sicilian landscape. Secondly, the biblical scene in which Moses strikes the rock has hardly ever been represented in sculpture. Michelangelo, however, designed a fountain with a Moses in a niche in front of the Vatican. As a follower of Michelangelo, del Duca could well have been acquainted with this. Thirdly, there is the similarity the Moses sculpture shows to the sculptures of the evangelists in the Church of S. Giovanni Battista at Campagno, on which del Duca worked in 1582.

The Papacqua fountain in Soriano was probably the first fountain to use a rock landscape, a theme that often recurs in seventeenth and eighteenth-century fountains, such as the Trevi Fountain in Rome. The nymphaeum at Soriano, carved out of solid rock, seems to have had a great deal of influence on the sculpture in the nearby monster garden at Bomarzo. Though this garden had been under construction since 1550 it was not until 1564, about the time of the completion of the Papacqua fountain, that sculptures carved directly from the local tufaceous rock also appeared. Two figures from the Sacro Bosco at Bomarzo even show remarkable similarity to those at Soriano. The Amphitrite/Demeter of Bomarzo is directly comparable with Amaltheia (both are in a sitting position with outstretched legs, and even the putti are similarly arranged). The Pan on a Hermes pillar at Bomarzo has a similar facial expression, with a flat nose and mild smile, to the one at Soriano.

Roman Campagna   *Villa Chigi-Albani*   5

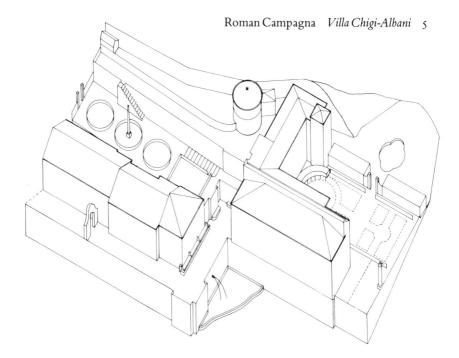

Cardinal Madruzzo was a good friend of Vicino Orsini as well as of Cardinal Farnese. They often visited one another and enjoyed 'rural life'. They showered each other with its produce and, furthermore, exchanged literature and possibly also recommended their architects and stone carvers (Ippolito Scalza and Fabio Toti among others) to one another. Directly after the completion of the Papacqua in 1564 del Duca came into the service of the Farnese family, for whom he built the casino of the nearby Villa Farnese at Caprarola.

VILLA CHIGI-ALBANI

Soriano (nel Cimino)

Open during exhibitions
   or with prior permission
Telephone: 0761: 729007

LITERATURE

S. Benedetti, 'Nuovi documenti e qualche ipotesi su Giacomo del Duca', *Palladio* (1970), pp. 3-22.
S. Benedetti, *Giacomo Del Duca e l'architettura del Cinquecento.* Rome 1972.
H. Bredekamp, *Vicino Orsini und der heilige Wald von Bomarzo*, 2 vols. Worms
   1985.
M. W. Casotti, *Il Vignola*, 2 vols. Trieste
   1960.
D. R. Coffin, *The Villa in the Life of Renaissance Rome.* Princeton 1979.
S. Lang, 'Bomarzo', *The Architectural Review* (1957), pp. 427-430.

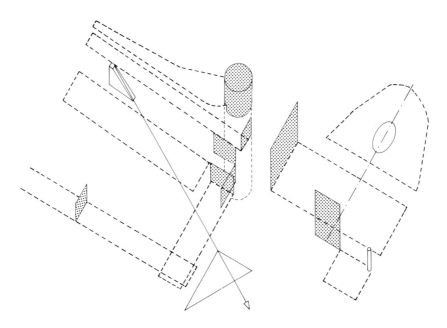

Villa Doria Pamphili

In 1630 Pamphilio Pamphili bought a small *vigna* outside the Porta S. Pancrazio on the Via Aurelia. It was the same spot on the Janiculum on which in ancient times the Emperor Galba's garden had been. Pamphilio's brother, Cardinal Giambattista Pamphili, was elected Pope Innocent x in 1664 and built a new casino in the north-east corner of the original site. It did not serve as a residence, but exclusively as a place for entertainment and the display of a collection of antique sculpture. Further to the west, on the Via Aurelia, an older house, the Casino della Famiglia (Villa Vecchia), was used as a residence.

The design for the new casino is attributed to the sculptor Alessandro Algardi and the master builder Giovanni Francesco Grimaldi, who completed the final design after provisional plans by Borromini and Rainaldi. In the original plan the casino had two side wings. At the same time as the construction of the casino the *vigna* was expanded by the purchase of ad-

Roman Campagna   *Villa Doria Pamphili*   1

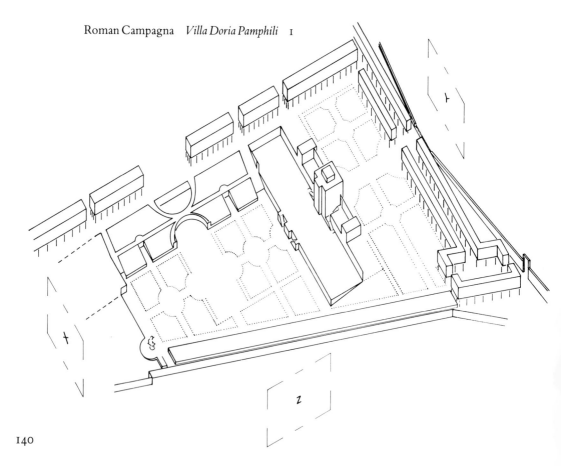

joining land and transformed into a country estate. With the new casino a terraced garden was laid out on the north-south alignment. West of it was an extensive *bosco* which was divided into two strips of land. The northern part along the Via Aurelia contained an orangery, fountains, sculptures, the old Casino della Famiglia with its own small garden, and a large field surrounded by trees. The southern strip consisted of a large, widely admired *pinetum* (pine wood) that gave the impression of an enormous columned hall. The terrain south of this *pinetum* and the casino garden were laid out as a menagerie. In it was a large oval-shaped lake, bordered by trees and with an island in its middle. The lake was connected to the fountain of the lilies (the Giglio fountain) and a water theatre in the *bosco* by means of a canal cut diagonally through the *pinetum*. A number of old Roman sarcophagi on the site were given a place in the *bosco*. The scheme in general was intended to compete in size and luxury with the other large seventeenth-century villa in Rome, the Villa Borghese.

The layout of the terrace of the *giardino segreto* was changed several times during the seventeenth and eighteenth centuries. In 1792 Francesco Bettini added a cascade to the Giglio fountain. In the nineteenth century the grounds of the villa were considerably expanded to the west, and in the east the site of the old Villa Corsini was incorporated. The villa suffered extensive damage during the French siege of 1849. In 1856 Andrea Doria Pamphili decided to transform the layout into the English style, with its associated variety of trees and shrubs. After 1945 the estate became the property of the state and the garden was opened to the public. In 1985 the casino was once again restored.

In what follows we shall discuss the plan and the spatial organization of the garden near the new casino as it appears in the engraving by S. F. Delino (which dates from around 1654). Another of the names of the villa was 'Belrespiro'. The casino is situated on the highest point of the site on the Via Aurelia. From there to the north, the south and, to a lesser extent, to the east, distant views predominate (fig. 1, 2). To the north there is a view of the Vatican and the dome of St Peter's set against the background of Monte

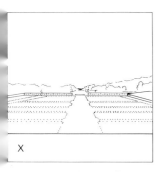

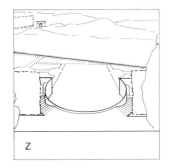

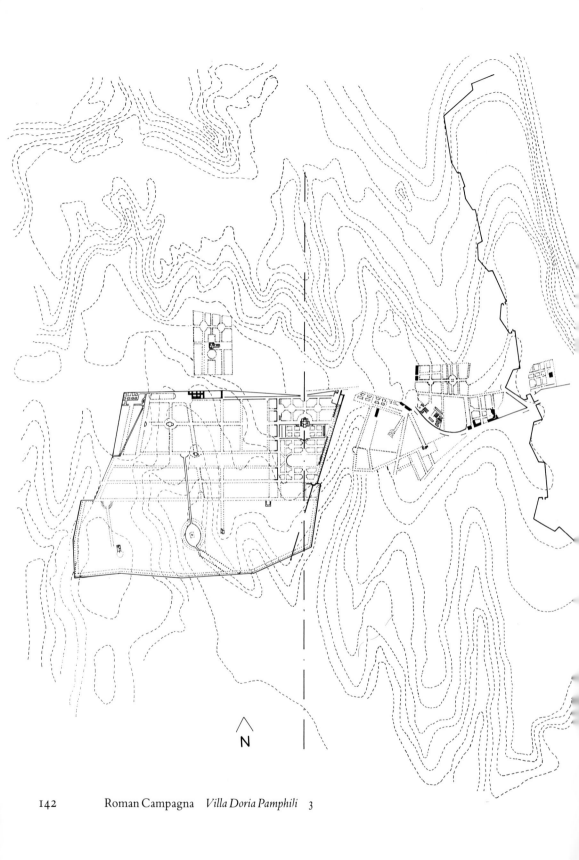

N

Roman Campagna   *Villa Doria Pamphili*   4

Mario. This view is separated from the rest of the city by the screening effect of the intervening hills. To the south the Campagna can be viewed up to the point where Monte Cavo is outlined above the Alban hills. On the flat top of this hill in the visual axis of the villa stood an old temple of Jupiter Latiarius.

Within the villa grounds this north–south visual axis was further developed as an axis of symmetry (fig. 3). The mirror symmetry of this axis is bounded by the east and west boundaries of the garden, and these were treated in different ways. The axis linked the rectangular terrace and the casino to the front and rear gardens. The direction of the axis is accentuated because the casino, as a unit, is pushed forward out of the plane of this terrace, while, at the rear, the loggia projects from the plane of the façade. Inside the grounds of the villa the main axis and the diagonal axis linked the garden with the large-scale *bosco*, the *pinetum* and the menagerie.

On the basis of the engraving by Delino a hypothetical reconstruction of the geometrical plan is possible. Similarities in the structure and dimensions of the floor plan (*piano nobile*) and the casino façade are striking (fig. 5). The square (module) which is derived from this can also be recognized in the villa plan as a whole, for example, in the way in which the cross axes are fixed. Furthermore, the vertical dimensions in the front and rear elevations can be traced to the depth of the front and rear gardens.

The casino was placed like a screen perpendicular to the north–south axis. In Algardi's original plan this was further accentuated by two side wings. From the steps on the Via Aurelia all attention is drawn towards the north elevation, which consists of three layers. The portico, whose arch continues into the second layer of the casino, accentuates the ceremonial nature of the entrance. The loggia above it opens the view to the north

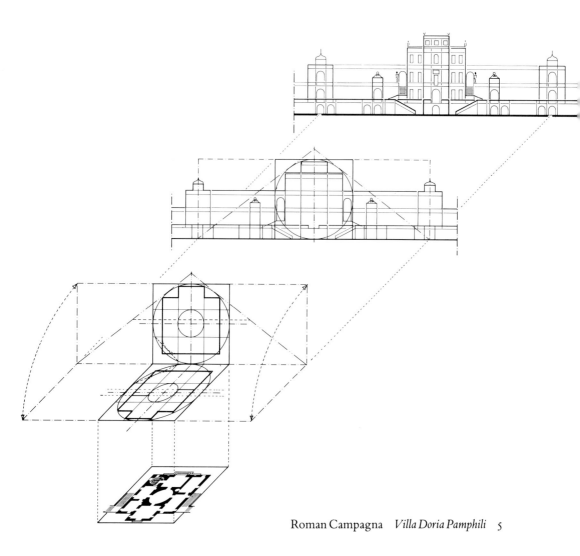

Roman Campagna *Villa Doria Pamphili* 5

over the aqueduct along the Via Aurelia. This view is framed by the screens of trees along the drive.

Through the portico a hall leads to the circular salon, with the most important rooms grouped around it. In the loggia to the south of the salon it becomes clear that the casino is set into the slope of the site. The loggia looks out over the rectangular terrace of the *giardino segreto* at the level of the basement, which houses the servants' quarters. From that point there is a view of the *giardino basso*, which is one level lower. Due to the narrowing and descending site this garden seems to continue into the *bosco*, the menagerie and, over this, into the Alban hills on the southern horizon. Looking back from the *giardino basso* the terrace wall with the grotto of the *giardino segreto* seems to form the base of the rear elevation, which thus seems to consist of five layers.

The most important view to the east is initiated in the rotunda of the unfinished *teatro* on the western edge of the *giardino basso*; this is the view over the deep valley, bordering the garden diagonally on its east side, to the old Villa Corsini. A triumphal arch now indicates the location of this vanished villa. Within the enclosed terrain of the villa, nature was represented by the sequence of garden, *bosco* and menagerie hunting grounds. The casino garden was a theatre, representative of the spatial continuity between the garden and the surrounding landscape. Inside the garden the views were framed by visual axes. Outside, the horizon was defined by buildings at the vanishing points of the visual axes.

VILLA DORIA PAMPHILI

Via San Pancrazio
Rome

Open: 9.00 to sunset
Casino not open to public

LITERATURE

I. Belli Barsali & M.G. Branchetti, *Ville della Campagna Romana*. Milan 1975.
M.L. Gothein, *A History of Garden Art*. New York 1979.
A. Schiavo, *Villa Doria Pamphili*. Milan 1942.

Villa d'Este

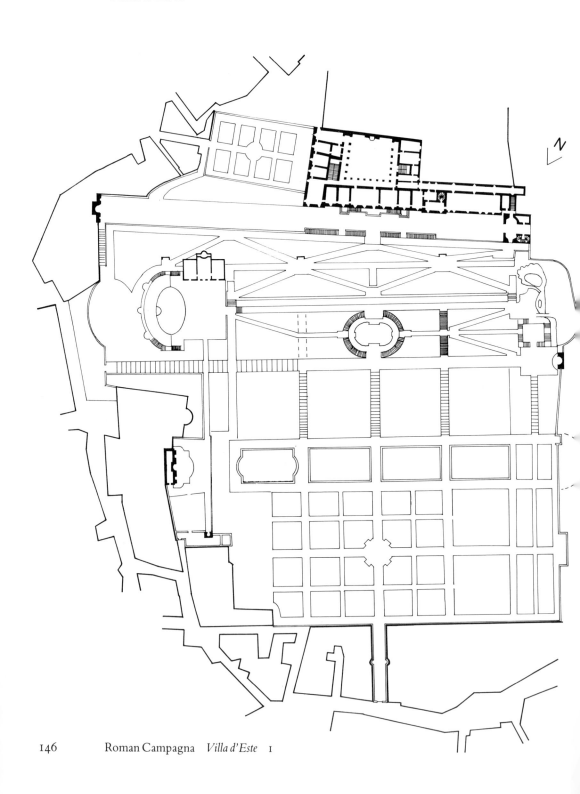

Roman Campagna   *Villa d'Este*   2

In 1550 Ippolito d'Este II (1509-72), cardinal of Ferrara and also a patron of the arts and a keen collector of antiques, was appointed governor of Tivoli, 30 km. to the north-east of Rome, by Pope Julius II. His residence there was a thirteenth-century Franciscan monastery, situated on a hillside. It was built on the western wall of the city, between the Porta S. Crucis and the Porta Romana, where the ground slopes down in a north-westerly direction to the Valle Gaudente. Because of its healthy air Tivoli had been a favoured resort for well-to-do Romans since ancient times. In the vicinity are the ruins of villas such as those of Hadrian, Quintilius and Varro. Cardinal d'Este, with these examples in mind, bought up gardens and vineyards on the hillside and a monastery, with the intention of transforming the whole area into a villa. The introverted character of the original monastery complex can still be felt in the *giardino segreto*, the former cloister garden, with its modest plan and restricted views of the outside world. In the developments which followed, the complex became more extensive and extrovert. Ippolito's wish was to surpass the achievements of his rival, Cardinal Farnese at Caprarola. Just as at the Villa Farnese at Caprarola, the Villa d'Este also contained an additional element: close to the small village of Bagni di Tivoli a *barco* was laid out in which an extensive hunting lodge was constructed. Ippolito was advised in the design of the villa by the archaeologist-architect Pirro Ligorio, who had studied the ruins of Villa Hadriana and who had assisted him with his archaeological purchases and excavations.

Around 1565 the sloping site was excavated and filled in such a way that terraces were created, with the city wall acting as a retaining wall. At the same time, an aqueduct from Monte S. Angelo and an underground canal from the River Anio were constructed. This ensured a constant water supply of 1200 litres a second. The terraced gardens were laid out during the next seven years. The addition of a double loggia on the garden side gave the monastery the appearance of a country residence. Several years later a dining loggia was built at the base of the building at the south-west point of the upper terrace.

After Ippolito's death the villa passed into the hands of his cousin Luigi. For most of the seventeenth century the villa remained the property of the Este family and the garden was well-maintained. During this period Bernini designed the Bicchierione (shell) Fountain and the waterfall between the water organ and the fishponds. During the eighteenth century the villa deteriorated; it was put up for sale in 1743 and in 1750 the antique statues began to be sold off. This is why in 1803, when the male line of the Este family died out and the complex came into Habsburg hands through Maria Beatrice d'Este, archduchess of Austria, almost all the antique statues had been removed from the building and the garden. Some of them can still be seen in the Museo Capitolino in Rome.

The villa continued to be neglected until 1850, when a German priest, Gustav Adolf von Hohenlohe, was allowed to live in the villa on condition that he maintain it. After the death of von Hohenlohe in 1896 the House of Habsburg again became responsible for the villa. After the First World War the Villa d'Este became the property of the Italian state. Although the garden has remained for the most part intact, most of the hedges, as well as the statues, have disappeared, the pergolas have been demolished, the fountains are overgrown with moss and ferns, and the cypresses have grown tall. Nature, freed from its restraints, has given to the garden a romantic 'patina'.

The original approach to the villa was from below, from the north-west, along the street which joins the Porta Romana (fig. 1). In this street there was an entrance gate on the main axis of the villa. Flanked by fountains and high walls one proceeded to the lowest terrace of the garden and a cruciform pergola from which the villa could not be seen. At the sides of the lowest terrace were four labyrinths. Where the two pergolas in the centre of the terrace used to intersect, a roundel of cypresses was later planted, and from here the villa is now displayed in all its magnificence. Since the slope is today hidden behind high cypresses and pines the building seen from the reflecting fishponds seems to be symmetrical, with its central part composed of an impressive series of vertical porticoes. The porticoes on the successive terraces of the garden form, in perspective, a single unity with the double loggia of the building. It also seems as if the path to the house continues along the main axis. On the second terrace, at the Fountain of the Dragon, it is impossible to continue along the axis, however, and one has to take the circular steps around the fountain. These lead to the third terrace, the Avenue of the Hundred Fountains. There one loses sight of the building, movement is directed sideways and one has to walk along the entire terrace in order to return to the main axis by means of one of the diagonal

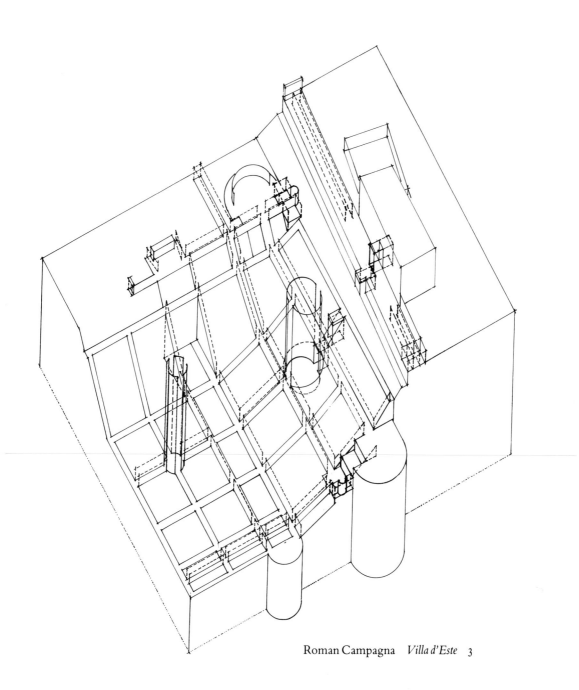

Roman Campagna   *Villa d'Este*   3

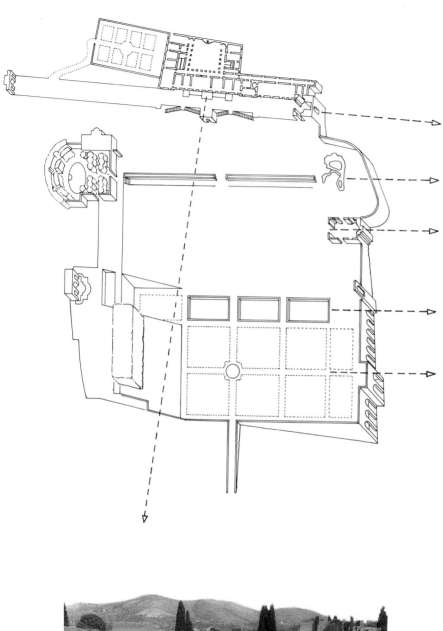

ramps. The main axis is discovered, almost by accident, at the Fountain of Pandora, and one can proceed by means of a set of steps to the fourth level, the terrace, in front of the house. Due to the manipulation of visual impressions and the enforced detour in its approach, the villa, which, as seen from the lowest level, appeared to be a comprehensible axial scheme, is step by step revealed as an ambiguous mysterious complex (fig. 3).

Today the garden is entered through the former monastery courtyard at the centre of the building on top of the hill. The plan of the house is detached from the axiality of the grounds. To reach the terrace at the foot of the building one has to walk in a south-westerly direction through a succession of rooms and, at the end, descend two floors by means of a spiral staircase. One comes out at an indeterminate point on the terrace, where there is hardly any incentive to enter the main axis. The building and the central axis are linked by means of the loggia on the *piano nobile*, attached asymmetrically to the central salon. The appearance of the garden axis on the balcony comes as a surprise. Because of the steep slope, this main axis, which seemed so dominant when seen from the garden below, is only of subordinate significance in the total concept. The garden as a whole is no more than a foreground to a much broader panorama. Moreover, the axis is not placed exactly at right angles to the garden elevation but points, at a slight angle, towards one of the Sabine hilltops on the horizon (fig. 4). In this way the villa is related to the enormous space of the landscape by a single wide gesture over the garden.

The natural slope of the terrain is formalized throughout the whole garden by the transverse direction. It is used to relate the garden to the outside landscape even at the scale of its constituent parts. On the highest terrace this relationship is brought under control architecturally by the portico of the dining loggia at the south-west end. This frames the panorama of the landscape towards the city of Rome, which can be seen in the distance on a clear day.

The Avenue of the Hundred Fountains forms a second important cross axis. It is terminated on the Tivoli side by the Oval Fountain with the water theatre and the grotto of Venus. On the city-wall side it is terminated by the Fountain of the Owl and the Rometta, a miniature version of Rome. A third important transverse axis is formed by the series of fishponds. Originally these were fed from the cascade of the water organ. The water would have disappeared into a lake outside the city wall by way of the Fountain of Neptune.

Within the garden visual contact with the landscape is not so much brought about by means of the main axis, which, seen from the garden, is closed off, but by means of the transverse axes. These divert attention away from the small town of Tivoli towards Rome. Both edges of the garden are elaborately treated, forming two independent series of attractions. The playful effect was enhanced by the very complex use of water elements, such as a waterfall, a curtain of water with rainbows, jets, reflecting surfaces, and the use of water-driven *automata* and *giochi d'aqua*. The water organ produced the sound of trumpets, the Fountain of the Dragon caused gun and musket shots to ring out and, in the Fountain of the Owl, bronze birds twittered until, suddenly, an owl appeared and began to hoot mournfully.

Thus separated from daily reality the visitor could imagine himself to be in an unearthly paradise. This, indeed, was probably Cardinal d'Este's intention. His coat of arms showed a white eagle with the three golden apples of the Hesperides. The Villa d'Este is an allegorical representation of the Garden of the Hesperides, which, itself, is a mythical interpretation of earthly paradise. Hercules had to perform his heroic deed within this garden: the retrieval of the three golden apples. The visitor can experience Hercules' struggle for the three divine virtues himself since the cardinal also expressed moral contradiction in the transverse direction of the garden. Thus the Grotto of Venus (Voluptas) at the Oval Fountain forms the counterpart of the Grotto of Diana (Virtus) below the dining loggia. The passage from Venus to Diana and vice versa is accompanied by the hundred stucco reliefs that portray the metamorphoses of Ovid in the Avenue of the Hundred Fountains. From the side, the scene of the battle is surveyed by the winged Pegasus, high over the Pegasus Fountain (above the Oval Fountain) on the hill of Tivoli, making ready to ascend Mount Parnassus.

This relationship between heathen myth and Christian philosophy completes Cardinal Ippolito d'Este's programme of connecting in an ambiguous way the exuberance of the villa ideal with the restraint of a monastery.

VILLA D'ESTE

Tivoli

Open: 9.30–sunset
Closed Mondays
Fee

LITERATURE

D.R. Coffin, *The Villa d'Este at Tivoli*. Princeton 1960.
M.L. Gothein, *A History of Garden Art*. New York 1979.
J.F. Groos, *Villa d'Este*. Delft 1987.
G. Jellicoe & S. Jellicoe, *The Oxford Companion to Gardens*. Oxford & New York 1986.
C. Lamb, *Die Villa d'Este in Tivoli*. Munich 1966.
P. Ligorio, *L'Antiquità*. Rome c.1560.
E. Panofsky, *Hercules am Scheidewege*. Leipzig 1930.
Venturini, *Le fontane del Giardino Estese in Tivoli*. Rome n.d.

Villa Farnese

From the beginning of the fifteenth century the lands around Caprarola had been in the hands of the Farnese family and were used for hunting by, among others, Cardinal Alessandro I Farnese. Around 1532, a few years after the sack of Rome, the cardinal commissioned Antonio da Sangallo to build a fortified country residence at Caprarola. From 1532 to 1536 Sangallo, together with Baldassare Peruzzi, designed this *rocca* in the form of a pentagon, typical of Tuscan fortifications. For reasons which are no longer known, building activity ceased for twenty years after Peruzzi's death in 1536. In 1546 Sangallo also died. Vignola, a pupil of these two architects, inherited the profitable connection with the Farnese family.

In 1556, as soon as Vignola had completed the Villa Giulia in Rome for Pope Julius III, Cardinal Alessandro II Farnese commissioned him to resume the building of a palazzo at Caprarola. For this the pentagonal foundation was taken as the starting point (fig. 1). Work on site commenced in 1557. Three years later the cardinal was already in residence and the Zuccari

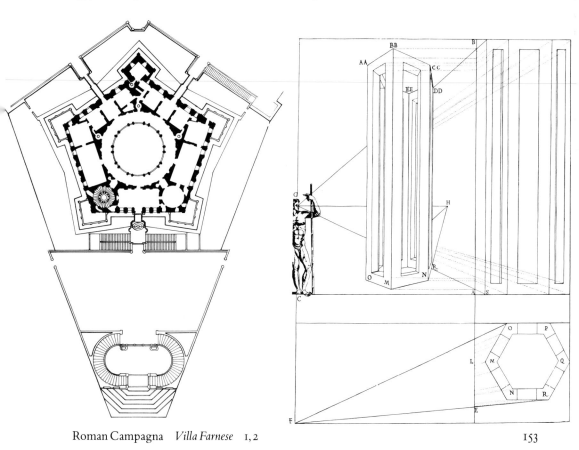

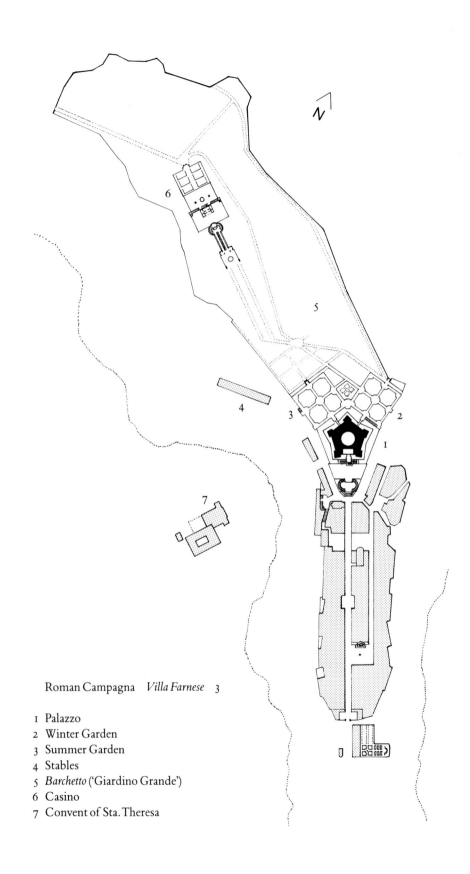

Roman Campagna *Villa Farnese* 3

1 Palazzo
2 Winter Garden
3 Summer Garden
4 Stables
5 *Barchetto* ('Giardino Grande')
6 Casino
7 Convent of Sta. Theresa

Roman Campagna   *Villa Farnese*   4

studio had started work on the paintings. By the time of Vignola's death in 1573 the building was complete except for the top storey. Of the two gardens the Summer Garden was finished and the Winter Garden was completed in 1579. According to Benedetti the steps in front of the front square were added at a later date by del Duca, who was also to design the casino in the Giardino Grande.

The Villa Farnese is not a true villa in the strictest sense of the word. It was used as a permanent residence and contained a large number of apartments for guests and their retainers. As such the building can better be described as a palazzo.

The formal scheme of the total architectural system is typified by a marked axiality. By this means the main compositional elements of horizon, city, forecourt, building, inner courtyard, garden, *barchetto* and landscape are all aligned with each other (fig. 3). These elements remain autonomous however; in reality they can never all be perceived at a single glance. The elements are only linked to each other when movement takes place. The true structuring principle is the architectural route. By this means the inner courtyard, situated within the closed volume of the palace, is incorporated into a series of open spaces. The architectural route becomes a necessary precondition for the comprehension of the system in all its complexity. This design, with the help of movement and perspective, puts an end to the concept of finite and continuous space: space becomes 'unreal' and discontinuous. Logical perception of perspective disintegrates and an illusionary perspective appears. Perspective stage sets, such as those designed for the theatre, by Serlio for example, are arranged in a calculated optical series. An ambiguous theatre comes into existence: the palace turns out to have more than one face – or rather mask.

The architectural drawings of Vignola published in his *Le due regole della prospettiva pratica* demonstrate how he was able to command and manipulate the structure of perspective (fig. 2). He distances himself from the position in which perspective is controlled by the eye. This position is transferred in his drawing to an individual who is situated in the drawing itself and who, in one case, takes on the appearance of a stage actor. By doing this Vignola goes beyond the limitations of early Renaissance perspective. In addition to the image first presented there is, concealed, another which is revealed by movement through the drawing.

Theatre at the Villa Farnese begins at the foot of the steps below the forecourt. There, where the narrow road which runs through the village opens out on to a small square, the observer is presented with an image of the building: a square façade, divided into three storeys, with the lower half heavily rusticated and the upper part smoothly stuccoed (fig. 6a). The whole has a harmonious structure. The middle section has, consecutively, from below to above, three, five and seven openings and is flanked by two continuous side elements. This image is, however, an illusion; it disappears as soon as one moves towards the object. It consists in fact of two screens which are linked together in perspective by the eye (fig. 6b). Screen 1 is the entrance to the grotto beneath the forecourt. Screen 2 is the front façade of the palazzo itself; the visual obstacle provided by screen 1, however, prevents a view of all but the top two storeys (fig. 5). In order to construct a new image of the real situation it is necessary to leave the axis and climb to a higher level by way of the two semicircular sets of steps, whose direction is transverse to that of the axial system.

On the forecourt a new scene is presented and the palazzo reveals its second face. Movement now leads to the building. Just before one enters the palazzo by way of a bridge across a dry ditch, an opening between two buildings on the south side of the square permits a view of an element in the natural landscape: the Convent of Sta. Theresa on the opposite side of the valley.

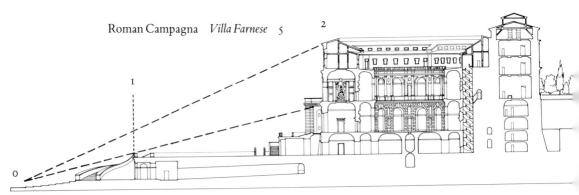

Roman Campagna *Villa Farnese* 5

Once inside the palazzo, after passing through the entrance hall one climbs the spiral staircase, whose dynamism is continued in the painted ceiling. The staircase begins beside the lobby in the basement. It was possible to enter the building by horse-drawn coach at the level of the forecourt. An entrance gate was located on the south-east side of the square. A circuit was provided in the basement of the building to enable the coaches to be turned round. The stair treads were designed to be climbed on horseback. At its upper end this staircase gives access to the circular courtyard in the centre of the palazzo. The apartments are situated in the solid, massive shell around this internal open space. Dynamism is brought temporarily to rest; here, time stands still and unity of place and time hold sway.

From the loggia of the Hercules Chamber possession is taken of distance. Looking back over the town of Caprarola, the Farnese domains seem to stretch out towards the horizon since a dip in the terrain at the edge of the town makes it seem as if the axial access route continues to infinity. The construction of this route split the town so radically in two that the inhabitants called the two halves Corsica and Sardinia.

In the Hercules Chamber the walls are painted with images depicting the four seasons and ten of the Farnese family's estates. The painted ceiling shows one of the two myths of Hercules, the hero with whom the Farnese rulers wished to identify. The murals in the remaining rooms form an iconographic programme. The spectator is involved in the drama of the real or imaginary acts of heroism of the Farnese family. The building is nothing but theatre: there is one room in which the echo scarcely fades away at all and whisperings are suddenly heard from unexpected corners. To the rear of the building there are two square gardens. They are higher up the slope than the palazzo and are connected to it by bridges. The Summer Garden and Winter Garden were originally laid out in different ways, creating an

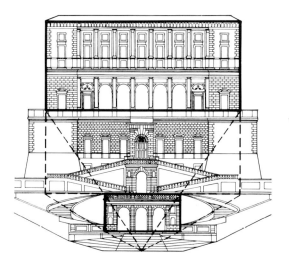
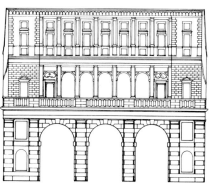

obvious asymmetry in the axial system. The differences were primarily derived from their respective situations. The Summer Garden, facing north to take advantage of the shadow of the palazzo, offered the possibility of relief from the heat by means of three fountains (one of which is the covered Venus Fountain). The Winter Garden, on the west side, had a wooden pergola which covered the link between the palazzo and a cool grotto. On the slope above was a viewing terrace.

A number of the fountains and the wooden pergola no longer exist, and the different arrangements in the plan as depicted in one of the murals at Villa Lante have disappeared. The grotto, however, still survives, as does the viewing terrace above. From here a view of the valley is offered diagonally across the geometrical pattern of the garden. Once again, a panorama becomes part of the system as an aesthetic image. If one looks over one's shoulder one imagines the surrounding Cimini hills to be incorporated into the domain of the garden. Although the extensive *barchetto* is surrounded by a wall, it gives the impression of merging into the wooded hills.

In the scheme of Caprarola it is possible to detect the source of the introduction of movement into the plan. A number of landscape elements outside the actual bounds of the garden are incorporated into the axially-determined hierarchical planning in a series of separate scenes.

The casino, situated further up the garden, is dealt with separately.

VILLA FARNESE

Caprarola

Open: 9.00-12.30, 14.30-17.30
Closed Mondays
Fee

LITERATURE

S. Benedetti, *Giacomo Del Duca e l'architettura del Cinquecento*. Rome 1972.
M. W. Casotti, *Il Vignola*, 2 vols. Trieste 1960.
D. R. Coffin, *The Villa in the Life of Renaissance Rome*. Princeton 1979.
C. Constant, 'Mannerist Rome', *A.D. Profiles 20* 49 (1979), pp. 19-22.
P. Portoghesi, *Rome of the Renaissance*. London 1972.

Casino Farnese

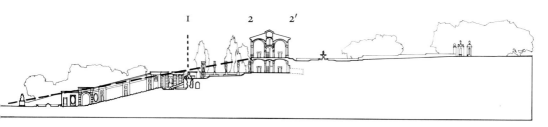

Roman Campagna   *Casino Farnese*   I

After the completion of the palazzo and the two square gardens behind it, Cardinal Farnese directed his attention towards the thickly-wooded *barchetto*, the Giardino Grande, behind the villa. Here, beside a path through the *bosco*, was the Fountain of the Goat (mythologically connected with the small town of Caprarola; the Italian word for goat is *capra*).

Immediately after the building of the stables (1581-84) along the road to Viterbo the cardinal decided to build an outdoor dining area in the woods. A friend, Cardinal Gambara of the nearby Villa Lante, remarked in a letter, however, that at their age it was more desirable to eat in the shade of a loggia, and he recommended that a casino should stand above the fountain; this would serve to offer both protection for dining in its loggia and a view, in which one might also enjoy the fountain, towards Caprarola. This advice was followed and in 1586 the construction of the casino, fountains and an intimate garden in the wood was almost finished. The design was probably by the Sicilian architect Giacomo del Duca (1520-1601), who was probably also involved in the completion of the Orti Farnesiani on the Palatine. Evidence to support the latter hypothesis is provided by a painting on the wall of the ground-floor loggia in the casino at Caprarola in which a casino is portrayed, the design of which appears to be a hybrid of the designs for the casino as actually constructed and the Orti Farnesiani at Rome.

Around 1620 the architect Girolamo Rainaldi (1570-1655) introduced some radical changes to the immediate surroundings of the casino. He added the rusticated grottoes at the entrance to the complex and changed the layout of the terrace in front of the casino. It was during these activities that the caryatids, designed by Pietro Bernini in the shape of satyr herms bearing vases on their heads, were also placed on this terrace.

A path leads through the wood to the casino from a small diamond-shaped garden concealed behind the two square gardens at the rear of the palazzo (Roman Campagna, Villa Farnese, fig. 3). The linear path follows the shape of the hills and has a bend in the middle. On leaving the densely-wooded path one encounters an open space at the foot of the cascade, and

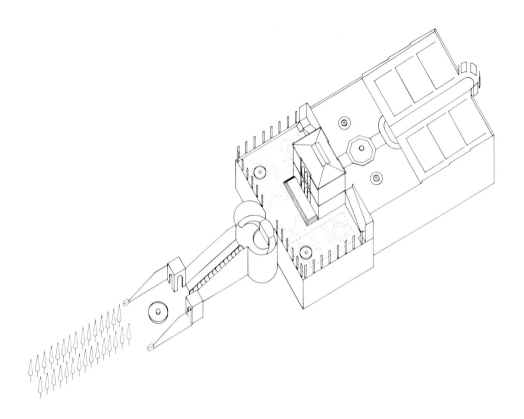

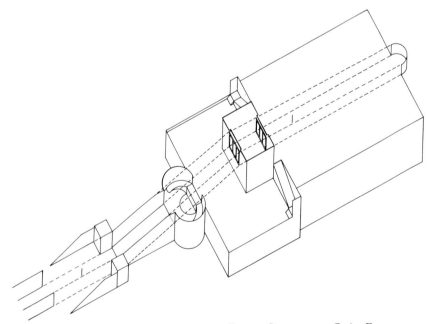

Roman Campagna *Casino Farnese* 2, 3

Roman Campagna   *Casino Farnese*   4

from here the casino looks like a small building with a loggia on a rusticated base. Like the palazzo, however, the casino also appears to have several faces (fig.1). In the design of the casino and the surrounding garden the scheme of the main palace is repeated. Climbing the steps alongside the Fountain of the Vase to the plateau on which the casino stands, the building seems to consist of two storeys (fig.3). It is surrounded by a closed garden room, whose intimate inward-looking character is reinforced by the later additions of the caryatids and the benches between them. This *giardino segreto*, traditionally placed adjacent to the main system, is here placed on the main axis. Yet in the way in which the perspective is designed, it remains 'invisible' until the last moment. The caryatids, the 'guardians of the secret garden', bear on their heads the imaginary ceiling of this hidden storey. From this garden a further ascent by way of the ramps or the casino leads to a still higher area, where there used to be a magnificent flower garden. There the casino suddenly takes on its original form: the one storey construction with loggia. The revelation of a moment ago is called into doubt.

As with the palazzo the symmetry at the rear of the casino is modified. From the flower garden one diagonal view is closed off (because of the sloping terrain and planting), while the other is opened out towards the panorama of the valley. Apart from these similarities between the casino and the palazzo, the organization of the ground plan of the casino complex is very similar to that of the Villa Lante at Bagnaia. At both villas there is a spatial widening, though at the Villa Lante it occurs while descending the slope and at the Casino Farnese while climbing it. The two grottoes and the extended walls at the bottom of the cascade, however, cancel out this difference to a certain extent. The bottom part of the casino complex seems to be a miniature version of the Villa Lante. The same elements recur in practically the same sequence: spring, the two river gods, the cascade (*catena d'aqua*), the two small buildings (grottoes), and the flat mirror pond in a square area. In this part, just as at the Villa Lante, the spatial widening follows the direction in which the water flows. Furthermore, whereas at the Villa Lante the garden continues between the two symmetrically-placed building volumes, the continuous movement at the Casino Farnese seems to be intentionally blocked. There is, nevertheless, a directional element: picking up the line of the forest path, continuing over the cascade, then rising until it pushes forward, through the loggias of the first floor and on to the highest plane (fig. 2). Here it is finally checked and shattered by a fragmented exedra. This direction is also accentuated in the detailing of the façade and in the roof of the casino.

THE 'BARCO' The complete Villa Farnese complex contained a third element. Cardinal Farnese owned a hunting ground, or *barco*, laid out in 1569, on the old road to Rome. A painting in the Casino Gambara at the Villa Lante shows a lake surrounded by straight rows of trees and, next to it on a small hill, a hunting lodge (fig. 5). This small building, designed by Vignola in 1569, is of a type similar to the Villa Vecchia in Frascati and the Casino Gambara in Bagnaia, which he designed in 1568.

CASINO FARNESE

Caprarola

Open: 10.00-11.30, 15.00-17.00
Closed Mondays

LITERATURE

I. Belli Barsali, *Ville di Roma*. Milan 1983.
S. Benedetti, *Giacomo Del Duca e l'architettura del Cinquecento*. Rome 1972.
D.R. Coffin, *The Villa in the Life of Renaissance Rome*. Princeton 1979.
J.C. Shepherd & G.A. Jellicoe, *Italian Gardens of the Renaissance*. London 1986.

Roman Campagna   *Casino Farnese*   5

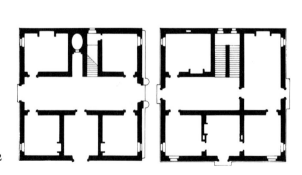

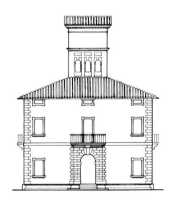

Villa Giulia

Preliminary work on the building of the Villa Giulia began in 1550, immediately after the election of Cardinal Giovanni Maria Ciocchi del Monte as Pope Julius III. In accordance with his new status he ordered the building of an extensive villa complex. Before his appointment he already owned a villa and several country estates along the Via Flaminia, just outside the Porta del Populo, the city gate on the north side of Rome. From 1550 onwards this property was rapidly extended to include the vineyards in the immediate surroundings until it comprised all the hills between the Aurelian wall and the Ponte Milvio. Within a relatively short time it could compete with the Villa Madama on the other side of the Tiber.

The villa site included a small strip of land along the River Tiber, and the building of a new harbour provided a direct connection between the villa and the Vatican Palace. A covered passage connected the Vatican with Castel Sant-Angelo, from where a ceremonial boat that transported the Pope and his guests to his country residence departed. From the mooring place a pergola led to a gate on the Via Flaminia that gave access to the garden grounds (fig. 1).

Some of the most famous architects of the time were engaged on the project. The original concept was probably developed by Giorgio Vasari

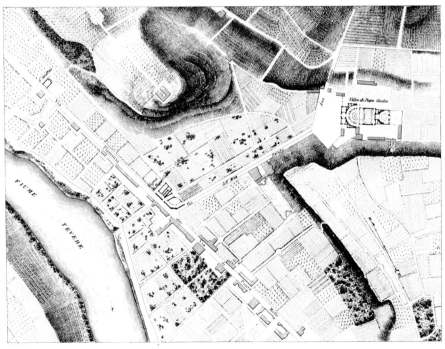

Roman Campagna   *Villa Giulia*   1

(1511-74), while Michelangelo, who was working at St Peter's, acted as adviser. Vignola and Ammannati, both still at the beginning of their careers, worked on the central part of the villa. Vignola was responsible for the building of the casino and for engineering the waterworks of the sunken nymphaeum. Ammannati was responsible for the nymphaeum itself and the courtyard connecting it to the casino.

The situation of the villa is remarkable. The house was not placed on top of a hill, but low in a side valley of the Tiber that ran in a north-westerly direction. The two directions, arising from a bend in the valley, meet each other at the point where a long entrance drive ends at the forecourt of the villa. As the avenue is laterally defined by trees, it only becomes apparent at the very last moment that it does not lie in the main axis of the villa but follows the bend in the valley. Because of this bend in the axis it seems as if the villa, no matter from which direction it is viewed, is situated in a broad enclosed valley (fig. 2). The villa is not, however, only an object against the background of the natural landscape; the landscape is also integrated into the architectural treatment of the villa plan, which extends as far as the eye can see. Nothing is left to chance. The slopes were completely covered with trees by the landscape architect Jacopo Meneghini. Ammannati reported in one of his letters that from 1550 onwards 36,000 trees of various species were planted.

The architecture of the villa, with its main building and a series of garden courtyards behind it, shows a clear allusion to the design of the Cortile del Belvedere of Julius II, while the semicircular enclosure of the first courtyard is reminiscent of the Villa Madama. Following these two large

Roman Campagna *Villa Giulia* 2

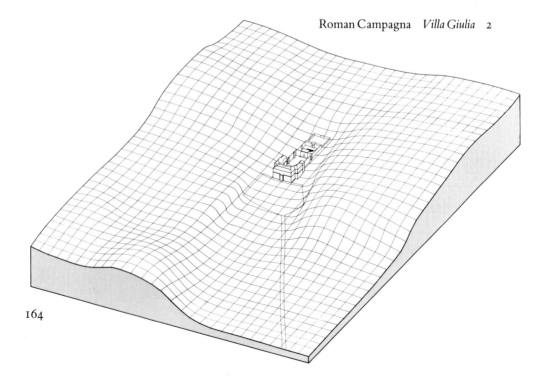

Roman Campagna   *Villa Giulia*   3

early Mannerist designs, which were built in the same area as the Villa Giulia, a spatial scheme was developed in which a synthesis between architecture and landscape arose, and which heralded a more mature period of Mannerism.

Whereas the building at the Villa Madama acts as a gateway to the garden, in the Villa Giulia the transition from building to garden is less immediate. The courtyards, as a series of voids, are developed to such an extent that the architecture of the building becomes the frame for the garden itself.

Vignola's fondness for the use of the façade as *decorum* is discernable in the contrast between the front and rear elevations of the house. The openness of the villa towards the landscape is not evident at first sight; the severe, closed front elevation of the villa is directed towards the square and has a clearly representative function. The triumphal arch motif in the centre of this façade is repeated in the rear elevation and thus forms the link between the two sides. The playful rear elevation has the character of an inner façade because the treatment of the concave shape refers directly to the interior of the Pantheon (fig. 5a, b). (Vignola also effected a transformation of the exterior of the Pantheon with his design for the Tempietto di S. Andrea, built in the grounds of the villa along the Via Flaminia. His fascination with the Pantheon was finally rewarded when it became his last resting place.) Facing this apparent inner façade the central section of the garden manifests itself as a series of inner spaces, and the sense of intimacy of both the building as well as the garden behind it is intensified. As an additional element the surrounding landscape also forms part of the composition. The interaction between the architecture of the house and the garden, as well as the surrounding landscape, are central to this design and has been treated in a great number of different ways.

The main elements are organized geometrically on the central axis in a linear series of screens and perspectives. From the building towards the hill the openings in the screens widen and the volume of the elements and the height of the walls decrease. This increasing transparency is also given material form by the gradual transition from stone to vegetation (fig. 4). From the hill towards the casino the extent of the vegetation diminishes, to end as thin as a lawyer of painted plaster at the colonnade, suggesting a green-covered pergola. It is only from the first floor of the building that there is an accurate view over all the walls and that the view over the central axis is directed towards the surrounding landscape, although the curved loggia had offered one an introduction towards the adjoining hills over the side gardens even before one had actually entered the garden.

In one of his letters Ammannati compares the building to a theatre and the garden to a proscenium and a stage. The play is initiated by the visitor himself; he is both spectator and actor in his progress through the plan. Movement is an essential condition for unveiling the spectacle.

Although the three middle garden courtyards are visually linked to each other on one axis, each consecutive space can only be reached by leaving the axis obliquely. Thus a tension between axis and route is created and even heightened by the vertical construction of the nymphaeum, which consists of three layers (fig. 6) and thereby forms a repetition of the tripartite division of the geometry of the entire garden layout (fig. 7). Opposite the semicircular colonnade in the main building an almost closed wall concealed this nymphaeum from the entrance. Only a small doorway in this wall (now replaced by three open arches) gave access to a loggia, offering a view over this sunken *giardino segreto* carved out of the rocks. Two paired ramps lead to the middle level, while two small staircases descending to the lowest level are hidden from view. From the intimacy of the lowest level of this hidden part of the garden, which is decorated with grottoes, a relationship with the broad valley is created by means of a sequence which broadens spatially and becomes increasingly transparent. The decorations too reinforce this sequence. The lowest floor is dominated by various water elements and by the surrounding mossy grottoes. On the edge of the middle level two enormous statues of river gods were placed in niches and four plane trees were planted around the open centre. On the highest level the

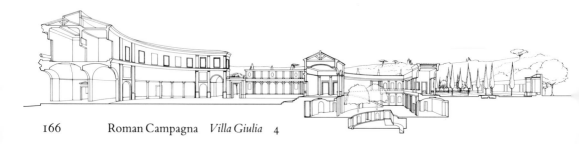

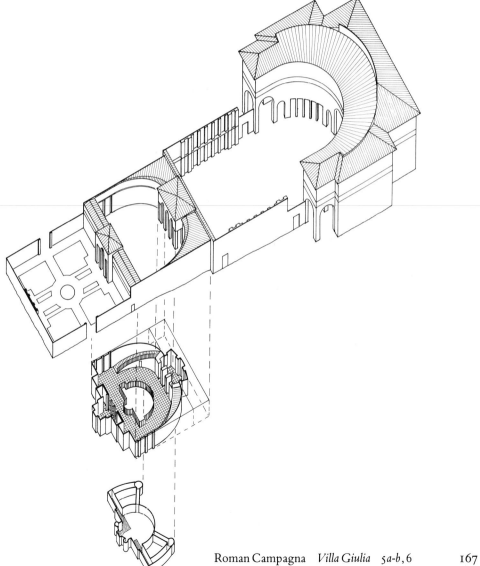

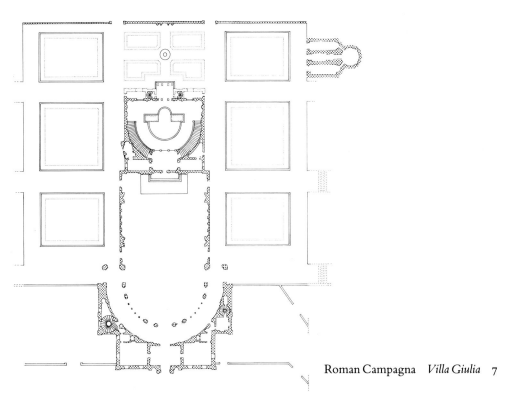

inner walls were painted with landscape scenes and the screen was broken open above the niches with two openings towards the sky; behind these birdcages were placed. Eventually the vegetation of the surrounding landscape became visible above the walls. In this villa the panorama is controlled as far as the horizon, not from above but from below.

The connection between the nymphaeum and the section at the very back was made by two small staircases, again hidden from view. These finally emerged next to the birdcages and were covered by small towers, whose shapes referred to the planned (but never executed) domes above the staircases of the main building. In the rearmost section the axis was stopped by means of a niche in the end wall, and it was only here, for the first time, that the full width of the plan was properly visible and emphasized. Movement was directed towards the sides, where there were several features along the boundary, including an ice cellar at the south side. The ridge of hills was also accessible from here by means of various paths that were articulated by accompanying statues or specific planting. In the wooded *barchetto* there were several arbours, birdcages and loggias marking the viewpoints from which one could see not only the villa itself in the valley below (fig. 8), but also the Vatican Palace, Castel Sant-Angelo and the Villa Madama. The lack of a panorama of Rome from the house was compensated for by the integration of these features into the plan of the villa.

The building of the villa was interrupted after the death of Julius iii in

1555. Some years later a number of changes were carried out by Pius IV, probably under the direction of Pirro Ligorio. The casino near the fountain on the corner of the Via Flaminia is also ascribed to him. Towards the end of the eighteenth century, however, during the restoration work carried out for Pius VI, some changes were made that seriously affected the nymphaeum; at its rear, for example, a loggia was added and the birdcages and the small staircase towers were bricked up. The villa also suffered greatly during the nineteenth and twentieth centuries from its constantly changing functions and from extensive changes in its urban setting: the wings added to the museum and the busy road around it now obscure the actual relationship between the villa and the landscape.

VILLA GIULIA

Museo Nazionale di Villa Giulia
Viale delle Belle Arti
Rome

Open: 9.00-14.00
Sundays: 9.00-13.00
Fee

LITERATURE

M. Bafile, *Villa Giulia, L'architettura – il giardino.* Istituto d'archeologia e storia dell'arte Opera d'arte, Fascicolo 14. Rome 1948.
I. Belli Barsali, *Ville di Roma.* Milan 1983.
M.W. Casotti, *Il Vignola*, 2 vols. Trieste 1960.
C. Constant, 'Mannerist Rome', *A.D. Profiles 20* 49 (1979), pp. 19-22.
P. Murray, *The Architecture of the Italian Renaissance.* London 1963.

Roman Campagna   *Villa Giulia*   8

Villa Giustiniani

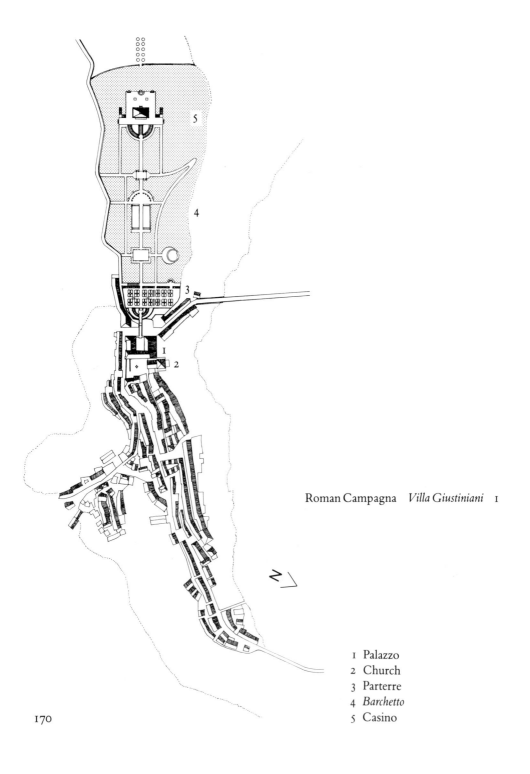

Roman Campagna   *Villa Giustiniani*   1

1 Palazzo
2 Church
3 Parterre
4 *Barchetto*
5 Casino

Roman Campagna   *Villa Giustiniani*   2

The history of Bassano goes back to the building of a castle there between 1150 and 1175. For more than two centuries this castle belonged to the Anguillara family, who extended it considerably between 1550 and 1590. It was probably during these alterations that the double loggia on the inner courtyard was added. This breaks the massiveness of the castle; the highest loggia looks over the courtyard wall. In 1595 Bassano became the property of Giuseppe Giustiniani. He died in 1599 and his only heir was his son Vincenzo Giustiniani (1564-1637), a rich Genoese nobleman who was a banker and a patron and collector of art. In 1601 he started alterations to the palazzo, finished in 1602 under the direction of the architect Pompeo Pozzichelli, and its transformation into a villa by laying out an extensive garden. Work on the garden lasted until 1610. For its design Vincenzo employed three architects, Carlo Maderno (1556-1629), Carlo Lambardi (1554-1620) and Girolamo Rainaldi (1570-1655). It is not known which architect was responsible for which section of the garden, but it seems that the design for the casino (also called *palazzina* or *rocca*) situated in it can best be ascribed to Lambardi. Although Maderno had more experience as an architect (having designed several villas in and around Rome) and Vincenzo greatly admired his work at St Peter's, Lambardi had already built two other villas in Rome for Vincenzo: one just outside the Porta del Populo (Via Flaminia) and the other 'al Laterano' (Via Boiardo). The elevational treatment and the floor plans of the latter resemble those of the casino in Bassano; they were built at virtually the same time (1607-18). In 1620 the villa owner also built a church, the Chiesa di S. Vincenzo, on a hill just outside Bassano. After Vincenzo's death the building of the church was continued by his adopted son, Prince Andrea Giustiniani. In 1854 the villa was bought by the Odescalchi family and has been their property ever since. The original design has, for

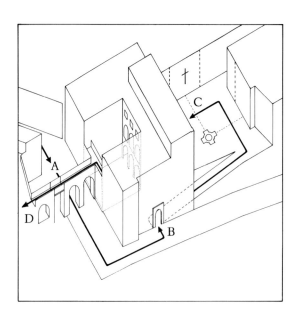

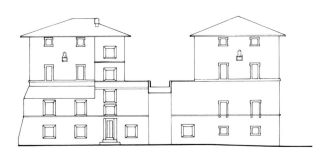

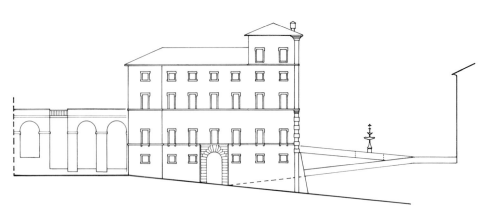

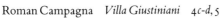

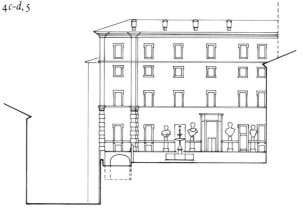

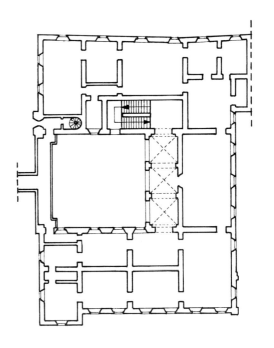

the greater part, been preserved, although the total complex is currently in a poor state.

The main building of the Villa Giustiniani is situated at the extreme end of the narrow hilltop on which the little linear town of Bassano lies (fig. 1). From this position the former medieval *castello* dominates not only the most important entrance to the small hill town, but also the entire urban context, by virtue of its dominant position on the square which connects it with the town. On this square the central axis seems to shift continually; sometimes it is the palazzo entrance that is central, and sometimes it is the fountain at the centre of the square marking the intersection of the axes of the town hall and the church (fig. 3). On one side the square is open, giving a view of the surrounding landscape. In this late-Mannerist villa rural life is placed in direct contrast to urban life. In its design, however, a new synthesis is achieved: the rural and the urban elements are reconciled to each other in a single formal structure. The linear structure of Bassano is continued in the design of this villa. The residential palazzo forms the focal point around which the garden and the village reflect each other (both are roughly equal in size); seen from the building they are complementary to each other.

At first sight this villa shows a great number of similarities to the Villa Farnese, built some decades previously at nearby Caprarola. The elements that are employed are the same: town, forecourt, residential palazzo with internal courtyard, bridge to parterre, *barchetto*, casino and landscape. Though it is likely that the architecture of Vignola and del Duca, with which the architects at Bassano were already well acquainted, served as a model for the design of the Villa Giustiniani, there are also distinct differences. In contrast to Caprarola one does not approach the Bassano villa axially. The approach road, with a bridge over the neighbouring valley, joins the axial system at right angles. A bend in the road, just before the palazzo, delays its perception until the last moment. It is only from the lower square that the building can be seen in its true proportions for the first time (fig. 3, position A). For this building, like Caprarola, seems to have different faces. By means of a complicated route the villa displays an unusual masquerade. From the square the building is presented as an enclosed, inaccessible *castello* with two clearly outlined towers (fig. 4a). The imposing bridge (leading to the garden) reinforces the fortified character. Going underneath the bridge and round the corner, the building has the appearance of a city wall (fig. 3, position B). The turreted character becomes less clear: whereas one side of the façade still slightly protrudes, the other side only suggests a tower by the modelling of the wall surface (fig. 4b). In the middle of the façade is a gate which leads by way of a ramp to the village square higher up. On this square (fig. 3, position c) the building looks like an urban palazzo (fig. 4c). Above the underpass the tower motif is repeated once more in the façade, only now in the lowest of low-reliefs.

Four busts (the four seasons) on the sides of the villa entrance form the symbolic introduction to the garden. After the public underpass the build-

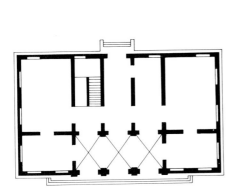

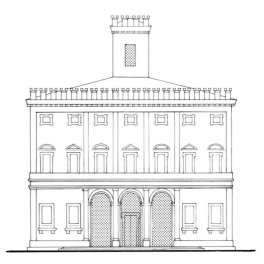

Roman Campagna   *Villa Giustiniani*   6

ing is entered for a second time; this time it is the private sections of the villa which are accessed. Climbing further up inside the building one enters the garden via a bridge. At the end of the bridge one climbs a set of steps to the parterre, and from there looking back (fig. 3, position c) the building gives the impression of a farm in the countryside (fig. 4*d*). Yet it is the same façade as the one already described in which the building appeared like a castle. 'Reality' is transformed by a change of viewpoint. Through the rotational routing system the building undergoes a metamorphosis and manifests itself in every direction in an appropriate manner. Indeed, the history of the villa can be read in this movement: the transformation from *castello* to palazzo and subsequently to villa. This development can also be traced in the plan: the enclosed courtyard was moved in the direction of the garden (the extent of the shift is the depth of the loggia, fig. 5) and is open to the garden on the first floor.

The design of the garden is characterized by a strong axial structure. Yet the design is clearly asymmetric (in contrast to the symmetry suggested in the engravings of Percier and Fontaine). In some places the natural situation is made to conform to the design, and at others the design is made to conform to the situation. The southern boundary of the site is defined by a wall, while at the northern boundary the *barchetto* merges without any clear, visual distinction into the natural landscape of the valley. On the parterre the view of the valley is designed as a specific feature: an extra area was added to enable one to enjoy the panorama towards the north-east. Just as in the designs of Vignola and del Duca, the view diagonally from this area was linked to the axial system.

In contrast with, for example, the Villa Farnese in Caprarola, the division between the axial system, in which the house is central, and the *barchetto* has for the greater part disappeared at the Villa Giustiniani. The main axis has been continued in the *barchetto* and is emphasized by an orthogonal path structure. The casino (fig. 6) is no longer placed independently in this part of the garden but on the axis of the palazzo instead.

In this respect the garden can better be compared with Pratolino's Florentine garden and the early French gardens visited by Vincenzo Giustiniani in 1606 during a long journey through northern Europe. During his visit to Gaillon in France Vincenzo had a room on the first floor, from the window of which he had long vistas of the garden below and a pavilion in the distance 'fatto con disegno portato d'Italia'.

In Bassano there were at one time, especially on the various squares along the long *allée*, small sculptures, such as vases and small animal figures; today hardly any remain. The best impression of the specific elements in the garden can be obtained from an account given by Vincenzo himself in a letter to a lawyer friend, Theodore Amidini: 'the garden of the squares above the grotto of the dwarf trees; the main avenue to the web groves; the covered walks, the gallery, the avenue of the pear trees, the avenue of the roses; the theatre of Navona; the piazza of the Rocca; Mount Parnassus; the avenue of Aesculapius; the barrel grove; the avenue of the fishpond; the hillock; the square piazza; the avenue of the hillside; the avenue of the riverbanks; the avenue of the stream; the avenue of the hazelnuts; the fir grove; the round piazza; and so on'.

VILLA GIUSTINIANI

Bassano (di Sutri) Romano

For admission apply to: Amministrazione Principe Guido Odescalchi, 81, Piazza S.s. Apostoli, 00187 Rome
Telephone: 06: 6789153/6798686

LITERATURE

I. Belli Barsali, *Ville di Roma*. Milan 1983.
A. Blunt, *Guide to baroque Rome*. London & New York 1982.
M.L. Simo, 'Vincenzo Giustiniani: his Villa at Bassano di Sutri, near Rome, and his «Instructions to a Builder and Gardener»', *Journal of Garden History* 1 (3) (1981).

Villa Lante

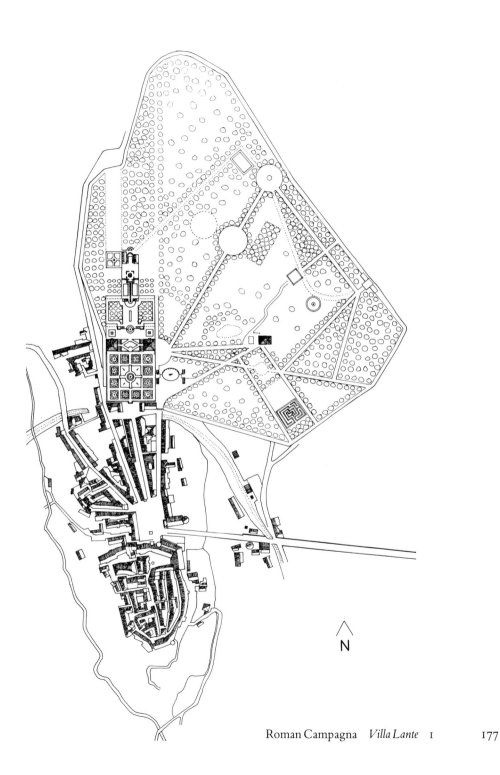

N

The Villa Lante was situated in hunting grounds on the edge of the small town of Bagnaia. From the beginning of the sixteenth century this *barco* had been enclosed, and the former hunting lodge where open-air banquets used to be held still stands in the centre. As soon as he acquired ownership of the estate in 1560, two years after his appointment as Bishop of Viterbo, Cardinal Gambara commissioned the building of a villa there. The design of the villa is usually ascribed to Vignola, but it is also possible that Giacomo del Duca worked on the project. At that time Vignola was working on the Palazzo Farnese in nearby Caprarola for Cardinal Alessandro II Farnese, a good friend of Cardinal Gambara. Financial misfortunes made it impossible for Cardinal Gambara to see the complex through to completion within his term of office. At his death in 1587 only one of the planned casinos, the Casino Gambara, had been finished. Two years later Cardinal Montalto came into possession of the villa. In 1598, twenty-five years after Vignola's death, the second building, Casino Montalto, designed by Carlo Maderno, was completed. Many of the fountains were destroyed or altered around that time, however, and some new elements were added. In 1656 the complex passed into the possession of the Lante family.

In the architectural system of the Villa Lante the interaction between architecture, town, landscape and nature has been realized in various ways. The entire design, as can be seen in sixteenth and seventeenth-century illustrations, is composed of two distinct parts: the parterre and the *barchetto*, which are moulded into a single concept by the enclosing wall (fig. 2). It

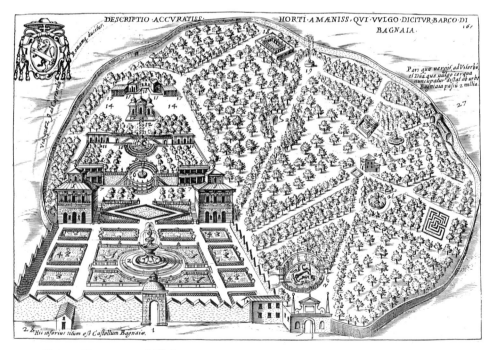

Roman Campagna *Villa Lante* 3

is remarkable that in later drawings the *barchetto*, regarded as an irrelevant detail, is omitted, whereas it is in fact an essential component of the villa concept. A similarly dualistic character can also be recognized in the four-teenth-century description of a garden by Petrarch; his *villetta* in France had two gardens, one dedicated to Apollo and one to Bacchus, alluding to the dualistic character of the dimensional structure. At the Villa Lante, too, both parts are in sharp contrast to each other and, at the point they are confronted, the dialogue between them becomes visible (fig. 1).

Each garden section has its own form and its own pattern of movement. The *barchetto* is labyrinthine; it represents free nature and consists of paths intersecting at random. Movement is guided only by visual stimuli placed at the intersections; one moves from feature to feature. The terraced parterre garden is composed axially; all movement takes place along this axis. Here geometry is the structuring principle and imposes its order on all the parts. The natural slope of the terrain is also assimilated and formalized. The dif-ference in height of 15 m. from the lowest to the highest point is bridged by a series of terraces. The steps and fountains burst through the screens which enclose these terraces. The dimensional grids overlap at the changes in level and the elements bridging the different levels have been erected specifically on the overlap (fig. 4).

On the upper terrace the *bosco* (a symbol of nature) feeds the spring, which flows from the cave terminating the upper end of the axial system. Analogous to the gradual calming down of the spring flowing from the nymphaeum flanked by two small temples devoted to the nine sacred Muses – patrons of art and science, and, therefore, muses of the intellect – is the emphasis on the rationality of the entire plan. The water itself bubbling up from its source is increasingly controlled on its downward course. The

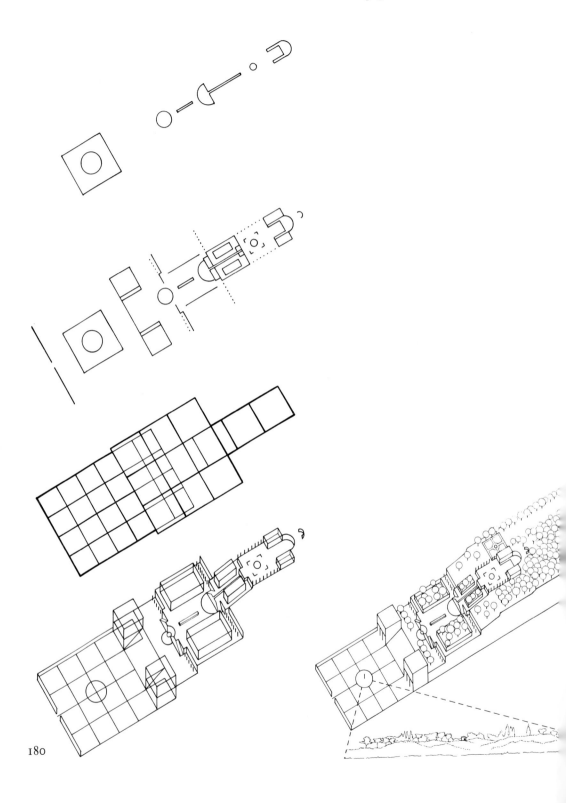

spring, which here literally, as well as figuratively, forms the axis of the garden, connects the terrestrial and the celestial, the erotic and the oceanic, between the highest and the lowest terraces by means of its two extreme appearances. Movement is determined by the direction of the current of the water flowing over the cascade.

The ambiguity created in the axis by the metamorphosis of the water between the reflecting pool and the cave can also be read as a theme present in the other elements of the plan. On the edges the *barchetto* penetrates into the parterres and is restrained by surrounding hedges. The influence of nature, symbolized by the *barchetto*, increases from below to above. At the highest level the marble columns of the (now demolished) aviaries still stand next to and between the 'columnar tree trunks'. The two-sided and ambiguous quality of this villa is expressed here both in the connection of, and in the sometimes apparently fluent transition between, the two parts of the garden. The two casinos play a relatively unimportant role. They have only a minor residential function and have, in effect, been reduced to garden furniture. They are situated on the lowest terrace and perform there their ancillary role. Formally, they are included in the strips along the edges and are thus placed in series with a number of other small buildings, including the two now disappeared aviaries on the upper terrace (a recurrent element in the work of Vignola and del Duca; compare the Orti Farnesiani and the Villa Giulia) which, screenlike, border the various terraces.

The difference in plan of the casinos is noteworthy. The Casino Gambara designed by Vignola shows, in plan as well as in elevation, a remarkable similarity to the hunting lodge at Caprarola and the Villa Vecchia in Frascati. These three buildings were designed in the same two years (1568-69) and built during the following five years. All three have the outward appearance of small country houses, with dovecotes on their roofs which have been transformed into belvederes. Inside, the casinos of the Villa Lante distinguish themselves from each other by, for example, the paintings in the loggias. In the Casino Gambara, designed by Vignola, there are frescos of the Villa Farnese at Caprarola, the Villa d'Este at Tivoli and of the Villa Lante itself. In the Casino Montalto the perspective is continued on to the sidewalls, and there is a *trompe-l'œil* of birds on the ceiling.

Unobstructed by the two casinos, the axis, along which the component parts of the geometrical garden have been ordered, stops at the ceremonial entrance gate at the town end of the garden. On the lowest terrace the direction of the garden is, as it were, turned, with the reflecting pool acting as a pivot so that the eye is diverted sideways, bringing the panorama into the formal design from across the boundary wall, which is low on the side of the *barchetto* (fig. 5). One cannot see the town itself from the lowest terrace, and it is only in the entrance gate that it is formally included. On the axis the panorama of the landscape is unfolded from the upper terraces. The small bench situated at the highest point, above the spring (fig. 6), functions as the beginning of the central axis and is the focal point connecting the panorama, the *barchetto* and the geometrical layout.

The immediate formal link with the town is made between the side entrance to the parterre, the entrance gate of the villa, and the *borgo* (castle) in the town. At a later date this formal connection between *barchetto* and entrance gate was incorporated into the somewhat oblique *patte d'oie*, whose central street is directed towards the ceremonial entrance of the lowest terrace.

VILLA LANTE

Bagnaia

June–September: 9.00–17.00
October–May: 9.00–18.00
Fee

LITERATURE

S. Benedetti, *Giacomo Del Duca e l'architettura del Cinquecento.* Rome 1972.

D.R. Coffin, *The Villa in the Life of Renaissance Rome.* Princeton 1979.

C. Constant, 'Mannerist Rome', *A.D. Profiles 20* 49 (1979), pp. 19-22.

J. Hess, 'Villa Lante di Bagnaia e Giacomo del Duca', *Palatino* 10 (1966), pp. 21-32.

J. Hess, 'Entwürfe von Giovanni Guerra für Villa Lante in Bagnaia (1598)', *Römisches Jahrbuch für Kunstgeschichte* 12 (1969), pp. 195-202.

J.C. Shepherd & G.A. Jellicoe, *Italian Gardens of the Renaissance.* London 1986.

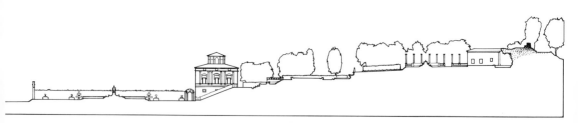

Villa Orsini

Pitigliano is a small town situated on the flat top of a steep crag on the south flank of Monte Amiata in Roman Tuscany. It has Etruscan foundations and is one of the oldest continuously inhabited settlements in Italy. In the Middle Ages and the Renaissance it was an important settlement on the border of the Papal states.

The Orsini castle, of thirteenth-century origin, was expanded by Niccolò III Orsini during the fifteenth century. Between 1540 and 1545 Gian Francesco Orsini commissioned Antonio da Sangallo the Younger to execute a number of urban schemes, one of which was the construction of an aqueduct. In 1547, when Niccolò IV Orsini, son of Gian Francesco, returned from a campaign, he ousted his father and seized power. In a subsequent campaign in 1552, in which he supported the French in the war against Siena, Niccolò reconquered the small town of Sovana, situated near Pitigliano, which more than a century before had been captured from the Orsini by Siena. With Sovana the nearby Etruscan necropoleis also came into his possession.

It was probably during the intervals when he resided in Pitigliano that Niccolò had some changes made to the castle and had a garden laid out on top of the hill immediately opposite the small town. After the death of the last descendant of the Orsini family in Pitigliano the garden seriously deteriorated. Perhaps in an attempt to forget the cruel rule of the Orsini the garden was left to degenerate and it almost disappeared from sight. Though there is now only a fragment left of the garden, there has, for some years, been a revival of interest in it. It appears to form, together with the Sacro Bosco of Niccolò's friend Vicino Orsini of Bomarzo, a unique part of Italian garden history.

At the northern end of the little town of Pitigliano is the mountain landscape with its deep ravines; at the southern end is a broad river valley with the fields, gardens and vineyards belonging to the inhabitants. In Sangallo's design for the square, laid out between the Orsini castle and the rest of the buildings on the full extent of the hilltop, this topographical contrast was reinforced. The totally introverted character of the medieval fortified town is broken by two 'giant windows' at the far ends of the piazza. The view of the two contrasting panoramas is framed. At the southern end it is framed by an architectural screen in the form of a triumphal arch, depicting the victory over nature; the view from the arches was of the pastoral man-made landscape. At the northern end stands an 'architectural' tree; a large solitary planc represents free, untamed nature, a sight of which it introduces; the rugged mountains can be glimpsed under its screen of foliage. In his design, probably one of the last before he died in 1546, Sangallo had intended a small sunken garden on the site of the tree. This was never executed however.

A similar polarity between the cultivated and the natural played a leading role in the garden, which was later laid out by Niccolò IV. The small mountain ridge on which the town was situated did not offer the possibility of laying out a garden of any size, and that is probably the reason why it was situated on the hill immediately to the north of Pitigliano (fig.1). The garden and the castle in the town were, therefore, separated from each other; their only link was a public road. There was, however, a direct visual relationship; from the square and from the castle there was a good view of the facing hilltop, which was more or less on the same level. A loggia, facing north, was added to the two upper floors of the castle.

There is presently little left of the garden; the last avenues of cypresses disappeared in the Second World War. To what extent there may have been a geometrical garden architecture, and what form it took, are not yet known. Only the small part of the garden which remains can, due to its labyrinthine structure and situation, best be regarded as a *bosco*.

Roman Campagna   *Villa Orsini*   1

N

Roman Campagna *Villa Orsini* 2

A number of sculptures and seats were created, partly balancing on the northern edge of the hilltop and partly below it against a steep wall of the ravine. They were carved in chunks of tufa stone and linked by an apparently random network of small paths, usually not wider than 30 cm., worn into the side of the ravine and sometimes with a number of steps cut into the rock. Both the garden features and the paths raise the question of to what extent they came into existence spontaneously and to what extent they have been 'manufactured'. This ambiguous position between natural art (wild untamed nature) and artificial nature (the cultivated garden) causes continuous reflection; a search for the essence of nature. The Renaissance concept of geometry as the expression of the 'hidden' order in nature is implicitly criticized by a confrontation with its wild physiognomy. The architecturally treated ravine side is entirely oriented towards the natural mountainous landscape and away from the urban context. There is only one exception; at the western end of the hilltop a reclining male sculpture, Orlando, holding a cornucopia, looks back towards the village.

The comfort of the seats on the edge of the ravine is relative. Completely isolated from everything and everybody, surrounded by the solid mass of tufa stone, the fear of falling or of not being able to resist the fatal attraction of the ravine is ever present. In one place, half-way down the slope, one of the seats has even taken on the appearance of a larger-than-life human figure (or was a visitor literally petrified on this spot?). A solitary sculpture in the form of a reclining female figure (thought to represent Orlando's wife) seems hardly able to resist the attraction of the depths and the call of untamed nature. In its immediate vicinity death is represented by an Etruscan tomb.

At the eastern end of the *bosco* there is a large, round viewing terrace on a

185

projecting part of the rock. At this point there is an unimpeded view over a landscape of ravines, three of which meet here; it is also the point where the small mountain streams Lente and Lupo join the River Prochio. The hill used to be called the 'hill of the crossroads' (Poggio Sterzoni) until 1575, when Orso Orsini, Duke of Pitigliano, strangled his wife, Isabella degli Atti, there. Since then it has been known as 'strangle hill' (Poggio della Strozzone). The shape and detailing of two small chairs, carved within a single frame, next to the entrance to this platform almost entirely correspond to a similar element on an Etruscan tomb at Norchia. Towards the edge a narrow meandering path goes down the rock into the valley. Carved in the rock under the round viewing tower there is a spacious and seemingly natural niche; here, every vestige of culture seems to have disappeared.

Although Niccolò's garden was laid out with less pomp and with significantly fewer sculptures than the Sacro Bosco of Vicino Orsini at Bomarzo, an at least equally forceful field of tension was created in which the natural and the artificial, the realistic and the visionary, the erotic and the oceanic, life and death were placed opposite each other and related to each other. Both gardens had a similar structure and location and were characteristic examples of *bosco* design at the height of Mannerism. It is significant that in both gardens contact was sought with a culture older than that of Ancient Rome by references to Etruscan tomb architecture. An appeal to the Etruscan ancestry of the Orsini family would raise them above those who claimed a link with classical Rome. With their gardens the Orsini turned away from 'the towns of towns' and, indeed, from all urbanity; both gardens were separated from residential life in the nearby town.

VILLA ORSINI

Pitigliano

Owner: Giuseppe Savelli

LITERATURE

H. Bredekamp, *Vicino Orsini und der heilige Wald von Bomarzo*, 2 vols. Worms 1985.

C. Lazzaro, *The Italian Renaissance Garden*. New Haven & London 1990.

G. Masson, *Italian Gardens*. London 1987.

J. Pieper, 'To make landscape visible (Piazza of Pitigliano by Antonio da Sangallo)', *Daidalos* (Dec. 1986), pp. 104-107.

P. Portoghesi, 'Nota sulla Villa Orsini di Pitigliano', *Quaderni dell'Istituto di Storia dell'Architettura* 7-9 (1955), pp. 74-76.

Sacro Bosco di Bomarzo

Due to its favourable situation along the important road linking Rome with Florence, 'Polimartium', the town of Mars, later known as Buon Martio, was already important in the Roman Empire. The fact that there are Etruscan remains in the immediate vicinity, at the foot of Monte Casoli, suggests that the small town's history goes back even further. During the Middle Ages the castle, built like an acropolis on top of the narrow hill, changed hands many times. From the beginning of the fourteenth century it was probably owned by princes of the Orsini family, who from the thirteenth century onwards owned a great number of estates between Rome and Siena. In 1502 the castle was left by Girolamo Orsini to his son Gian Corrado. Both princes expanded and embellished the building, and probably one of them had a Renaissance garden laid out in the valley at the bottom of the hill. In 1542, when Gian Corrado died, his inheritance was divided between his two sons, Maerbale and Pier Francesco I. The latter, who called himself Vicino, became the owner of the Bomarzo estate.

Vicino Orsini (1523-84) was a friend of the three cardinals who had built villas in the same neighbourhood: Cardinal Madruzzo at Soriano, Cardinal Gambara at Bagnaia, and Cardinal Farnese at Caprarola. He belonged, like

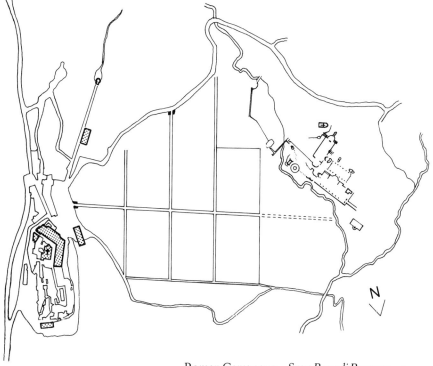

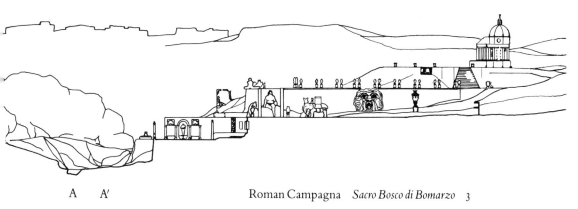

A   A'   Roman Campagna   *Sacro Bosco di Bomarzo*   3

INDEX OF ELEMENTS

1 pool in the 'front wood'
2 springs adjacent to the original
   entrance
3 two sphinxes with inscriptions
4 the leaning house
5 Love Theatre with obelisks
6 Pan, Jupiter, Hecate and retinue
7 Isis/Aphrodite-fountain with masks
   of Jupiter/Amon
8 boat-fountain with dolphins
9 nymphaeum (bathhouse of Venus)
10 benches with female satyrs and two
   lions
11 the three Graces
12 remains of a column pedestal
13 tree trunk carved in the rock
14 Pegasus fountain
15 muzzle of an Orc
16 giant tortoise with Lady Fortune
17 site of an earlier dam
18 reservoir
19 bench
20 Roland and Amazone
21 tower and bench
22 Psyche, fettered to a rock
23 giant sea creature/fish
24 Poseidon/Neptune/Tiber
25 urn and vase field
26 dragon fighting with lions
27 elephants with warriors
28 Demeter
29 Hellmond
30 giant vase
31 the Golden Fleece
32 bench
33 Kerberos (Cerberus)
34 Persephone
35 field (flower garden), surrounded by
   pine cones and acorns
36 a pair of heraldic bears
37 Echidna
38 pride of lions
39 Chimare/Harpy
40 viewing platform
41 temple
42 imitation Etruscan temple tomb
43 sculptured rocks
44 Mask of Madness/Aztec mask

them, to the most important literary circle of the time. Furthermore, he was married to Giulia Farnese, a cousin of Pope Paul VIII and Cardinal Farnese; in the cardinal's service he had fought as a soldier in various North European countries, including Germany, Flanders and France.

After Vicino returned from a campaign in 1547 and when, shortly afterwards, his wife died, he laid out the first section of what he later called the 'Sacro Bosco'. With only a few interruptions he was to work on this 'Garden of Monsters' at the foot of the Colle Cardon until his death. Later in 1645 the country estate was sold to the Lante (della Rovere) family, who sold it to the Borghese family in 1845. The garden was neglected, however, and only rediscovered, completely overgrown, by Mario Praz and Salvador Dali in 1949; their film about the garden made it famous. Since then the *bosco* has received more and more attention and has often been the subject of studies attempting to explain this 'miraculous' phenomenon of Italian garden history.

The uniqueness of the Bomarzo garden lies in the fact that Vicino Orsini's attention was entirely devoted to the planning and development of the *bosco* as an independent unity in which the spatial organization, the working method, and iconographic programme were different from those usual in garden architecture up until then. The hierarchical Renaissance concept of the garden, in which geometry expressed the 'hidden order' of nature, was criticized in the *bosco*, which was arranged like a labyrinth.

In the final plan of Bomarzo the urban and the rural are placed opposite each other. From the castle only odd fragments of elements in the *bosco* can be seen across the valley and, conversely, the castle can only be seen occasionally through the trees from the *bosco*. The contrasting poles were connected by means of the main central axis of a geometrical garden that formed an intermediary (fig. 1). At both ends of the axis there were monumental entrance gates which emphasized the individuality of the three related elements: the town with its castle, the geometrical Renaissance garden, and the *bosco*. In addition, the elements were also made independent of each other by two natural barriers: the change in level of the hill near the town, and a small river near the *bosco*.

One entered the *bosco* by way of a bridge over this river (fig. 2). The original entrance was formerly indicated by two stone sphinxes, on the pedestals of which mysterious inscriptions posed riddles to visitors. The sphinxes were, however, like the adjacent series of double busts of Hermes, moved during the twentieth century and placed, out of context, near the present entrance further south. On passing the original entrance the first element the visitor came across was the consciously crooked 'leaning house' between the entrance and the 'Love Theatre', subverting the lack of geometry and orthogonality. Vicino seems to be paying homage to Cardinal Madruzzo here: at the corner of the leaning house a bear (the Italian word for which is *orso*, a reference to Orsini) carries the coat of arms of the cardinal. From the theatre the *bosco* was expanded in a number of phases with further elements,

Roman Campagna *Sacro Bosco di Bomarzo* 4

in all probability without any premeditated plan. Initially the garden followed a more or less geometrical plan. This was increasingly abandoned,
however, during later phases, when more and more elements were carved
out of the chunks of tufa stone which were available on the site. A series of
inscriptions was added to the elements as a separate stage of the plan and,
finally, a large number of the colossal sculptures were painted in bright
colours.

The labyrinthine structure, in which it was only the route chosen that
ordered the various objects, makes an unambiguous reading of the objects
and the inscriptions (as bearers of meanings) impossible; they stand in
a continually changing relationship to each other. Moreover, there are a
number of statues which in themselves are so ambiguous that it is almost
impossible to speak of them as having an unequivocal theme. It is possible
that a new concept was being developed in Bomarzo whereby the object
was intended to absorb a number of, possibly even contradictory, themes,
and that it was from a synthesis of these that a new and clear (frequently
Manichaean) meaning was created. (It is probably on account of this that
there has been something of a revival of interest in this garden in the post-
modernist period.) What results in the Sacro Bosco is a visual and fluid
portrayal of a world that criticized the Renaissance concepts of hierarchy
and order.

One of these ambiguous objects is the small temple consecrated to Giulia Farnese and built on the hill above (fig. 3). The front of the chapel has a
tympanum and, behind this, a round cupola (fig. 10), and clearly refers to the
Pantheon in Rome. The rear of the building, where the octagonal-faced
structure, in which there are four oculi, supports the cupola (fig. 11), strongly
suggests the cathedral built by Brunelleschi in Florence. As a result, the

Roman Campagna   *Sacro Bosco di Bomarzo*   5, 6

position of the Sacro Bosco, which at first sight seems such an unworldly, illusionary creation (owing more perhaps to a world of dreams), becomes clearly defined, as much geographically as mythically, situated literally and figuratively between Classical (Papal) Rome and the Tuscan Florence which drew on the ancient civilization of the Etruscans.

Despite the fact that the evidence is not always so clear, it is still possible to distinguish some other themes which determined the design of the garden; a number of them are considered below.

SELF-KNOWLEDGE AND SELF-FULFILMENT   The design of the garden was used as a means of acquiring knowledge about oneself, one's emotions and one's character. Vicino regarded the route through the plan as a journey through the labyrinth of the soul, and art as a means to recognize this soul. This is confirmed by the inscriptions at the castle: 'know thyself' and 'if thou knowest thyself, thou knowest, without doubt, all', as well as that on the pedestal of one of the sphinxes (fig. 5) at the entrance to the *bosco*: 'He who does not visit this place with raised eyebrows and pursed lips will fail to admire the seven wonders of the world'.

'ORDER, RATIONALITY AND REALITY' VERSUS 'CHAOS, IMAGINATION AND INSANITY'   Central to this theme is the inscription on the pedestal of one of the sphinxes that guarded the entrance. In this inscription the visitor is asked whether the wonders of the *bosco* 'have been wrought by imagination or by art [i. e. skill]'. A sense of astonishment certainly plays an important part throughout the entire design. Near the original entrance to the *bosco* the visitor is confronted with the so-called leaning house (fig. 6). If one enters the small building and stands upright on the sloping floors the walls

Roman Campagna   *Sacro Bosco di Bomarzo*   7, 8

seem almost to be on the point of collapse and the visitor's normal sense of order is disturbed. On the other hand, if one accustoms oneself to the distorted windows the position of the horizon, and thereby of the world in general, is called into question.

In another part of the *bosco* stands the statue of the fighting colossus (fig. 7) which, according to the nearby inscription, is the Colossus of Rhodes – one of the seven wonders of the world. The statue is probably also a reference to Orlando (Ariosto's *Orlando furioso*), who went mad after the loss of his loved one and was no longer able to distinguish between reality and imagination. It is sometimes regarded, however, as a portrait of Vicino himself.

The theme of insanity returns in the nearby 'Mask of Madness'. On a globe on top of this giant head balances a miniature version of the Orsini castle (which Vicino called the 'Atlas Castle'). Just as in the case of the leaning house the stability of Vicino's construction is doubted.

NATURE VERSUS CULTURE   The theme of nature versus culture runs throughout the entire design and is clear in the treatment of water: the tiny natural stream which borders the eastern side of the *bosco* was contrasted with a large artificial lake which also served as a reservoir for the nearby fountains. By 1573, however, this artificial Ocean had disappeared as a result of the dam bursting during a heavy thunderstorm. The Pegasus fountain (fig. 8), which was a symbol of patronage and a feature of almost every other important garden at that time, was built on a tilt in Vicino's garden; the water from the fountain flowed into the river which ran below, and thereby symbolized the merging of culture with nature. Vicino's attitude towards city culture becomes clear in his statement: 'towns are the enemies, woods the friends of my thoughts'.

Roman Campagna   *Sacro Bosco di Bomarzo*   9,10

ETRUSCAN CIVILIZATION   Vicino not only rejected towns in general, but the 'Town of Towns' – Rome – in particular. By reverting to Etruscan tomb architecture (fig. 9) a link was sought with a culture older than that of Ancient Rome. An appeal to the Etruscan origins of the Orsini family would enable them to rise above those who looked to classical Rome. Vicino was also interested in other non-Roman civilizations, such as those of Egypt, Africa, America and the Far East – civilizations from 'strange' exotic countries, some of which had only recently been discovered and become focuses of interest.

LIFE AND DEATH   This theme is central to the entire garden, most conspicuously in the small temple (fig. 10, 11) dedicated to Vicino's dead wife, Giulia, in the various appearances of the female goddess of fertility, sometimes combined with the goddess of the underworld, but most of all in the entrance to the underworld: the Mouth of Hell (fig. 4). In contrast to the frightening exterior the interior of the mouth is pleasant and cool, and a small bench has been carved out in the stone. Sitting on this bench one could use the tongue as a table for picnics. The transposition from eating to being eaten, living and dying, plays a role here. Moreover, in this ambiguity Vicino's aversion to the Catholic Church was clearly demonstrated.

SEXUALITY, EROTICISM, SEDUCTION, SENSUALITY   The erotic aura of many of the sculptures, such as those of Aphrodite, Chimare, Echidna, Demeter, Persephone and Psyche, is felt all over the *bosco*. The theme is also clearly expressed by the 'love battle' between the two giants (fig. 7), and the text 'I can do no more, I am doing as much as I can', which perhaps expresses Vicino's fear of losing his virility as he grew older.

194

Roman Campagna *Sacro Bosco di Bomarzo* 11, 12

LOVE   According to the humanist Francesco Sansovino, a friend of Vicino, it was not only the temple on the hill which was dedicated to Giulia; Vicino had dedicated the entire *bosco* to her, including, of course, the Love Theatre (fig. 12). The shape of this theatre, being based on that of Bramante in the Cortile del Belvedere next to St Peter's, again seems to be an oblique reference to, and a criticism of, the perversions of the Papacy.

The themes mentioned here give only an indication of what is depicted in the elaborate iconographic programme in the Sacro Bosco. The themes are all directly related to the person of Vicino Orsini himself. Not only did he develop them, inspired by texts such as those of Cardano, Ariosto's *Orlando furioso*, Rabelais' *Pantagruel*, and the *Hypnerotomachia Poliphili* of Francesco Colonna, he was also involved in their realization. The architect sculptor Simone Moschino and the sculptors Raffaello da Montelupo and Fabiano Toti were probably responsible for the execution of the plans.

SACRO BOSCO DI BOMARZO

Bomarzo

Owner: Giovanni Bettini
Open: 8.00–17.00
Fee

LITERATURE

H. Bredekamp, *Vicino Orsini und der heilige Wald von Bomarzo*, Worms 1985.

A. Bruschi *et al.*, *Quaderni dell'Istituto di Storia dell'Architettura* 7–9 (1955), pp. 1–76.
J. B. Bury, 'Review Essay: Bomarzo Revisited', *Journal of Garden History* 5 (1985), pp. 213–223.
M. J. Darnall & M. S. Weil, 'Il Sacro Bosco di Bomarzo: Its 16th-Century Literary and Antiquarian Context', *Journal of Garden History* 4 (1984), pp. 1–94.
S. Lang, 'Bomarzo', *The Architectural Review* (1957), pp. 427–430.

Frascati *Introduction* 1

1 Aldobrandini
2 Belpoggio
3 Borghese
4 Falconieri

5 Grazioli
6 Lancelotti
7 Mondragone
8 Muti
9 Torlonia
10 Vecchia

4 Frascati

The villa as decorative item   198

Aldobrandini   202

Belpoggio   207

Falconieri   211

Lancelotti   215

Mondragone   220

The villa as decorative item

One point of focus in the development of the *villeggiatura* around Rome is the group of villas draped against the hills around the village of Frascati, situated about 20 km. to the south-east of the city of Rome. Many villas were concentrated in this location, then called Tusculum, even in the time of the Roman emperors. Cato, Lucullus and Cicero had their country seats there. The village was destroyed in the Middle Ages and its classical villas laid to ruin. After the election of Alessandro I Farnese as Pope Paul III (1534-49) and the establishment of his country retreat in Frascati, there was renewed interest in the area, particularly among the Roman prelates.

Between about 1548 and 1598 many cardinals built relatively modest villas there. In a second period of building between 1598-1650, associated with the Counter-Reformation which followed the Council of Trent, owners competed with each other to embellish and extend their villas.

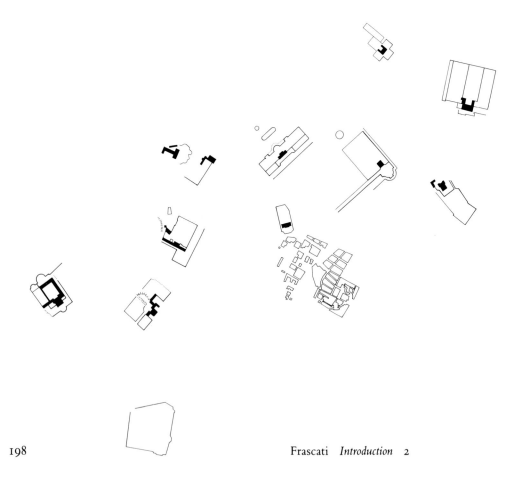

In the beginning the main point of staying in the country had been to enjoy nature; now it came to be seen as the struggle to achieve the perfect arcadian utopia as a reconfirmation of that religious and secular power which had been questioned by the forces of reformation. The execution of this perfection in arcadian ideals took place in a variety of ways. In the Veneto district, where the construction of the Palladian villa was inextricably linked to the Venetian neo-feudal policy of colonization, the villa became a symbol within the agricultural system, the *santa agricoltura*, a symbol of the reinstitutionalization of the god-given patriarchal relationship, with the landowner as *padrone*.

In the Frascati villas (fig. 2), which were built by church prelates themselves, the depiction of power and authority was added as a component of the *villeggiatura*. The stage-management and the architectural treatment are determined to an important, if not dominating, degree by the need to present and make the restored power of the church explicit. The early type of Tuscan villa, in which the interaction between villa and landscape took place in the garden, was thus adapted to a new function. A type of villa

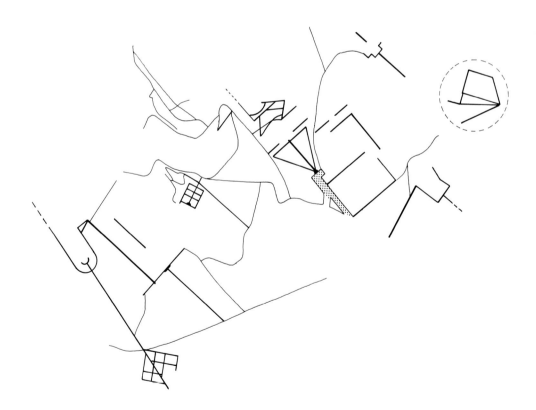

came into being in which the situation of the complex against the hills, the position of the house on the terraces, and the design of the façades were given monumental significance. The garden at the rear was a subordinate private area, and the ceremonial landscape definition was taken over by the execution of the façades of the house and the front terraces.

Frascati is situated about 300 m. above the level of the River Tiber. The land slopes away to the north-west, where Rome is visible on the horizon. To the south-east the slope increases steeply, climbing over several kilometres to a height of 670 m. From the slope the villas have a panoramic view of the sunlit Roman Campagna. The background is the dark forest set against the hills. In general the house embraces the difference in height between the north and the south side. The shadowed, flat north façade contains a balcony or loggia. Opposite the sunlit south façade the slope of the hill is caught by a retaining wall with a nymphaeum. Here, opposite the entrance to the house, the water which runs off the hills is collected. In a number of places parts of the forestation have been cut away to permit a better view. The plans of the villas as they looked after the extensions and embellishments of the first half of the seventeenth century begin to show the 'competition' between two different ways of organizing the space: the terrace and the axis.

The terrace is a geometrical surface and is used as an architectural foreground, balancing on the edge of the panorama, forming an open space and binding it to the villa. In particular, those villas on the ridges which stand out from the slope and which have a panorama of at least half (i.e. 180 degrees) of the horizon form a single terrace which also runs around the sides of the house (e.g. the villas Mondragone and Aldobrandini). Seen from below, the striking proportions of the villa façades form a monumental unity with the walls of the terraces.

The improved presentation of the villas was, moreover, supplemented by an avenue leading in a totally straight line up the slope. Following this line the house and terrace are arranged symmetrically. Approaching the villa, the driveway ensures a frontal, ceremonial approach to the complex. The length of the avenues seems to be in tune with the view from the entrance to the house up the hill. An interesting detail, supplied by Franck, is that the avenue ends at the point where the treetops are just below the level of the terrace. Because of this, one looks over the avenue from the terrace. The actual entrance to the villa is however not at the front. One is led around the terrace to the rear of the house and the *piano nobile*. This entrance is usually linked to a more accessible access route paralleling the slope of the hill. The longest axis, at the Villa Mondragone, is 700 m. long.

Even though the avenues remain in the foreground and one can look out over them, their layout outside the actual territory of the garden and their placement in the panorama indicate that this is no longer an open space, valued equally in all directions. The panorama itself has been ordered and given visual direction. In the link between foreground and background the house appears as a set piece against the dark, forested slope. The regular spacing in the orientation of the individual villas is striking. The symmetrical axes run down the slope virtually parallel to each other into the distance (fig. 3). This arrangement makes it clear that mutual visibility and views of the town of Frascati are of less importance here. These axes have no formal end, but instead a virtual one; their point of reference is the point on the horizon where the city of Rome stands.

In this orientation to the panorama all the villas are similar. Because of this they no longer have different points of view. Unlike Florence or Rome there is no circuit with changing panoramic views. There is actually only one view and one direction from which to look out over the panorama. Furthermore, the significance of the city within the panorama is diminished by the fact that only the outline of Rome appears on the horizon. This space is hierarchical and monothematic. In this monothematic concept of space the garden has lost its role as the focus of the stage-management. In the Frascati villas the garden has been relegated to the rear, between the house and the slope, and therefore is much more of a component in the confrontation between the monumental and ceremonial side of the complex and the walled and private part of the garden.

Within the typology of the Frascati villa advanced by Franck the axial connection of the villa's elements places the *bosco* against the slope. The structure largely conforms to the plan of, for example, the Veronese Giardino Giusti in the seventeenth century, and generally resembles the Villa Barbaro of Palladio. In the latter a purpose-planted forest on the hillside is used to give the villa the necessary background and thereby the required cerebral significance when seen from the approach road. In the Frascati villas the *bosco* joins with the hill to create a common background and the binding element in the monumental stage-management. Despite competing with each other in terms of the wealth they display, the separate villas hereby preserve their mutual affinity.

The development of the Frascati villa took place within this spatial framework. The Villa Lancelotti in its original form can be taken as a model for the type of spatial use in Frascati, while the Villa Aldobrandini is its most refined Mannerist example.

LITERATURE

C. Franck, *Die Barock-villen in Frascati.*
   Munich 1956.
G. Jellicoe & S. Jellicoe, *The Landscape of*
   Man. London 1975.

Villa Aldobrandini / Belvedere

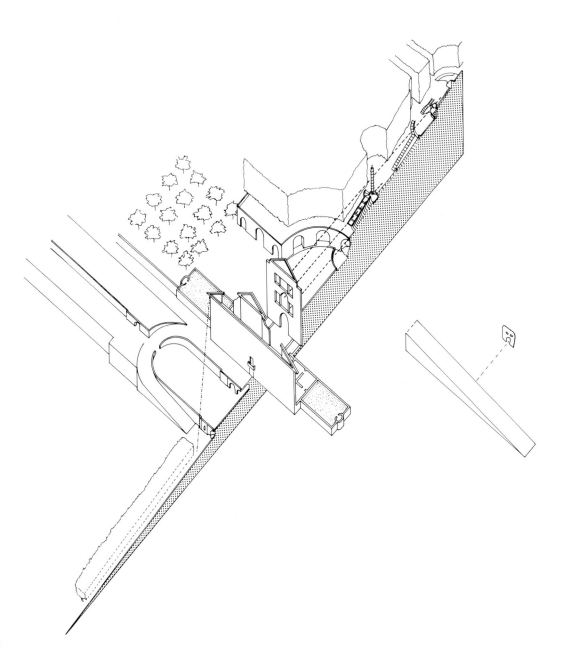

Frascati *Villa Aldobrandini* 2

In about 1560 Pier Antonio Contugi had a small villa laid out. The villa was subsequently bought by Pope Clement VIII, who in 1598 gave the villa to his nephew Cardinal Pietro Aldobrandini in gratitude for his part in the recapture of Ferrara. In 1683 the villa passed into the hands of the Pamphili family and later came into the possession of the Borghese family.

After the final land purchases had been carried out the building of the house was started in 1598, in accordance with the designs of Giacomo della Porta. Papal revenues had increased so much as a result of the annexation of Ferrara that the costs of building the villa could satisfactorily be met from them. Della Porta died while the villa was still under construction and Carlo Maderno and Giovanni Fontana, who were also responsible for the construction of the cascade and the water theatre, took over supervision of the work. Maderno designed the cascade and the water theatre, whereas Fontana, aided by Oratio Olivieri, was responsible for the engineering. Fontana was a famous aquatic artist, having made his name at the Villa d'Este, and it was he who designed the hydraulic effects.

The building of the Villa Aldobrandini was decorated with a richness exceptional in those days. The walls of the drawing room, situated in the centre of the main block on the *piano nobile*, are covered with large tapestries and the ceiling is decorated with frescos ascribed to Zuccari. The southernmost hall on this floor is decorated with Chinese wallpaper and the ceiling was painted with scenes from the Old Testament. The most important paintings, however, were in the two small buildings next to the water theatre. In one of them, a chapel dedicated to St Sebastian, the frescos were painted by Domenico da Passignano. (These were so badly affected by damp, however, that they were removed and they now hang in the National Gallery in London.) In the other, the Stanza dei Venti, a garden room with an artificial hill and sensational aquatic effects was created.

Frascati   *Villa Aldobrandini*   3

In the layout of the Villa Aldobrandini the section in front of the building and the part behind it are entirely independent of each other. The
building itself functions as a screen between the front and the rear (fig. 1); it
separates culture from nature. The town is controlled by means of the view
and is itself dominated by the enormous façade of the house. Partly hidden
behind the house lies the wild overgrown *bosco*, only accessible to the owner
and his guests. In engravings by Dom Barrière, Falda and Specchi it is clearly shown how the building forms a protruding part of the hill and how the
slope of the hill is continued in the projection of the roof (fig. 3). In front of
the house is a bare slope with the approach avenue on the axis of symmetry.
This avenue, flanked by clipped trees (now so grown together as to form
a tunnel), directs the view from as well as towards the building, giving
the house its monumental backcloth-like significance with regard to the
village. The entrance was originally marked by the intersection of two
avenues forming two sides of a triangle and their bisector, formed by the
main axis. The growth of the village and the construction of the garden wall
and entrance gate, designed by Carlo Bazzicchieri, destroyed this triangular
configuration.

   The entrance avenue leads to a niche in the lowest retaining wall of the
two-storeyed front terrace, which projects on to the slope like a bastion. An
unexpected combination of images takes place at the highest point of the
avenue: the niche and the upper part of the building are visually linked by
perspective (fig. 5) in accordance with the principles developed by Vignola
and del Duca (see the Villa Farnese at Caprarola). This carefully constructed
image disintegrates as soon as the axial approach is departed from and a
movement is made towards the sides.

From the highest level of the front terrace there is no direct passage to the terrace at the rear, which is connected to the house one floor higher on the *piano nobile*. In spite of the strongly axial structure, movement is interrupted for the second time. At the east side of the villa there is a domestic entrance from a narrow side road, which leads straight up the hill. Two *boschi* of plane trees situated on the transverse axes unite the front and the rear in a simple manner. The western side-terrace, which continues to the edge of the hillside, offers a view of the villas Torlonia, Grazioli, Muti and Belpoggio. On the rear terrace, opposite the south façade of the house, is the spectacular semicircular water theatre. In the centremost of the five niches Atlas shoulders the globe and is submerged in a curtain of water. Only a glimpse of the garden above the nymphaeum can be seen from the terrace. The connection with this *bosco*-like garden is made by means of a ramp on the western side-terrace, again deflecting movement sideways, away from the axiality of the villa. (Next to this ramp, hidden in the woods, there is a giant head similar to those in the Sacro Bosco at Bomarzo, fig. 6.)

The succession of fountains, cascades and grottoes in the main axis, and the two flanking columns are connected to the different levels of the house. The central part of the south façade, which projects slightly, consists of stacked loggias, from which a constantly changing perspective of

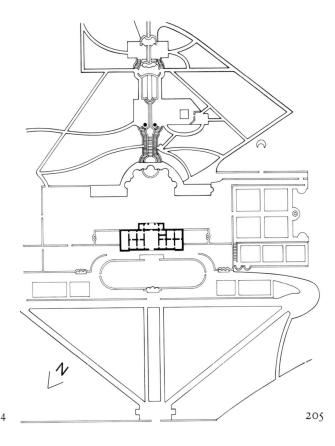

Frascati   *Villa Aldobrandini*   5   Frascati   *Villa Aldobrandini*   6

the water attractions can be seen. Only from the highest loggia can the garden be viewed as a whole. Here one is on the same level as the eternal spring, from which the water courses flow down the slope, and in communication with primeval nature. The upper cascade is shaped so as to counteract perspective (fig. 4). It seems to be projected on to a screen between the two water columns and is thus perceived from the house as a flat plane.

Looking in the opposite direction from the slope, the house is seen through constantly changing frames. Only the central part with the loggias is visible, as a set piece between the two columnar fountains. The house seems to control every part of the slope. At the level of the spring, where the horizon of the Roman landscape becomes visible over the house, the contrast between culture and nature is cancelled. Even here we are being deceived. The loggias and the eaves are treated in such a way as to play tricks with perspective. There is no longer a belief in the mathematical ordering of the world; faith is no longer confirmed but challenged in the Aldobrandini perspectives.

VILLA ALDOBRANDINI/
BELVEDERE

Via del Cardinal Massaia 18
Frascati

For admission apply to the Principe
Aldobrandini

LITERATURE

C. Franck, *Die Barock-villen in Frascati.*
Munich 1956.
G. Masson, *Italian Gardens.* London
1987.
J. C. Shepherd & G. A. Jellicoe, *Italian
Gardens of the Renaissance.* London
1986.

Villa Belpoggio / Pallavicini

The Villa Belpoggio took its name from its location on a beautiful hill (*poggio*) on the Via Tuscolana, the entrance road to the small town of Frascati. Building started in about 1605 and the client was Ottaviano Vestri. After 1620 ownership of the villa passed to the Ceri family, then to the Borromeo family, and after that to the Visconti. In 1724 the villa was bought by the Pallavicini, who in 1733 commissioned Pompeo Battoni to decorate the interior of the chapel with a painting of S. Filippo Neri in adoration of the Virgin. For almost two centuries the villa remained in the hands of the Pallavicini. In 1932 the upper part of the complex was occupied by the Suore del l'opera Pia della Providenza. The villa was completely destroyed during the Second World War. A new building, now used as a school, was erected on the site of the house, but the gardens were never restored. Of the original complex there are now only remnants of a few of the fountains and the former entrance.

A number of aspects of the spatial organization and landscape setting characteristic of the Villa Belpoggio do not occur in those Frascati villas which have survived. They illustrate the way in which the 'Frascati concept' could be applied to a villa which, because of its specific situation, did not lend itself to such a treatment.

Percier and Fontaine show a model of the plan in which the position of the *bosco* is 'corrected' and brought within the orthogonal matrix of the plan (fig. 1). It should be remembered that when analysing villa plans Percier and Fontaine simplified the plans, which they drew into a (preferably symmetrical) orderly geometrical pattern. When the plan of the villa, as represented by Franck, is compared with the eighteenth-century reconstruction by Percier and Fontaine we note a remarkable difference in the way in which the *bosco* is depicted within the complex. In Franck's version, which shows the situation in 1932 (and which can still be reconstructed by examining the present features of the terrain), the *bosco* is twisted with respect to the main

Frascati   *Villa Belpoggio*   1

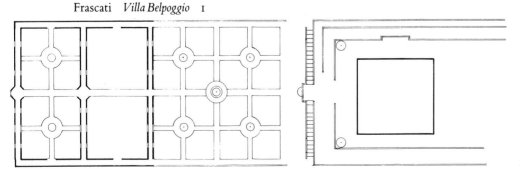

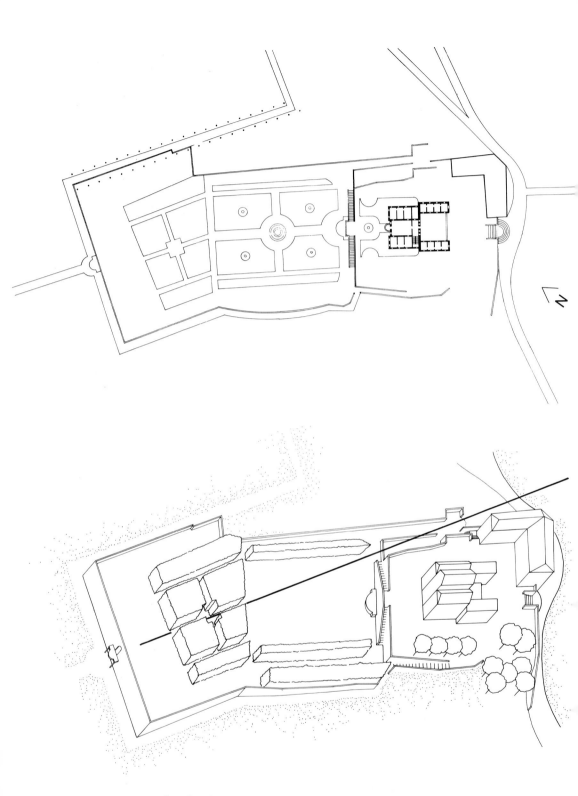

Frascati *Villa Belpoggio*   2, 3

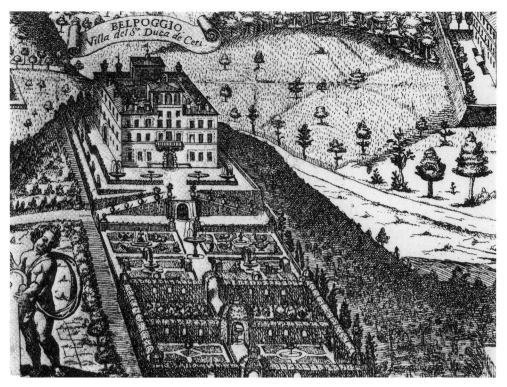

Frascati *Villa Belpoggio* 4

direction of the complex and follows the direction of the contours of the adjacent valley (fig. 2). One can question to what extent this somewhat curious twisting of the rear of the garden has to do with the setting of the villa in the landscape.

The villa is not situated on a sloping site as, for example, the Villa Aldobrandini or Villa Mondragone were, but on top of a small hill. The entrance is also different from the usual Frascati villa; it is situated on the north side, where, generally speaking, the *bosco* was supposed to be connecting the villa to the slope. The entrance was directly connected by a set of steps to the terrace on which the monumental rectangular house was placed. The building was provided with towers which overlooked the valley and the hills on the far side. From the terrace, steps led down to the parterre that was terminated to the south by the *bosco*. This parterre was of lesser importance, conforming to the Frascati concept; it was enclosed on four sides and played an insignificant part in the setting. From the plateau around the house the garden was integrated into the vista over the *bosco* and thus related to the valley. It would appear that there was a small square in the *bosco* from which the view was directed back over the parterre along the slanting edge of the terrace and an opening in the enclosing parterre hedge towards the hills to the north which formed the background of the most important

Frascati villas. Because of the twisting of the *bosco* and its retrospective effect in the plan, the direction of the valley and the presence of the hills are as unambiguously formalized as the scenic elements with which the villa is made to interact. The problem of the reverse situation is solved by designing the scenery on several levels: from the towers flanking the house the unrestricted vista, in other words the stage-management of the whole panorama; from the terrace the view of Rome over the *bosco*, in which the plan is related to the direction of the valley; and, finally, from the *bosco* not the usual retrospect towards the house but, on the contrary, towards the spot where the villa should have been were it to have been included in the series of Frascati villas located along the northern slopes (fig. 3).

VILLA BELPOGGIO/
PALLAVICINI

Frascati

Destroyed

LITERATURE

C. Franck, *Die Barock-villen in Frascati.* Munich 1956.

Villa Falconieri / La Rufina

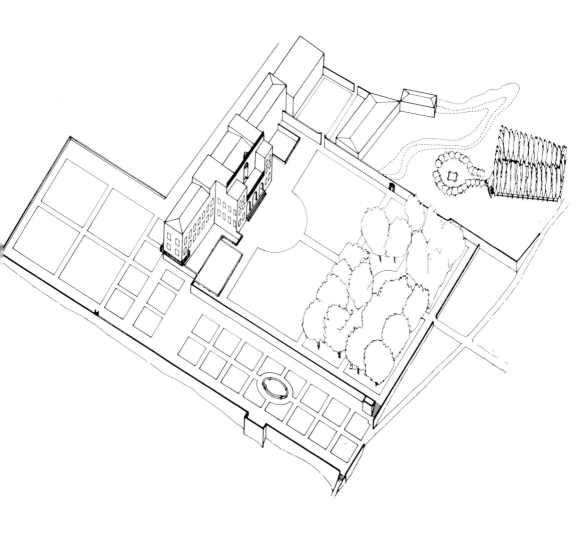

Though the Villa Falconieri in its present form is one of the most recent of the Frascati villas it was, in fact, the first to be built. In 1546 Cardinal Alessandro Ruffino acquired the site and in 1548 he built a casino on it. The cardinal was probably related to Pope Paul III, the then owner of the village of Frascati, which he was restoring and decorating in preparation for his becoming probably the first to establish a small summer residence there. A small chapel, dedicated to St Mary Magdalene, had to be demolished to make way for the construction of the villa. The villa is therefore sometimes referred to as the Villa Maddalena.

The first casino consisted of an almost square rectangular block with four corner towers (fig. 2). On three sides loggias provided views of the landscape. The entrance was on the western side, as was the large front terrace and the entrance arch. To the north of this terrace and about six metres lower was another terrace, which stretched along the entire perimeter of the site and stood out on the hillside like a bastion. In 1563 Cardinal Ruffino was forced by lack of money to sell the villa to Francesco Cenzi. Later it came into the hands of Duke Paul I of Sforza. It subsequently passed to Cardinal Gonzaga, who in 1650 sold it to Falconieri. Falconieri was to herald a new chapter in the history of the building by appointing Borromini in 1660 to undertake a far-reaching rebuilding of the villa complex.

The entrance to the villa was replaced by a monumental gateway on the western side and two wings were added to the northern and southern sides of the house (fig. 1). The extension on the northern side caused the disappearance of a loggia, but no loggia was created to replace it at the end of the wing, which therefore remained subordinate to the new symmetry of the house. There was, however, a balcony, and the room located there was transformed by paintings into an imaginary garden with a fountain in its centre;

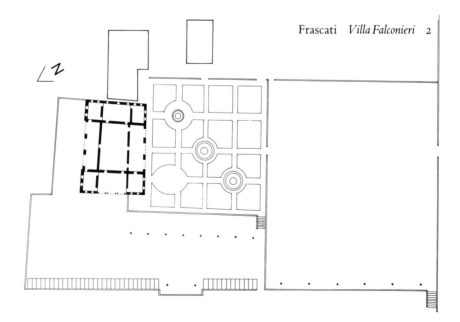

Frascati   *Villa Falconieri*   2

Frascati *Villa Falconieri* 3

it was in this manner that contact with an exterior was re-established on the northern side. The entire *piano nobile* is richly decorated with murals by Carlo Maratta, Cirro Ferri and Pier Leone Ghezzi, who was chiefly responsible for painting the illusionary architectural perspectives.

The two eastern towers remained visible as vestiges in the façade, which was lengthened on two of its sides. This gives the principal rooms a view of the valley, separating the Villa Falconieri from the grounds of the Villa Mondragone, rather than towards the north as was usual in the Frascati villas. In the first design the casino had already been shifted to the eastern perimeter of the site, but, owing to the lack of a distinct direction in the building volume, the view to the north was equal in importance to those from the loggias on the other sides. The ceremonial approach avenue characteristic of the later Frascati villas was a feature neither of the first nor the second versions of the plan. On the contrary, Borromini's actions led to an increased emphasis on all elements leading towards an east-west axial organization (fig. 4). Neither did the eighteenth-century additions deviate from this. The now unused 'Falcon gate' was erected in 1729 at the point where the old approach road to the villa curved away from the main street. The present entrance gate, dating from around 1900, was placed on the axis of the casino entrance.

The layout of Villa Falconieri is, therefore, somewhat different from that of the other Frascati villas. The organization of the garden follows the system outlined by Franck: the house, a parterre with clipped hedges, and a *bosco* immediately bordering on to the parterre. In the *bosco*, which was probably planted during the extension of the villa, is the now famous trapezium-shaped cypress pond. The sequence of the elements of the villa in a north-south direction shows that there is, indeed, a front terrace, a parterre, a nymphaeum, and a *bosco* on the axis; only an intervening casino, in which the view of Rome should culminate, is missing from the series. Its function is partly taken over by the retaining wall between the front terrace and the parterre, where the paintings of visitors arriving by horse-drawn coach suggest the entrance level. The spatial organization here is at right angles to the entrance axis.

The reason why the siting of the house does not comply with the Frascati scheme (for which the layout of the Villa Lancelotti served as a model and which received its most perfect form in the Villa Aldobrandini) is probably because the villa was built before this scheme had been formalized, and in addition it would seem that the foundations of a Roman villa, the remains of whose mosaic floors are preserved in the cellars, were used during later extensions.

The villa was almost entirely destroyed during the Second World War and subsequently plundered. Restoration has been in progress since 1954, and from 1959 onwards the villa has been the property of the Ministry of Education.

VILLA FALCONIERI/LA RUFINA

Centro Europeo dell'Educazione – CEDE
Frascati

For admission apply to CEDE

Frascati   *Villa Falconieri*   4

LITERATURE

C. Franck, *Die Barock-villen in Frascati.*
Munich 1956.

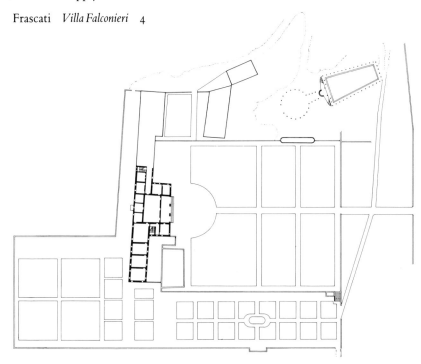

Villa Lancelotti / Piccolomini

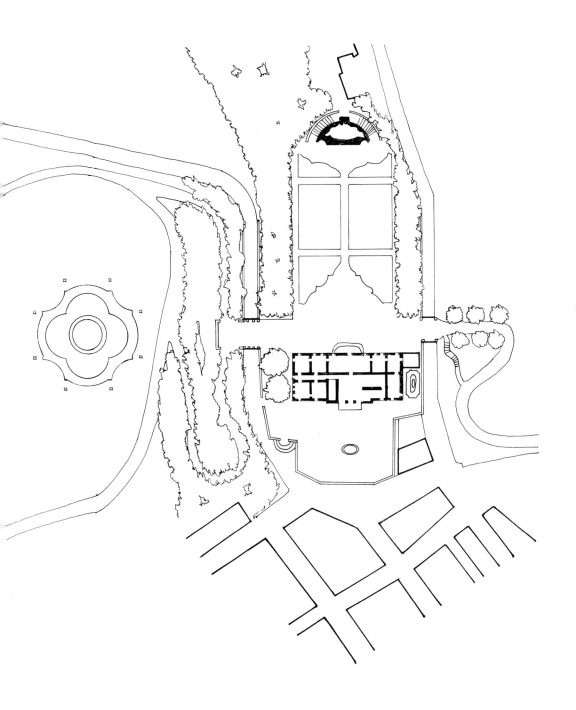

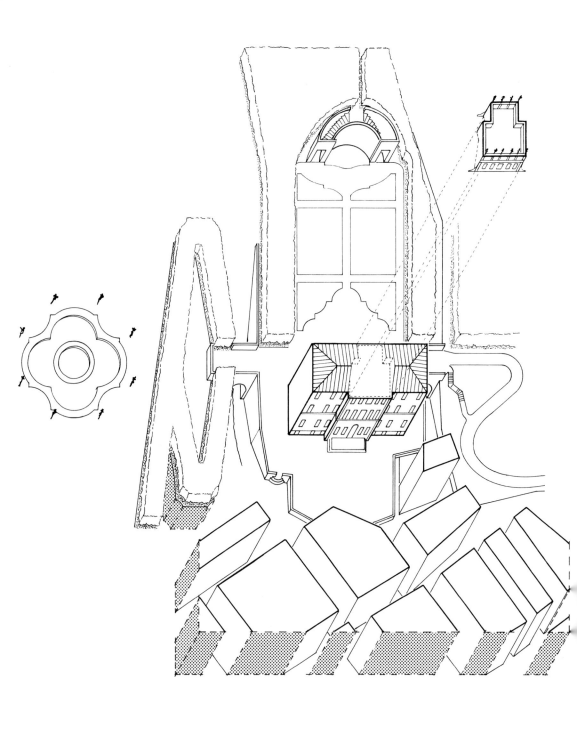

Frascati   *Villa Lancelotti*   3

In contrast to the pattern of development usual in the Frascati villas this villa does not seem to have been built as an extension to a casino in an existing garden layout. Here probably the gardens and later the further surroundings have been added to the palazzo built by the Visconti during the sixteenth century at the edge of the city. The building distinguished itself from the existing type of town palazzo in that it was set back from the street and a garden laid out between the building and the street.

After the palazzo had changed ownership several times (the Bonani, the Mattei and Cardinal Gonzaga were among those who at one time owned the villa) it came into the hands of the papal banker Roberto I in about 1620. Under his management the change from an urban palazzo to a villa was brought about. Behind the side of the building, facing away from Frascati, there was already a flower garden, terminated by a nymphaeum. This garden was transformed into an open-air room by the provision of a double row of holly oaks on both sides, which concealed the garden from outsiders. The front garden was converted into a terrace, which, unfortunately however, could only offer a view of the buildings of the town and not of Rome as was characteristic of the Frascati villas.

After the marriage of Roberto I's daughter the villa was handed over to the Piccolomini. During the eighteenth century the purchase of surrounding farmlands continued and the house was also considerably enlarged and provided with a new elegant façade. Inside the house two of the rooms were provided with frescos by Annibale Caracci. Later, in 1863, an antique mosaic from Camaldoli was relaid on the floor of the hall. Over the central part of the living quarters a roof terrace was constructed, raised above the ridge of the roof and crowned with statues. In about 1870 the villa came into the possession of the Lancelotti, who acquired the Villa Ruffinella at the same time and had a combined entrance gate for both villas built on the Piazza Borghese. The two side gardens linked to the rear terrace by bridges over the two adjacent roads were also laid out during this period. With these additions the villa was given its final shape.

Although the Villa Lancelotti is one of the larger at Frascati as far as the grounds are concerned, the actual building remains the most modest of the Frascati villas. The villa can serve as a model for the basic plan of the other Frascati villas. The sequence of terrace, house, parterre, nymphaeum, and the termination by means of a *bosco* pushed up against the slope is characteristic of the type of villa on the north flank of the hills (fig. 1). In these villas the view of Rome was formalized and the monumentality of the villas emphasized in the landscape by means of the ceremonial entrance avenues, the pronounced terrace walls, and the imposing north façades. The possibility of exploiting these situational aspects was not available, however, at the Villa Lancelotti. As it is only visible from the front terrace the elegant

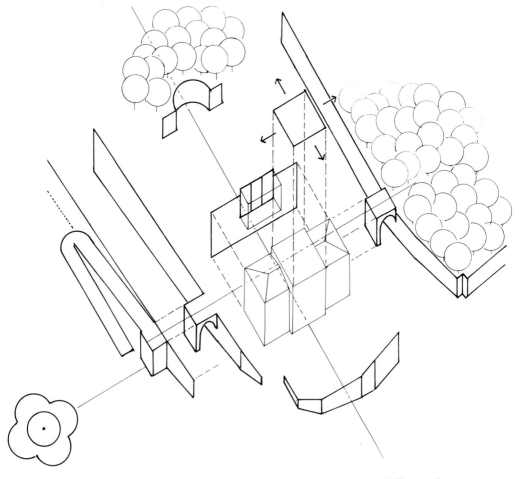

treatment of the north elevation is here more a reference to a formal meaning than an effective display to the valley of the monumentality of the villa. The ceremonial entrance avenue is absent and, apart from the situational impracticability of creating one, it would have made little sense. The nymphaeum which terminates the parterre is integrated into the retaining wall, but the ground behind it was not raised sufficiently to suggest that the villa is anchored into the hill. A thick wood was planted behind the wall in order to achieve this essential effect. Owing to the specific situation of the complex the view of Rome could not be realized. This view was added to the villa by the construction of a roof terrace on the raised central part of the house (fig. 2). The addition of the two side gardens and their connection to the parterre by the bridges over the lower roads releases the villa from its situational shackles. The view in all directions from the roof terrace therefore has tangible consequences in the plan. The grounds to the east and west of the villa are made part of the formal interaction with the landscape (fig. 4).

The three successive stages of development remain visible in the present situation: the naturally introverted character of the urban palazzo, still recognizable in the way in which the terrace and the north elevation relate to the urban morphology; the later developed 'Frascati' concept, in the relationship of the house to the parterre and the enclosing *bosco* on the south side; and, finally, the lateral development which links the villa with the surrounding landscape. This is finally 'condensed' in the construction of the roof terrace, where the successive stages are spatially linked.

VILLA LANCELOTTI/
PICCOLOMINI

Frascati

For admission apply to the owner

LITERATURE

C. Franck, *Die Barock-villen in Frascati.* Munich 1956.

J. C. Shepherd & G. A. Jellicoe, *Italian Gardens of the Renaissance.* London 1986.

Villa Mondragone

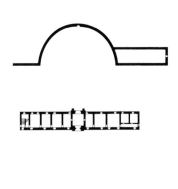

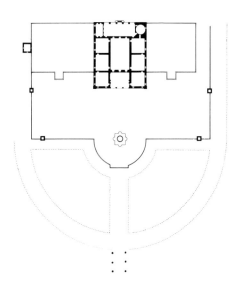

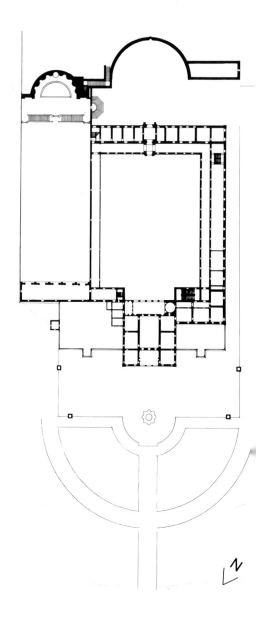

Frascati *Villa Mondragone* 2

In the period of about fifty years between the commencement of building operations and the completion of the successive building phases Villa Mondragone developed from a relatively modest casino into the gigantic building complex that can still be seen, high up on the north-west slopes of Tusculum. Its origins can be traced to 1573, when Cardinal Marco Sitico Altemps bought the site above his recently completed Villa Vecchia. According to tradition the country estate of Quintilius had stood on this site in Roman times. The Cardinal gave the commission for the building of a casino to the architect Martino Lunghi, who, as assistant to Vignola, had also worked at the Villa Vecchia. Construction work went so smoothly that the casino was ready for occupation as early as 1575. The stage setting was exceptionally beautiful. Nowhere along the slopes around Frascati would it have been possible to have found a site with such a majestic view. The hill and the villa were named Mondragone (Monte Dragone), after the dragon in the coat-of-arms of Pope Gregory XIII, a friend of the Cardinal.

The casino was laid out conventionally, in accordance with the first version of the Villa Falconieri. It was designed as a rectangular block with four corner towers (fig. 1a). On the south side facing the slope was a double loggia, the lowest part of which served as an entrance hall. On the north side on the main floor were the papal rooms (*appartamente papale*), oriented towards the view. The Cardinal's rooms were on the lower floor and were connected to a large terrace which projected from the slope with the servants' rooms and the kitchens underneath it. The smoke from the kitchens, which emerged from the tall stone chimneys on the terrace, suggested the smoke-billowing nostrils of the Monte Dragone. In the central section there was a high hall that received light from the upper loggia and the terrace above the southern rooms.

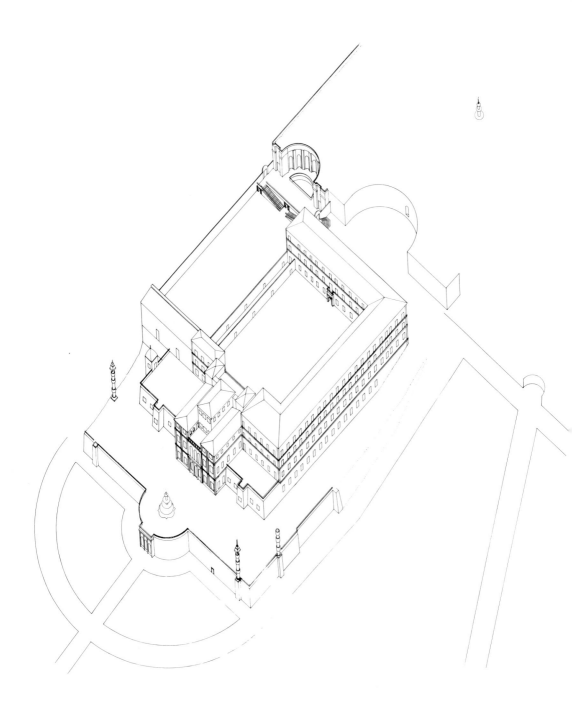

There is a remarkable similarity between the layout of the building at the Villa Mondragone and that of Palladio's Villa Cornaro. In both cases there is a tripartite division with a central bay in which a hall and the front and rear loggias are placed. The location of the staircase is also similar in the way in which it connects the main floors through the two superimposed loggias. This tripartite division, which in the Palladian villa is a standard element in the composition, also occurs in the elevation of the Villa Falconieri. It seems as if Palladio reverted to the plan of the traditional type of early Frascati villa for the spatial treatment of his Veneto villas.

The special character of the Villa Mondragone lies in the handling of the building's section. The casino was placed just over the edge of an enormous terrace. Two ramparts, like lateral terraces, were accessible from the papal accommodation on the *piano nobile* and were probably laid out as gardens. The size of the casino remained relatively modest compared with the vastness of the terraces, which received no further treatment. The boundlessness of the panoramic view of the *campagna* projected itself in the confrontation between this casino and the emptiness of the terraces.

Shortly after the completion of the first phase, which was regarded as an outrageous curiosity at the time, Cardinal Altemps ordered a new building to be constructed on the south side of the main terrace between the hillside and the casino to house his illegitimate son, Roberto, who had just been married to Cornelia Orsini. As a result of the construction of this elongated, three-storeyed Palazzo della Retirata, an entrance terrace was created in front of the semicircular retaining wall. This gave access through an archway to what thus became the more enclosed terrace of the existing casino (fig. 1a). The ceremonial cypress-lined avenue, which shared a communal entrance archway with the Villa Vecchia, was probably already in existence at that time; the proper entrance was still situated on the south-facing slope however.

In the subsequent forty years after the completion of this building phase there were no alterations made to the villa. In 1613 it was sold. The owner at that time, Giovanni Angelo Altemps, Duca di Galasse and the son of the finally-legitimized Roberto, was forced to sell the villa. It passed into the hands of Scipio Caffarelli. After his appointment as cardinal, Caffarelli adopted the name of Borghese. With him came the architectural staff of the Borghese family and a series of building activities followed which gave the villa its present appearance. The complex was considerably enlarged by the Dutch architect Jan van Santen (Giovanni Vasanzio), who, after the death of his predecessor, Flaminio Ponzio, also worked for the same client at the Villa Borghese in Rome from 1613 onwards. A long western wing was added which linked the original casino to the Palazzo della Retirata. The main block, which remained visible in the new plan, was provided with an adjoining annexe on the west side. In the interests of symmetry an annexe and an open corridor were also built on the east side, thereby creating an enclosed courtyard (fig. 1b). The autonomous character of the free-standing casino in the panorama, which projected itself from all sides on to the terraces, was destroyed as a result. Over the low corridor the view to the east remained unobstructed. Falda's etching, depicting the seventeenth-century situation, even shows this linking element as having the appearance of only a raised garden wall pierced by windows. On the other side of this corridor was a hidden sunken garden, which could only be entered on the north side via the water theatre designed by Fontana. Opposite this nymphaeum, with its perspective scenes, a portico screens off the view towards the valley almost completely.

As a result of the successive stages of building activity a disunity arose between the internal organization of the villa and its landscape setting. In its original setting the villa was oriented towards all sides. Because of its protruding position it formed a link between the Roman Campagna and the Frascati hills. In the transformation of the villa the function of the terrace has now been taken over by the extensive building mass. The interaction between landscape and villa was once formalized and activated in the dual relationship of the terrace (garden) to both the house and the view, but now a situation has arisen in which one of the determining elements in the creation of this interaction, namely the terrace, has disappeared.

Externally the villa takes on the appearance of a large, closed volume, terminated by the terrace on the valley side (fig. 3). Today the link with the horizon is projected on to this terrace by means of the ceremonial avenue of cypresses and the pentagonal garden on the other side of the road (fig. 4); the original continuation of this axis between the two higher lateral terraces on to the upper terrace has been broken however. At the same time this has caused the treatment of the courtyard to become distinct from the way in which the complex is treated in the landscape. The upper terrace, which had once been determined by the axis between the casino, the archway in the Palazzo della Retirata, and the semicircular retaining wall in the slope,

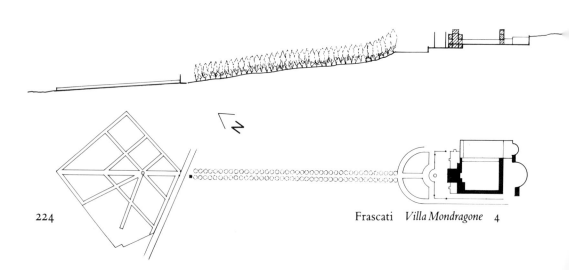

Frascati   *Villa Mondragone*   4

and which had also formalized the manipulation of the panorama, is now bounded on three sides and the view to the east is diverted ninety degrees over the lower side garden. Whereas in the Villa Lante at Bagnaia the twist in the direction of the organizing action forms the culmination of the spatial system and the landscape is brought into the garden as a complementary component and connected to the formal layout, the opposite occurs here. The spatial relationship of the villa to the landscape is broken into two separate components without ever being reunited within the broader landscape setting.

This disunity is not integrated into a new panoramic concept. The Villa Mondragone is, in the aggressive way in which the building – with its 365 rooms celebrating the introduction of the Gregorian calendar – juts out from the hillside, unquestionably the most imposing of the Frascati villas. At the same time, however, the dividing line, which is determined not so much by the scale of formal actions as by their intent, and which marks the transition from stage-managing the landscape to dominating it, has been exceeded. In the Frascati villas the intention to dominate coexists with the original concepts of the villas. This can be seen most clearly in the separation of the ceremonial entrance avenue from the actual entrance to the villas, an ambiguity that can also be observed in a number of Palladio's Veneto villas. At the Villa Mondragone it is almost impossible to find the entrance. The route from the access road is, partly because of the decline of the shared entrance with the Villa Vecchia, mainly determined by incidents, which, admittedly, can give a picturesque walk up the hill past the west side. This can never have been the intention of the original layout. In order to accommodate the geomorphological fact of considerable changes in level, however, the entrances had to be adapted, and the tension between the architectural plan and the unruliness of the situation have, apparently, led to a disunity that could finally only be solved by the total subordination of nature to the design.

VILLA MONDRAGONE

Monte Porzio Catone
Frascati

The villa has been converted into an international study and congress centre for the Universita degli Studi di Roma

LITERATURE

C. Franck, *Die Barock-villen in Frascati.* Munich 1956.
G. Masson, *Italian Gardens.* London 1987.

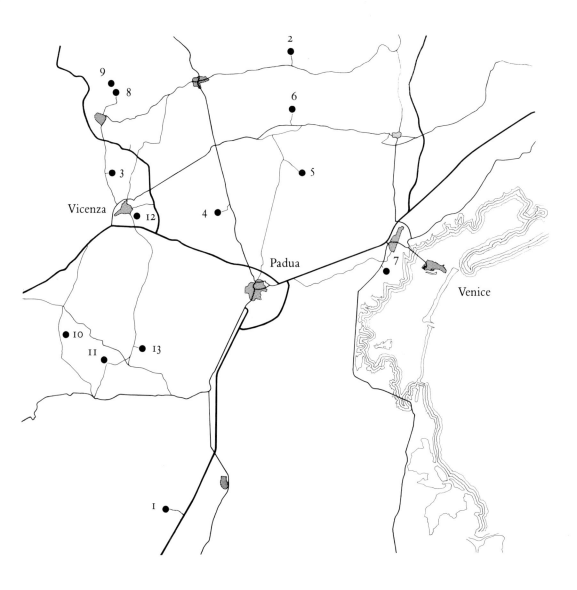

Veneto *Introduction* 1

 1 Badoer
 2 Barbaro
 3 Caldogno
 4 Contarini
226 5 Cornaro
 6 Emo

 7 Foscari / La Malcontenta
 8 Godi
 9 Piovene
10 Pisani
11 Poiana
12 Rotonda
13 Saraceno

5 Veneto: Palladio

Palladio: the agricultural villa   228

Barbaro   242

Contarini   246

Cornaro   251

Emo   255

Godi   259

Piovene   262

Rotonda   265

Palladio: the agricultural villa

A voluminous amount of literature has been published on the work of Palladio. Here we shall confine ourselves to an examination of the fabric (*fattorie*), which is considered important to the development of Palladio's individual architectural grammar, and the way in which it was integrated into the rural landscape.

Although the majority of Palladio's villas are situated in a flat landscape, there are some examples which are built on an incline or a hill. Of these the early villas of Godi and nearby Piovene (attributed to Palladio) will be examined together. We shall also refer to the Villa Barbaro and especially the Villa Rotonda, the last and most famous of Palladio's villas and one in which the biaxially symmetrical plan reflects its relationship to the surrounding landscape in the spatial structure of the house and surrounding terraces.

Of the villas situated in a flat landscape Villa Emo is included as an example of a completed single-storey plan based on one axis. In addition, this plan shows a great number of the elements of Palladio's vocabulary, which were used to relate the house, the gardens and the landscape to each other. The Villa Cornaro is representative of those villas which had two main floors of equal importance and it was built entirely according to the design Palladio published in his *Quattro libri*.

The Villa Contarini will be dealt with as a final and somewhat isolated example. This extensive complex can no longer be called an agricultural villa in the strict sense of the term. A series of drastic conversions and additions in the course of the seventeenth century transformed it into an entertainment centre. The effect of Palladio's efforts on the sixteenth-century condition is also contestable. Nevertheless, a discussion of the villa is not out of place here since the Villa Contarini fits into the series of villa-farms designed by Palladio in the Brenta valley which are concerned with landscape setting.

THE PROGRAMME OF THE VENETO VILLA   After the collapse of overseas trade and a series of military defeats towards the end of the quattrocento Venice had to fall back on its own region, the Veneto. The main thrust of economic policy was directed towards the development of agriculture. This offered sufficient opportunity for the investment of the capital gained through overseas trade. As part of this agricultural development the city of Venice pursued a policy aimed at opening up and reclaiming the marshy hinterland in as short a time as possible, exploiting the large pool of unemployed labour in the city for that purpose.

The Veneto villa differs from villas elsewhere in Italy, in part because of the economic circumstances which determined their function. For most of its history the Italian villa had been intended as a place of peace and relaxation in the midst of nature, and as a refuge from busy town life. The Veneto villa, however, was a working farm. The programme of the villa was influenced by the need to lure the Venetian aristocracy into the countryside. The renewed interest in farming coincided with the publication of a series of treatises on agriculture which extolled the virtues of country and farming life. Half-way through the sixteenth century the *Discorsi della vita sobria* by Alvise Cornaro, a prominent Venetian landowner, was published. Cornaro advocates the *vita sobria*, the ancient ideal of simple country life. The cultivation of the land was a divine occupation, comparable with the Creation. Agriculture was virtuous, so it was difficult to conceive of anything more virtuous than money earned by tilling the land. Treatises such as these laid a sound ideological foundation for involvement in farming. With the increased status thus provided it became worthwhile to settle down in the countryside as a landowning farmer. A number of agricultural villa designs were also described in these treatises. The *Liber ruralium commodorum*, which originally dated from 1305, was republished in Venice in 1495 and provided with illustrations. The author, Pietro de Crescenzi, described his villa as an economically independent community consisting of the landlord, the manager of his estates and the agricultural labourers; physically it took the form of '[...] an enclosed courtyard with one side pierced by the entrance road. The exit is immediately opposite. In the middle of the courtyard, along the road dividing the property and set back a little from the road, the landowner's house should be built with the façade facing the road [...]'

From these treatises it may be concluded that the villa was a functional unity which had to meet the demands of farming, the country idyll and aristocratic status. Initially these demands were met by a type of building that afforded status, namely the urban palazzo. This phase is illustrated by the work of the architects Sansovino at Pontecasale, Sanmicheli at S. Vigilio and Falconetto at Luvigliano.

It was only in the sixteenth century that the Veneto villa developed into a new type of building, accommodating all the aspects of the programme. Palladio's contribution was to develop an architectural scheme in which it is possible to control the agricultural programme by means of rational planning in relationship to the ideological needs of the new land policy. He designed a standard vocabulary in which the articulated components of the villa could be used to produce different combinations according to the individual wishes of the clients.

THE PROGRAMME OF THE HOUSE   The external appearance of the villa is sober, in accordance with the ideal of the *vita sobria*. According to Palladio the houses of antiquity were also built without decoration. Palladio dropped the idea of the villa as a unique object and created instead a series of objects (fig. 2, 3); in the course of doing this his personality disappeared to a certain extent from the work. In this kind of architecture, without

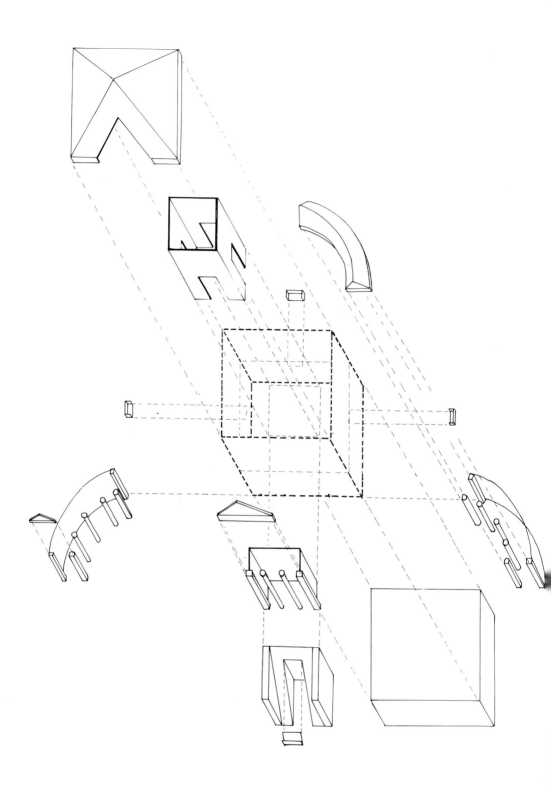

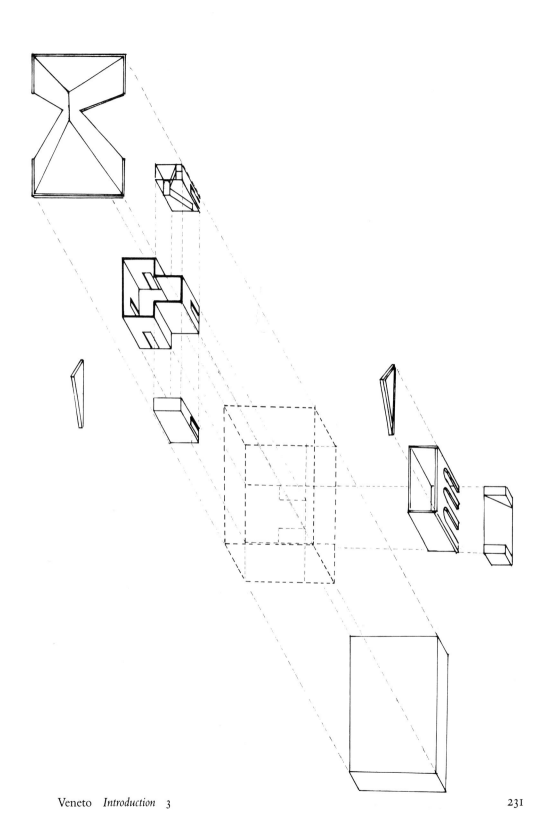

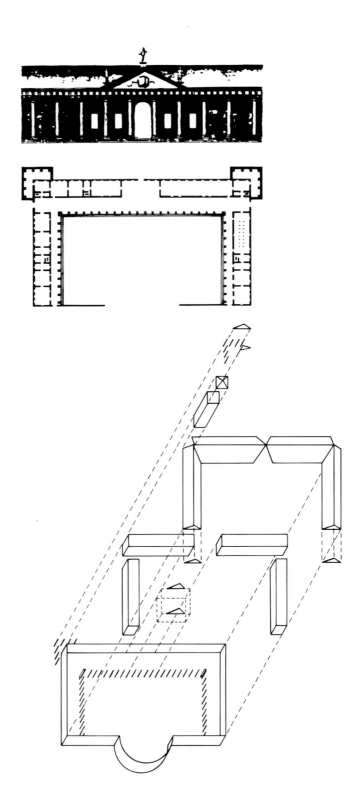

autobiographical caprices, the client had to renounce private decoration. Richness, however, showed itself primarily in the interior, with walls decorated with frescos in which the picture painted is one illustrating villa life, the landowner, his possessions and his erudition.

THE HALL   The ideal hall is square; it is used for feasts, performances, weddings and receptions. The hall, on to which the private rooms of the house open, Palladio termed a public space, analogous to the town square on to which several streets open. The hall in the villa is the centre of administration and entertainment, analogous to the forum in the ancient city. The arrangement is self-evident: the villa is centrally situated in the country estate and the hall is the heart of the villa; the hall and the loggia are the crowning glories of the whole.

THE LOGGIA   From the loggia the landowner looked out over the forecourt, through which the harvest was brought and in which games were held. It gives access to the living quarters and is used to beautify the house. It serves many purposes; it is a place to eat, to walk, and a place of recreation. The loggia is related to the hall behind it, in height, width and the number of floors. The loggia and the hall are the centre of the composition. If there is only a loggia in the front elevation the hall is slightly extended at the rear, and opposite the main entrance is a door or window, which serves to frame the view of the landscape.

THE TEMPLE FRONT   The temple front emphasized the main entrance to the house and adds considerably to the status of the building (fig. 4). The use of a temple front in domestic architecture is intended to suggest the divine status of the landowner. Since the front side is more prominent than the rest of the house this was also the best place to put the family's coat of arms, which is usually carved in the centre of the temple front.

THE STEPS   The steps leading up to the *piano nobile* lend distinction to the house. The introduction of the raised *piano nobile* subordinates contact with the garden to the view of the landscape from the loggia. According to Palladio the raised main floor has two advantages. In the first place it no longer requires any servants' quarters, which are now housed in the basement. Secondly, it is a more pleasant place to be because the floor is raised above the damp soil; it also commands a better view of the farmlands and can itself be seen to better advantage from the distance. The physical dominance of the villa achieved through its central position and the raised position of the main floor symbolizes total control of the landscape.

THE FORECOURT   The original layout of the gardens is unknown. Old engravings suggest that the forecourt was an open space. The low flat ponds, which hardly rise above the grass, and the low walls round the

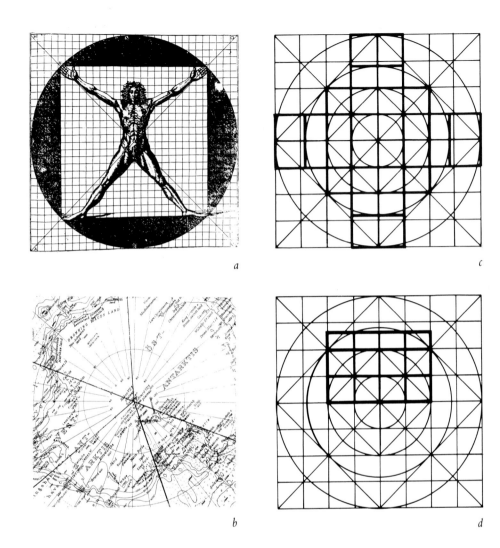

a

c

b

d

Veneto   Introduction   5

c Villa Rotonda
d Villa Badoer
e Villa Tricino
f Villa Foscari

The villa plans illustrated in these figures do not take into account the situational context in which these villas were to be placed. They are reduced to schemes, which Palladio subsequently developed in the landscape as the main feature within the series of architectural elements that characterized his designs; in this way these schemes were anchored to their situational context.

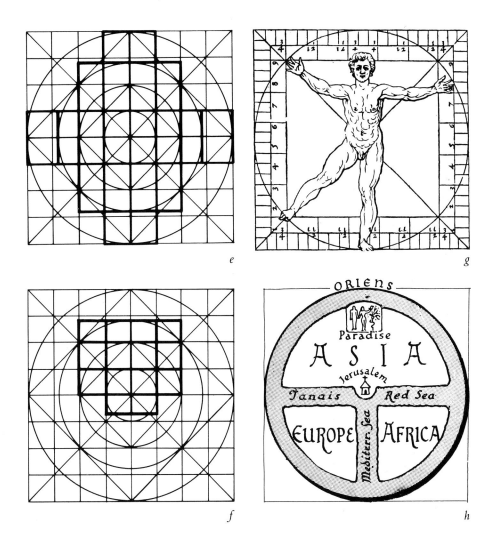

e

g

f

h

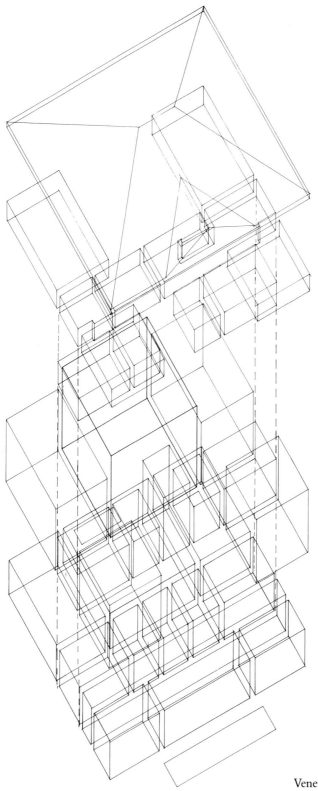

courtyard suggest the same. An open forecourt ensures that the villa can be seen from afar and that it commands a view of the fields. The forecourt was a public space on to which the barns, the dwellings of the agricultural workers and the stables opened.

THE PLAN   Wittkower suggests that the villa plans belong to a single geometrical scheme (fig. 5). Nevertheless, one can distinguish three types of villa on the basis of the zoning of the plan. In type 1 the plan consists of four equal zones. In type 2 the plan consists of three zones in a 2:3:2 relationship. In type 3 the plan consists of three equal zones.

Within this zoning the rooms are organized and proportioned according to the rules laid down in the *Quattro libri*. There are seven possible relationships between the length and the width. These proportions are determined by numerical series which could vary from villa to villa. The series are in turn generated from a basic number, representing either the length or the width or both and from which the height could be derived. The unit of measurement employed in these series was the Vicentine foot; the number of feet a particular space measured is written in the plan. The thickness of the walls is important in the geometrical scheme. This can be deduced from the way in which the temple front is joined to the wall.

Because the heights of the spaces are dependent on the length and the width there is a compositional relationship between the spaces of the villa. The central hall is the largest and highest space. As a rule the smallest and lowest spaces, the *mezzati* (mezzanines), are situated round the staircase. Although the spaces are of different heights they are combined in one composition, one volume. The various cross-sections through the Villa Emo demonstrate this clearly (fig. 6, 7c, 7d). The way in which the large and small spaces are combined resembles the *Raumplan* of the twentieth-century Viennese architect Adolf Loos, who claimed to be the first to think in terms of spaces rather than plans. Both architects also held that the house should have a sober exterior and that only the interior should betray the personal taste and richness of the client.

The location of the staircase was very important in the spatial composition of Palladio's villas. The houses with one main floor have only small staircases because these staircases served no important function; they were only used by servants and lead internally to the cellar, the *mezzati* and the loft. Houses with two main floors have spacious oval staircases in well-lit stairwells immediately behind the façade. In these houses the hall is a tetrastyle, a square hall with four columns. The staircases connect the two floors in such a way that the first floor was also entered by means of a loggia.

THE LANDSCAPE   The *raison d'être* of the Veneto villa was the reclamation of the countryside, in which the villa owner, in his role of divine *padrone*, occupied a central position. The villa was the centre from which the extensive farmlands were managed. The fields were mainly cultivated according

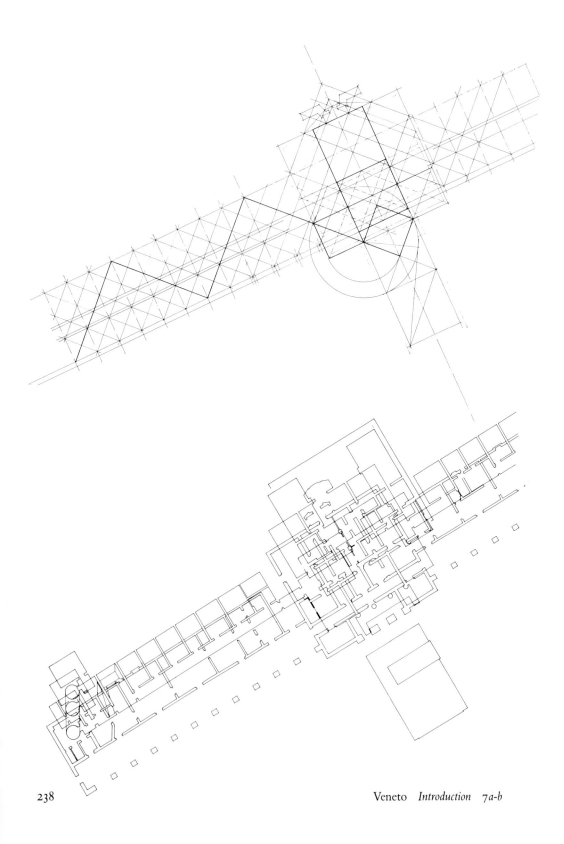

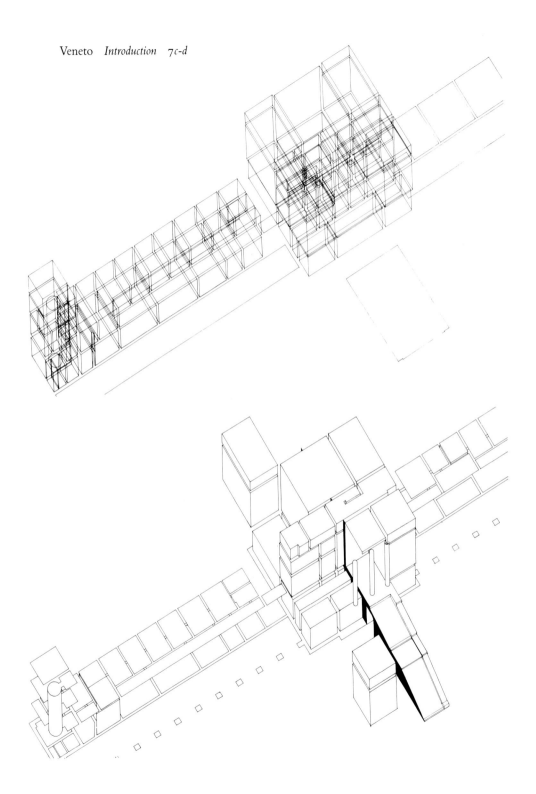

to the so-called Roman *centuratio* system, which still existed in a rudimentary form. This system consists of square plots of about 625 by 625 m. The villa sites conform to the pattern of this system.

The way in which the relationship between the landscape and the villa was created should be considered against the background of ideas about landscape and nature. In Palladio's villas there was no garden as understood in the fourteenth and fifteenth-century Italian villa tradition. In so far as there is a garden it is a ceremonial introduction to the steps leading to the *piano nobile*. The gardens in front of the house either decorate the courtyard or are substituted for it if the outbuildings are too small to constitute a courtyard by themselves. The flat bare lawns or gravelled areas which fill these squares impede neither the view of the villa itself nor the view of the farmlands from the villa. The kitchen gardens are situated on the edge and, as in the Villa Barbaro, camouflaged by high hedges and rows of trees. The trees at the front have a representative function. The few elements used in this part of the garden – low walls, gates and trees – direct the view towards the horizon. Across the garden, house and landscape are linked to each other in an aestheticization of the view; vistas from the loggia and the hall are channelled along avenues towards the landscape. Landscape and villa are therefore joined together in a single architectural structure by means of these avenues. The separate elements formalizing this arrangement are set up along the axes thus formed. Various elements can be left out or added to bring about the *integrazione scenica*. According to Palladio the road is also an element of this *integrazione scenica*. It is an environment in itself, a little higher than the fields it crosses, shaded by trees and offering pleasant views.

The arcadian idyll, the original motive behind villa life, was subordinated to the tough reality of the agricultural economy. Delight in nature within the enclosed domain of the villa was done away with. What had been lost on the outside could be regained in the interior. In the frescos covering the walls of the reception rooms the ideal of rural life could be recreated and the landscape restored to its arcadian significance. Arcadia, as the perfect illusion, was thus added to the villa.

LITERATURE

J.S. Ackerman, *Palladio.* New York 1986.
R. Bentmann & M. Müller, *Die Villa als Herrschaftsarchitektur.* Frankfurt 1970.
A. Palladio, *The Four Books of Architecture.* London 1965.

L. Puppi, *Andrea Palladio. Das Gesamtwerk.* Stuttgart 1977.
R. Wittkower, *Architectural Principles in the Age of Humanism.* London 1949.
M. Wundram & T. Pape, *Andrea Palladio.* Cologne 1988.

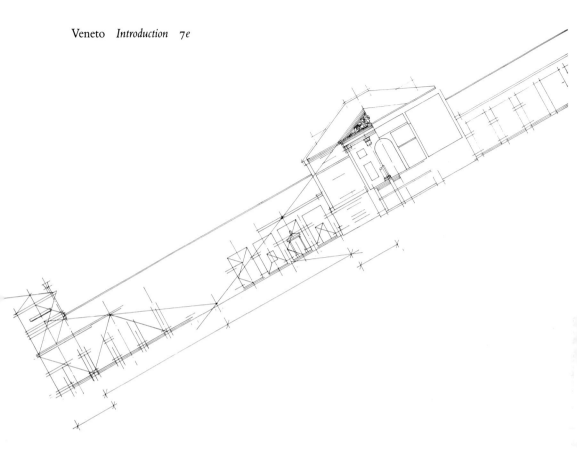

Villa Barbaro

The Villa Barbaro was built for the prominent humanists Daniele and Marc'Antonio Barbaro. Palladio was given the commission in 1549, the year in which he also began to collaborate with the two brothers, both of whom were experts on architecture. In 1556 Daniele was to publish an annotated version of Vitruvius, for which Palladio provided the illustrations. He is also supposed to have accompanied Palladio on his journey to Rome in 1554. Marc'Antonio was actively involved in the erection of several public buildings from 1574 until his death in 1595.

A number of aspects of the Villa Barbaro that seem rather out of place in Palladio's *œuvre* should probably be ascribed to the influence of the Barbaro brothers. The frescos in the hall were painted by Veronese between 1560 and 1562, in all probability without Palladio's involvement: the painter is not mentioned in the *Quattro libri*. In the murals of Veronese the ruins of antiquity formed an important motif, representing immortality and symbolizing the life of the ancient villa whose example the landowners wished to follow. In the frescos he made use of pre-existing architectural drawings of ruins of Naples and Rome. Veronese was not so much interested in presenting a faithful reproduction of these as suggesting an ancient landscape. In one of the frescos the Villa Barbaro is situated in this imaginative Ancient Arcadia.

In reality the villa is situated at the foot of the Dolomites, on a slight rise on the dividing line between the hills and the plains. At the front of the villa is a long avenue at right angles to the contours, fringed with a double row of trees, which directs the view towards the horizon (fig. 2). The usual *centuratio* division of land does not exist at the Villa Barbaro, but the landscape is organized by the avenue and thus integrated into the plan. A few remains of the walls and fireplaces of an earlier medieval *castello* are also integrated. A distinction between the living quarters and the outbuildings is made in the composition. In the *Quattro libri* the elevation of the main block is smoothly rendered, whereas the elevations of the outbuildings are rusticated. The central block is pulled forward in relation to the side wings and they are connected on the *piano nobile* (fig. 3).

The way in which the axis comes to an end on the hillside parallels, to a certain extent, the Villa Godi. At the rear of the main block at both villas there is a terrace terminated by a central nymphaeum. Its treatment at the Villa Barbaro, however, is considerably more sophisticated.

Palladio himself states: 'That part of the fabric which advances a little forward has two orders of rooms. The floor of those above is even with the level of the court backward, where there is a fountain cut into the mountain opposite the house, with infinite ornaments of stucco and paintings. The fountain forms a small lake, which serves for a fishpond. From this place the

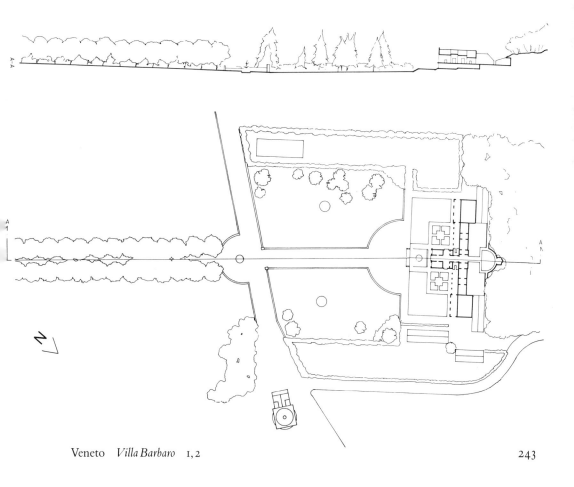

Veneto *Villa Barbaro* 1, 2

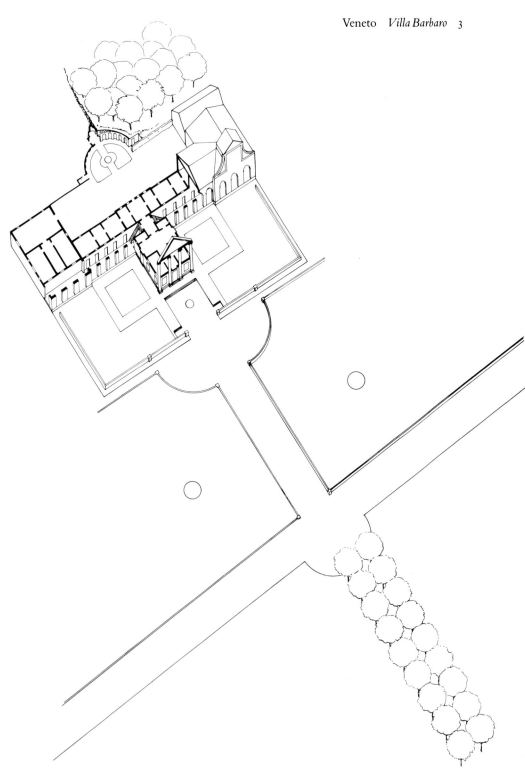

water runs into the kitchen; and after having watered the gardens that are on the right and left of the road, which leads gradually to the fabric, it forms two fishponds, with their watering places upon the highroad; from whence it waters the kitchen gardens, which are very large, and full of the most excellent fruits and of different kinds of pulse.'

The emphasis laid on the functional significance of the pool in the water circulation of the complex and on the fertility of the kitchen gardens and orchards on both sides is striking. Apparently Palladio thought it desirable to emphasize the agrarian connotations of the villa, which, because of its grandeur, might have been pushed into the background.

The treatment of the front elevations also seems to have been in conflict with Palladio's own design methods. It appears that an earlier version of the Villa Barbaro, in which the *piano nobile* was reached by way of the usual external staircase, was rejected by the clients. That is why a certain ambiguity in the position of the *piano nobile* is apparent in the lower floor of the built version, an effect reinforced by the use of the double order which, in other villas designed by Palladio, is only applied when there are two equal residential floors.

The actual entrance to the *piano nobile* is at the side of the main block and under the arcade. This has the effect of emphasizing the approach to the villa from the side, but in so doing allows the central approach avenue only a ceremonial function. A comparison with the layout of the Frascati villa can be made here. The planting of the *bosco* on the hillside behind the villa is also identical to the way in which the Frascati villas manifest themselves as set pieces against the background of the hill. It seems as if these similarities with the ceremonial treatment of the villas around Frascati were determined more by the influence of the two clients than by the vocabulary of Palladio. Though the villa does show evidence of exceptional architectural refinement, it falls short of the tension between architecture and landscape present in Palladio's other work, as seen *par excellence* in the layout of his masterpiece, the Villa Rotonda.

VILLA BARBARO	LITERATURE
Maser	*Quattro libri*, Book I, plate XXXIV
Open Tuesdays, Saturdays and Sundays: June-September 15.00-18.00; October-May 15.00-17.00 Fee The *tempietto* is open to the public on Tuesdays, by prior arrangement only	C. Constant, *The Palladio Guide*. London 1987. A. Palladio, *The Four Books of Architecture*. London 1965. L. Puppi, *Andrea Palladio. Das Gesamtwerk*. Stuttgart 1977.

Villa Contarini/Camerini

The Villa Contarini was built on the foundations of a medieval castle. It was strategically situated at a ford over the Brenta and formed an outpost of the town of Vicenza. From there the approaches and the farmlands belonging to the town could be controlled. In 1413, more than a century before the large-scale cultivation of the Veneto, the castle with its adjoining farmland was adapted as a country house by the Contarini, an influential Venetian aristocratic family. The house was ideally situated to be converted into an agricultural centre for sixteenth-century recolonization activities. It was situated on important roads and a navigable river. The palazzo was demolished around 1545 to make way for a new, efficiently organized agricultural farm, constructed according to the model that Palladio had introduced to the Veneto with his agricultural villas. The client was either Francesco (then Mayor of Vicenza) or Paolo Contarini.

A drawing of 1543 suggests that Palladio may have worked on this first version of the Villa Contarini, but decisive proof is lacking. A map of 1556 gives precise information about the new villa. On the foundations of the former castle an almost square terrace was constructed on which a two-storey block was built, flanked by two small towers (fig. 2a). To each side of this terrace side wings were added and used as a granary and for the storage of agricultural machines. In front of the building was a walled yard, where the main entrance of the villa was located, and on the east side a number of pre-existing outhouses. In 1557 the Contarini appealed to the Magistro dei Beni Inculti for permission to extend the waterways. The channel between the old moat and the Brenta was widened to become the first step in an extensive irrigation system, which still provides the farmlands situated north of the villa with water (fig. 2b). The new canal was dug round the site behind the villa. After two right-angled bends it continued in a northerly direction. At the spot where the canal finally turned north once stood the Palazzo Supplicante, from where the progress of the farms could be controlled.

A number of metamorphoses in the further history of the Villa Contarini reflected changing attitudes towards life in the country. As a result of the loss of Cyprus, a principal grain supplier, in 1558, Venice had become almost entirely dependent on the agricultural production of the Veneto, from which, even more than before, it demanded an efficient organization and as great a yield as possible. Parallel with this, however, a strong urge to prove their aristocratic dignity developed among the patrician families, in whom political and economic power was concentrated.

While the large farmers maintained personal control over the development and working of the farm, there was, within the organization of the villa, a more emphatic distinction between the lofty villa life and the mundane existence of agricultural labour. Farming became an excuse for the

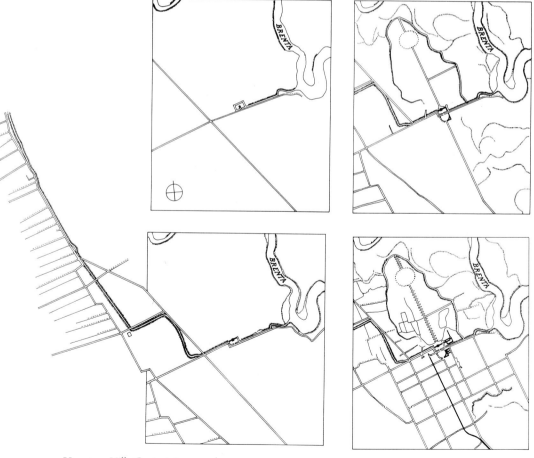

Veneto *Villa Contarini* 1, 2 a-d

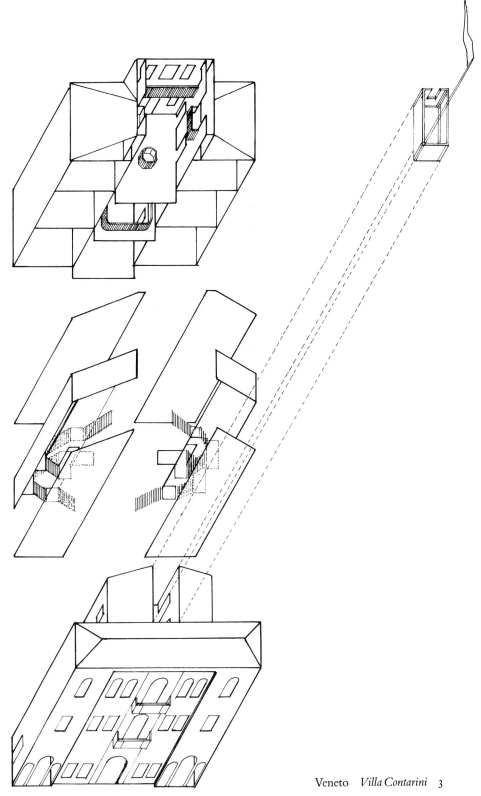

life of a gentleman and the villa a *visitá della nobilitá e della ricchezza*. In this respect the changes made to the Villa Contarini from the beginning of the seventeenth century were almost all geared towards effacing the agricultural function and to sweetening the aristocratic country life. The old farm was given a facelift and a number of facilities were added in order to make possible lavish feasting and the housing of a large number of guests. When the central block, the residence of the landowner (fig. 3), had been adapted to meet the new demands, the east wing was enlarged accordingly and provided with a new front façade; the villa was also considerably extended on the south side.

A map of 1788 gives the first accurate representation of the results of the conversions. Apart from the west wing the villa was shown in the same condition as that in which it can be seen today. The enlarged east wing no longer served as a barn, but functioned as library, fresco gallery and exhibition space for the Contarini's collection of antique stone sculptures and inscriptions. A statue terrace was built on the roof, the fishpond was enlarged, and the villa was extended by the construction of the stables and coach house which were necessary for the owner's equestrian pursuits. A

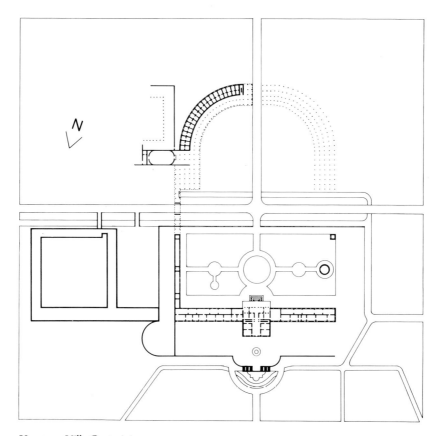

complex was built to the south of the villa containing a ceremonial entrance avenue, a chapel, a guest house and several annexes (fig. 2 c). The guest quarters and the chapel were connected to the east wing of the villa by a high-level corridor. Vision is emphatically directed towards the villa by the quarter-circular building, which was probably projected as a semicircular one, the 'missing' quarter taking the form of a double row of trees on the other side of the avenue (fig. 4).

To complete the design the axis was mirrored behind the villa, where an avenue of the same length, ending in a hippodrome, was constructed. The forecourt was provided with a Baroque garden and two fountains, thus finally achieving Doni's sixteenth-century ideal, although the dream was disturbed by the west wing of the villa, which still had the appearance of a barn. A few years later, however, this was also to be harmonized with the east wing; the difference in the way the front façade was treated continued to contrast, however, with the ruralness of the rear elevation (fig. 5). Finally, an arcadian landscape with a lake, winding paths, and an artificial hill (with a collection of casually but deliberately scattered antique stones) was laid out to the north of the villa (fig. 2 d). With this staging of an orderly illusion of nature within the grounds of his villa the landlord could then finally be released from his sixteenth-century role of agrarian aristocrat and enjoy the life of a gentleman living in the midst of nature.

VILLA CONTARINI/CAMERINI

Piazzola sul Brenta

Open: 9.00–12.00, 15.00–18.00
Closed Mondays
Fee

LITERATURE

C. Constant, *The Palladio Guide*. London 1987.
A. Palladio, *The Four Books of Architecture*. London 1965.
L. Puppi, *Andrea Palladio. Das Gesamtwerk*. Stuttgart 1977.

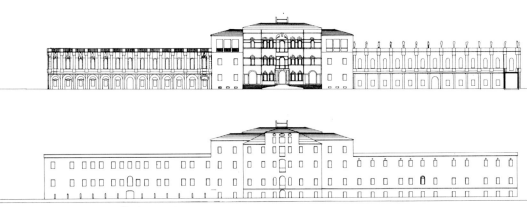

Villa Cornaro

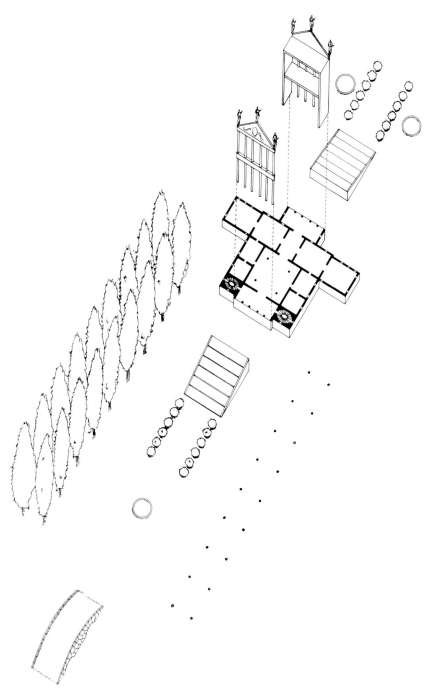

Giorgio Cornaro commissioned Palladio to build this villa in 1551 after he had inherited part of the family property at Piombino Dese on the death of his father. In 1554 the house was occupied, although it was not finally completed until 1590 when the side wings were added. Frescos by Mattia Bartolani and stuccoes by Cabianca were added in the eighteenth century. The villa has been carefully restored and still contains many of its original features.

The villa has two equal floors, and this is reflected in the architectural treatment of the façade. The hall is an example of a tetrastyle, a square hall with four columns. The columns in the Villa Cornaro are made to lean a little in order to reinforce the perspective effect and make the hall seem higher. Just as at the Villa Pisani at Montagnana the staircases are oval shaped and situated next to the façade. The stairs are positioned on both sides of the loggia at the rear and connect the upper and lower floors, so that the upper floor is also accessible from the loggia (fig. 3).

In this design the service wings are integrated into the building volume. They were placed in such a way that, on the street side, a broad frontage was created and, on the garden side, the impression was given of a pavilion placed in the garden (fig. 4). As at the Villa Pisani, where the street elevation is made almost flat, the urban context is here, too, accommodated in the treatment of the building volume. The front loggias were added to the façade like a double balcony and give views in three directions. The loggias at the rear are pushed into the block, thus giving protection from direct sunshine (fig. 1). At the rear the view over the fields outside the enclosure is reinforced along the axis of the villa by a double row of trees, a fountain and a grass bridge. The grass bridge, whose five arches span the ditch bordering the site, was an invention of Palladio, who thus achieved an uninterrupted continuation over the water of the grassy path. This version of the Palladian bridge was often used later in English landscape gardens, the most famous example being that at Stourhead.

VILLA CORNARO

Via Roma 104
Piombino Dese

Open Saturdays only, or by appointment: May–September 15.30–18.00
Fee

LITERATURE

Quattro libri, Book II, plate XXXVI

C. Constant, *The Palladio Guide*. London 1987.
A. Palladio, *The Four Books of Architecture*. London 1965.
L. Puppi, *Andrea Palladio. Das Gesamtwerk*. Stuttgart 1977.

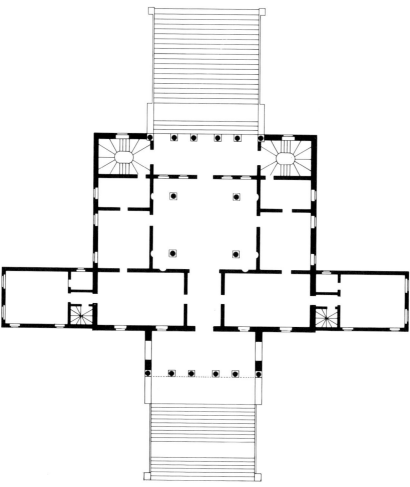

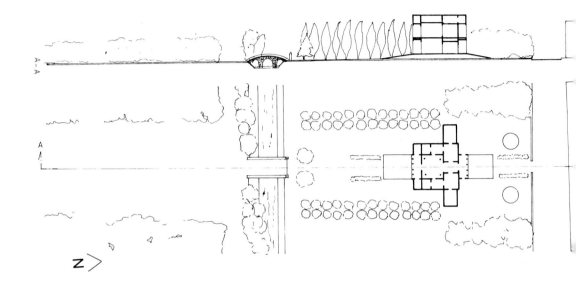

A-A

A
A

N

Villa Emo

In 1539 Leonardo Emo di Alvise inherited part of his uncle's property in Fanzolo, which had been obtained by the family as a result of their land reclamation work. He was at that time seven years old. In 1559 Leonardo decided to build a residential complex at the centre of his farmlands and commissioned Palladio to effect his plans. The frescos in the interior of the hall, the loggia and four adjacent rooms were completed between 1560 and 1565 by Giambattista Zelotti. A mixture of heroic Roman deeds, heathen legends and scenes from Christian history was portrayed between Corinthian columns painted in perspective. The restrained character of these frescos certainly reflected the wishes of Palladio himself, who did not wish to see architecture dominated by decoration. The description of the villa in the *Quattro libri* is fairly concise. In contrast to his usual practice Palladio here gives the dimensions of the rear garden. This covers a rectangle and is dissected by the small river, from which the situation derives its charm. Part of the garden was later remodelled as a 'natural landscape' with groups of trees.

The main axis of the Villa Emo follows the direction of the existing *centuratio* division of the land. This direction was emphasized by the projection of the axis in long tree-lined avenues at the front and rear of the main building, anchoring the villa in the centre (fig. 3). From some distance away the position of the villa in the landscape is clearly marked. From close by, however, the buildings are hidden behind high hedges and the entrance gate. From the front terrace the broad steps lead to the *piano nobile*, and from the loggia there is a view back, over the garden and its enclosure, of the landscape that from this position is ordered by the projection of the central axis. The steps to the loggia are considerably longer and less steep than those depicted in the *Quattro libri* (fig. 4). This gives the impression of a forecourt sloping right up to the loggia, reinforcing the central position of the building volume. The development of a transverse axis through the centre of the galleries was fairly exceptional given the general predisposition to monoaxiality. This axis passes through a side entrance of the garden and is stopped by a chapel on the opposite side of the road (fig. 1). The outbuildings are kept separate from the house (the asymmetrical one-winged Villa Garzoni at Pontecasale, designed by Sansovino, one of Palladio's predecessors, could have functioned as a model for the Villa Emo). The outbuildings also remain separate programmatically, and there is no direct entrance from the central *piano nobile*. The loggia is recessed into the main block and its side walls have murals. This re-emphasizes the concentration on the single direction of the main axis and, thus, on the negation of the side wings. It is only in the front elevation that the continuation of the gallery brings house and outbuildings into a unified whole.

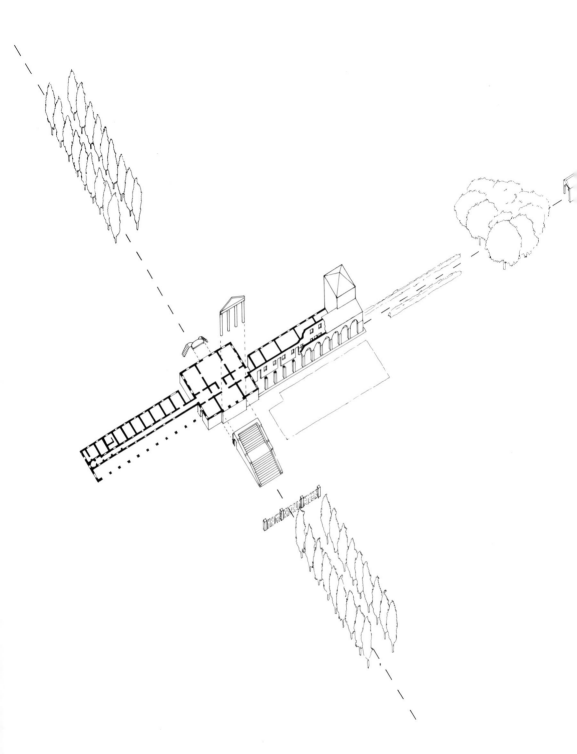

Veneto *Villa Emo* 2

The difference in the treatment of the front and the rear elevations is striking. Just as at the Villa Piovene at Lonedo, an absolute separation seems to be suggested between the symbolic significance of the front and the 'rustic' agrarian character of the back of the buildings. The impression of the *padrone*'s dignity continues from the front into the interior of the living quarters and is added as a separate element to the architectural system. This difference is continued in the solution to the landscape setting. The kitchen gardens are at the back and, on this side, one looks out along the axis imposed on the landscape over a wide, open stretch of land between rows of trees which seem to merge imperceptibly into the agricultural fields. The rows of trees in front of the villa are planted much more closely together and thus form an avenue, which, like the embodiment of a meridian, maps the landscape and brings it under control.

The ideological agrarian programme, which postulated land reclamation on the basis of the re-feudalization of the Veneto, can be seen in what is probably its most complete form at the Villa Emo. In his solution to this programme at the Villa Emo, including the villa's setting in working farmlands, Palladio provides his most complete and advanced example of the agricultural villa. The tension between the formal architectural vocabulary and the reference to traditional Veneto farm elements, which in the Villa Godi had led to a certain ambiguity and at the Villa Rotonda had resulted in complete formal control of the landscape, is here transformed into an almost nonchalant dialogue between the two components. That these components remain independent and identifiable within the total scheme does not only put matters into perspective but also even leaves room for the suspicion that the maestro might be making a somewhat ironic insinuation about the dignity of his client.

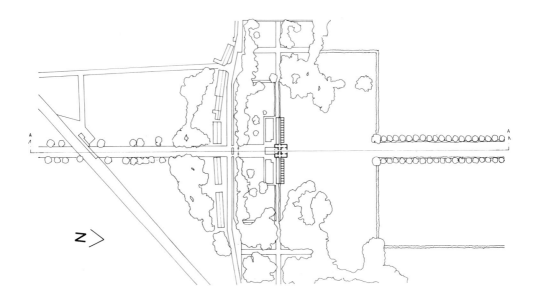

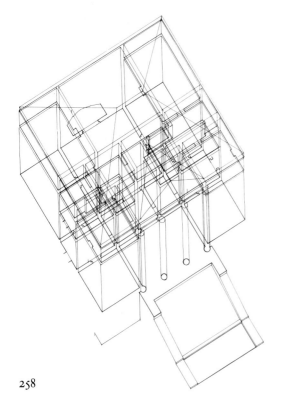

VILLA EMO

Fanzolo di Vedelago

Open Saturdays, Sundays and holidays:
  June-September 15.00-18.00;
  October-May 14.00-17.00
Closed January and February

LITERATURE

Quattro libri, Book II, plate XXXVIII

C. Constant, *The Palladio Guide*. London
  1987.
A. Palladio, *The Four Books of Architecture*.
  London 1965.
L. Puppi, *Andrea Palladio. Das Gesamt-
  werk*. Stuttgart 1977.

Villa Godi/Malinverni

Villa Godi was the first villa Palladio worked on as an independent architect. The client, according to the *Quattro libri*, was Girolamo de Godi. The plan is dated 1537. Building activities commenced in 1540 and the villa was completed in 1542. It is possible that the Pedemuro workshop, with which Palladio had connections as stonemason and architectural adviser, was involved in the building. Several years prior to the construction of the villa a *barchessa* (farm) had been built on the site. The incorporation of an already existing structure probably determined the position of the complex and caused some irregularities in the plan. Between 1549 and 1552 Palladio carried out some changes in preparation for the painting of frescos – in the south wing by Gualtiero (1552) and in the central hall and north wing by Zelotti (1552-55).

When the executed plan of the villa is compared with the version represented in the *Quattro libri* by Palladio a number of remarkable differences are apparent. The outbuildings as shown in the published version would probably not have fitted on to the site, and the terrace at the front has been radically altered in relation to the frontality of the main block. In the unexecuted plan the front side of the terrace was enclosed by a wall with a central entrance, and one approached the villa by way of a square, surrounded by a gallery of columns (fig. 1). The axiality of the plan would have been emphasized even more by the raised and frontally-treated central part of the main block. From the valley the villa would probably have manifested itself as an enclosed block, above which only the upper part of the front façade would have been visible. The raised part, with its culminating triangular pediment, would have had the function of emphasizing the central entrance and the articulation of the scheme in its situation.

The version constructed shows a totally different situational treatment. It shows, for example, clear similarities to the way in which the Villa Barbaro was situated on the hillside and where the villa entrance has also been moved out of the central axis. The front terrace is supported by a semicircular retaining wall, only the top of which is visible from the villa, allowing the central axis of the villa to dissolve into the distant hills. The steps to the *piano nobile* of the central block were narrowed, reinforcing the horizontal appearance of the front façade. Due to the absence of the raised and central middle part, the three resulting sections became more independent of each other within the horizontally-treated total volume. This is emphasized by the location of the windows. In the built version there are four windows in the side blocks instead of three as in the published plans. The two central ones are shifted towards each other, giving the side blocks a symmetrical structure of their own which is supported by the location of the chimneys. The outermost windows were placed more towards the edges, giving the impression that the block continues round the corner and articulating rather the volume than the frontality of the façade.

It is interesting to note that the *Quattro libri* were published considerably later than the building of the Villa Godi. This has led to the assumption that in the presentation of his design Palladio was more concerned with its formal structure than with how it was actually built, and that he adjusted this early villa, which does not conform to the standardized type, in order to make it fit into the series of his other designs.

At the rear the similarity with the Villa Barbaro is once again obvious. In both villas a nymphaeum and a pool are used to define the villa in the slope, although the semicircular wall at the Villa Godi remains a free-standing element and at the Villa Barbaro it actually separates the slope from the rear terrace. In fact the design for the Villa Godi has an ambiguous character. Its situation almost approaches the arcadian ideal; the villa is situated in the hills, with a view of the river winding through a broad valley edged with a luxuriant growth of trees. In its formal treatment, however, it anticipates the agricultural villa type and the standardization of the elements with which it was fixed in the landscape by Palladio. There is clearly a tension between the vernacular and the seeds of the formal architectural system, which was to be further perfected in the plan of the nearby and spatially related Villa Piovene.

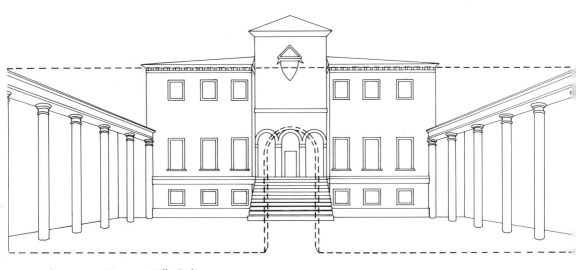

Veneto   *Villa Godi*   2

VILLA GODI/MALINVERNI

Lonedo di Lugo Vicentino

Open Tuesdays, Saturdays, Sundays and
  holidays: 15 March–October 14.00–
  18.00, except July–August 15.00–19.00
Fee

LITERATURE

Quattro libri, Book II, plate XLXVIII

C. Constant, *The Palladio Guide*. London
  1987.
A. Palladio, *The Four Books of Architecture*.
  London 1965.
L. Puppi, *Andrea Palladio. Das Gesamt-
  werk*. Stuttgart 1977.

Villa Piovene

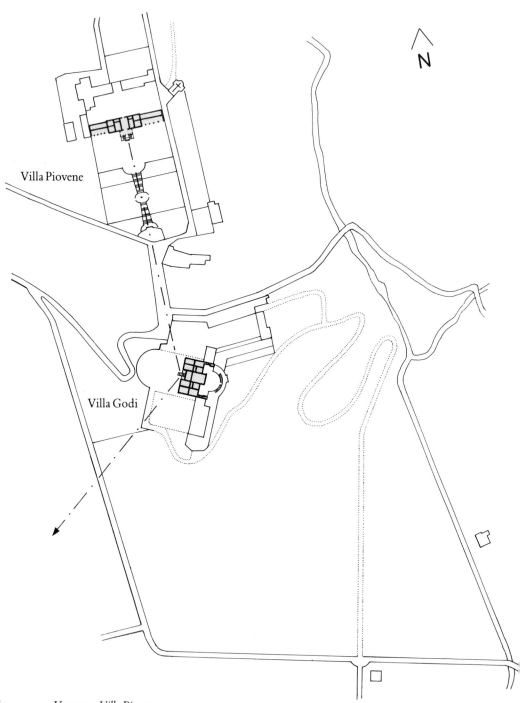

Villa Piovene

Villa Godi

Veneto   *Villa Piovene*   2

This villa was first ascribed to Palladio by Bertotti Scamozzi in 1778; it is not mentioned in the *Quattro libri*. Vagueness about the complex building history is probably the reason for the uncertainty about the extent to which Palladio was responsible for the plan. The commission was probably given to Palladio in 1539. It is known that in 1541 Tomasso Piovene was owner of the villa, which then consisted of the central part of the main block. The present size of the main block results from the addition of two rooms on each side. The projecting portico with the steps to the *piano nobile* probably dates from 1589 and can no longer be ascribed to Palladio. Muttoni was responsible for the entrance gate, the monumental steps, the terraces at the front, and the colonnades at the side of the house. These additions were completed in 1740. In the first part of the nineteenth century Antonio Piovene, the then owner, added a romantic landscape garden, situated away from the main complex opposite the side entrance of the villa.

The formal entrance to the villa is at the front at the bottom of the monumental axial staircase. A rear entrance is achieved by means of a gate in the enclosing garden wall. On one side the rear court is bounded by the solid façade of the main block with its adjoining wings, and on the opposite side by an ancillary building. To anyone who has seen the villa crowning the monumental steps from the ascending route, the contrast with the rustic, hardly formalized elevation of the side facing the rear court is so absolute that it seems as if they belong to two different buildings. A similar contrast is also to be seen at the Villa Emo, which, however, is only to be approached from the front. At the front of the Villa Piovene the adjacent service wings have been opened out into column galleries. On the terrace the villa seems to be floating in space: it is from the loggia that the panorama unfolds.

From the edge of the terrace the view is directed over the steps with their connecting parterres, at the far end of which the Villa Godi is given the central position in the axis. Because of the oblique position of the Villa Godi in this axis, the view is deflected in the direction of the valley (fig. 1). The erection of the Villa Piovene so close to the Villa Godi and also its relationship to it can be explained by the rivalry between the two families. The duality of the two villas is evident, but which of the two succeeds in achieving hegemony of the space is left unresolved. If the loggia, which can no longer be ascribed to Palladio, and the eighteenth-century colonnades are disregarded, there is even a similarity in the front elevation of both villas. The cultural jealousy, which seemed to have determined the Villa Piovene's position, is given a hidden meaning. Nowhere in Palladio's work is there such an emphatic mutual reference between two villas. The prospect of the Villa Godi is an essential component of the Villa Piovene's spatial system, thus making the *alter ego* an essential link in the setting. This makes the reference to a hierarchy ironic. It is only in relationship to each other that the game of spatial hegemony can be played.

VILLA PIOVENE

Lonedo di Lugo Vicentino

Garden only: 9.00-12.00, 14.00-18.00
Fee

LITERATURE

C. Constant, *The Palladio Guide*. London 1987.

A. Palladio, *The Four Books of Architecture*. London 1965.

L. Puppi, *Andrea Palladio. Das Gesamtwerk*. Stuttgart 1977.

Villa Rotonda / Capra

In 1566 the papal prelate Paolo Almerico returned to his native Veneto after having served a number of successive popes in Rome. He asked Palladio to build him a summer residence on a hill about 500 m. outside Vicenza.

Palladio wrote that 'The site is as pleasant and delightful as can be found, because it is upon a small hill, of very easy access, and is watered on one side by the Bacchiglione, a navigable river; and on the other it is accompanied with most pleasant risings, which look like a very great theatre, and are all cultivated, and abound with most excellent fruits, and most exquisite vines, some of which are limited, some more extended, and others that terminate with the horizon; there are loggias made in all four fronts; under the floor of which, and of the hall, are the rooms for the convenience and use of the family.'

In the *Quattro libri* the villa is included in the chapter on urban villas because it did not have an agricultural function and, though not situated in the town itself, was, nevertheless, in the immediate vicinity of one.

In 1569 the villa was ready for occupation. It was only completed, however, after Palladio's death, by the architect Vincenzo Scamozzi, who, among other things, replaced the semicircular dome in Palladio's conception with a less pronounced vault over the central hall. The design of the dome is supposed to be based on that of the Pantheon. This was intended to be a reference to the owner's status. The *oculus* on top was originally open (as in Scamozzi's Villa Pisari La Rocca at Lonigo): a water outlet in the floor of the hall leads to a well in the basement. The present main entrance and the buildings flanking both sides of the southern access avenue were also added by Scamozzi in about 1620. Of the artists who worked on the decorations, Palladio mentions only Lorenzo Vicentino, who was responsible for the statues on the pedestals of the loggias.

The situation of the Villa Rotonda was described by Palladio as a large theatre which presented a changing but always beautiful spectacle on each side; this explains his decision to provide the villa, designed as a belvedere, with identical loggias on all four sides (fig. 3). In planning the interior of this four-sided symmetrical construction a round central hall presents a logical solution. As corn lofts were unnecessary, because the villa did not have any agricultural function, the hall was continued up to the roof, with a gallery over the *piano nobile*, and later, at the end of the seventeenth century, painted with illusionistic architectural and sculptural elements to look like an open-air *tempietto*. The semicircular dome would have made the villa a salient feature in the landscape and would have fixed it in the centre of the panorama that unfolds on all four sides (fig. 1). It is therefore regrettable that Scamozzi did not have the courage and the sensibility to construct the dome according to Palladio's design.

Due to its centralized shape it is usually suggested in descriptions of the villa that it is situated on top of the hill as an isolated object. The villa does indeed stand out in the landscape because of its location on a plateau and also because it is rotated forty-five degrees to the north, independently of

Veneto *Villa Rotonda* 2, 3

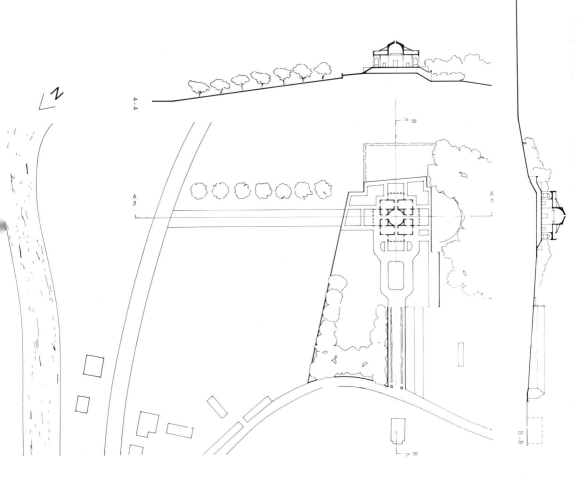

the local topography, in order that all façades of the house should receive some sunshine each day. Closer examination, however, reveals that despite its apparent autonomy the villa has been placed in the landscape with the utmost care. When the complex is approached, the villa is revealed gradually. The entrance facing the north-west loggia is recessed into the hill. Looking back over the entrance from the loggia a chapel can be seen on the axis on the opposite side of the road at the edge of the town. By means of this axis, linking the house, the entrance and the chapel, the formal relationship with the town is established. A walk around the villa reveals how its setting in the landscape is differently handled on each side. From the Strada della Riviera, below the north-east terrace, it can be seen how the villa is connected to the buildings on the edge of the town by the retaining wall of the terrace, although it juts out from the line of the other buildings. It is linked to the road and parallel river by means of a grassy raised embankment at right angles to the terrace wall. This raised feature at the north-east side of the villa is complementary to the recessed entrance and, on the edge of the terrace, makes explicit the relationship between the built-on land and the open landscape.

Walking along the Strada della Riviera the landscape rolls on behind the villa, as if in a film, but at no single point does the picture lose touch with the wooded slopes of Monte Berico. Cut out of the woods is the *giardino segreto*, which can only be reached from the basement. It is only on the east side, where the loggia discloses the most unobstructed view of the landscape, that the villa separates itself from the edge of the wood and is elevated in its surroundings. This is, therefore, the only side on which the retaining wall along the edge of the plateau meets the lower part of the site directly, without modifications or additions.

In the circuit round the villa the situative conditions seem to be reflected in the shape of the terrace and the treatment of its edges. Because of the villa's asymmetrical location on the terrace, the changing perspective effects, and thus its different and shifting positions with regard to its background, are projected into the terrace wall. The entire system of differentiating the landscape setting of the villa would, finally, have been anchored and unified by the semicircular dome, rising high above the house. This function is now only reflected in the repetition of the loggias on all four sides of the house.

The way in which the all-round symmetrical plan of the house is stage-managed in the landscape by means of the different treatment of the plateau in each of its four directions and its influence on the terrace walls confirms the mastery of this last villa project by Palladio. Precisely because there was no agricultural programme the landscape could be integrated without ideological prejudice into the composition as an independent component. The natural plasticity of the landscape, and not the reference to symbolic meanings, determines its interaction with the villa. Here Palladio reached the limits of the possibilities of confronting the landscape

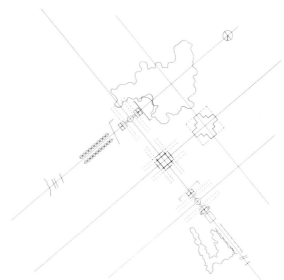

with an entirely controlled, formal architectural system in a stage-managed panoramic setting. This could result in two possible developments. One line of development was a further subordination of the landscape to a central perspective structure, as can be seen in French garden architecture, and the other – and this is anticipated in the setting of the Villa Rotonda – is the severing of the cosmic unity between landscape and architecture, which is fundamental to the development of paradigms in Enlightenment thought, dealing, as it does, with the contrast between nature and culture.

The architecture of Palladio, especially in this project, stood at the frontier between two worlds and was to prove of service to both of them. The final significance of the Villa Rotonda in the architectural theory of the last three hundred years lies, then, in the fact that the credo of Western thinking about the contrast between ratio and *genius loci* was here made concrete in an architectural manifesto which was actually constructed and which still exists as an example of an architectural achievement marking not only the point where ideologies diverged but, furthermore, a fundamental contradiction in modern Western thought.

VILLA ROTONDA/CAPRA

Vicenza

Garden and building: Wednesday
  10.00–12.00, 15.00–18.00
Garden: Tuesday and Thursday
  10.00–12.00, 15.00–18.00
Fee

LITERATURE

Quattro libri, Book II, plate XIII

C. Constant, *The Palladio Guide*. London 1987.
A. Palladio, *The Four Books of Architecture*. London 1965.
L. Puppi, *Andrea Palladio. Das Gesamt-werk*. Stuttgart 1977.

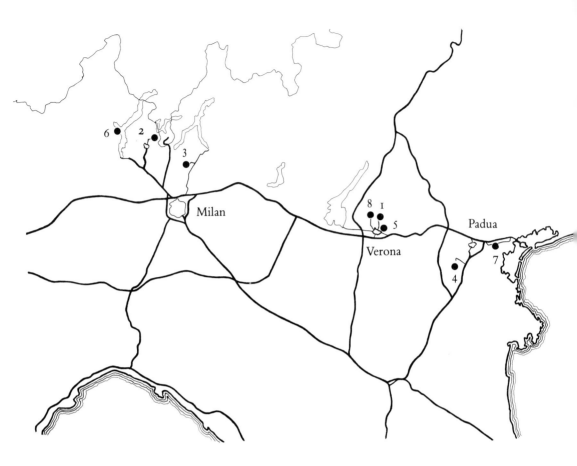

North Italy   *Introduction*   1

1 Allegri
2 Cicogna
3 Crivelli

4 Dona dalle Rose
5 Giardino Giusti
6 Isola Bella
7 Pisani
8 Rizzardi

6 North Italy

The North of Italy   272

Cicogna   273

Crivelli   277

Dona dalle Rose   280

Isola Bella   283

Pisani   286

The North of Italy

The three foci of Italian villa architecture were of course Tuscany, Rome and the Veneto. There are, nevertheless, examples elsewhere that cannot be omitted from any discussion of the Italian villa. In northern Italy especially, historically well-situated on the trade routes to the north and with important agricultural areas in the river valleys, there are several ceremonial and agricultural villas which justify a visit not only on their own merit, but also because in a number of these, later developments in villa architecture probably found their first form.

Isola Bella, centre of the empire of the Borromeo family, stretched along the shores of the Lago Maggiore, should be mentioned; the Villa Cicogna-Mozzoni, a well-kept jewel that has been in the possession of the Cicogna-Mozzoni family for more than five hundred years; the Villa Crivelli, once the proud centre of extensive agricultural possessions but at the moment in a poor state of decay; and finally, the villas Dona dalle Rose and Pisani, two idyllic spots to which the patricians from Vicenza and Venice travelled by boat for a festive stay in the *campagna*.

At first sight only the relatively arbitrary geographical location is noticeable. A closer look, however, reveals apparent similarities between the villas. Both the Villa Cicogna-Mozzoni and the Villa Dona dalle Rose are arranged on a crossing of axes, at whose ends the panorama is unfolded. This is an ordering which was not found in other regions at that time, and one in which the Mannerist principle of movement in the plan is projected on to the geometrical matrix without separating the view axis from the direction of movement.

While the Villa Pisani at Stra is an example of French influence on Italian villa design, the Villa Crivelli is a case on its own and demonstrates how the seventeenth-century French garden with its centrally developed perspective, can be integrated into the Italian tradition of panoramic stage setting in which the landscape outside the garden is not excluded but functions as an essential component in the interaction between the villa and the landscape. In this context the Villa Isola Bella is an exception. Without wishing to detract from its magnificent setting on the island in the Lago Maggiore, it is clear that the final realization of the complex has been determined primarily by an exaggerated tendency to monumentality.

LITERATURE

J. Chatfield, *A Tour of Italian Gardens.* New York 1988.

G. Masson, *Italian Gardens.* London 1987.
J. C. Shepherd & G. A. Jellicoe, *Italian Gardens of the Renaissance.* London 1986.

Villa Cicogna/Mozzoni

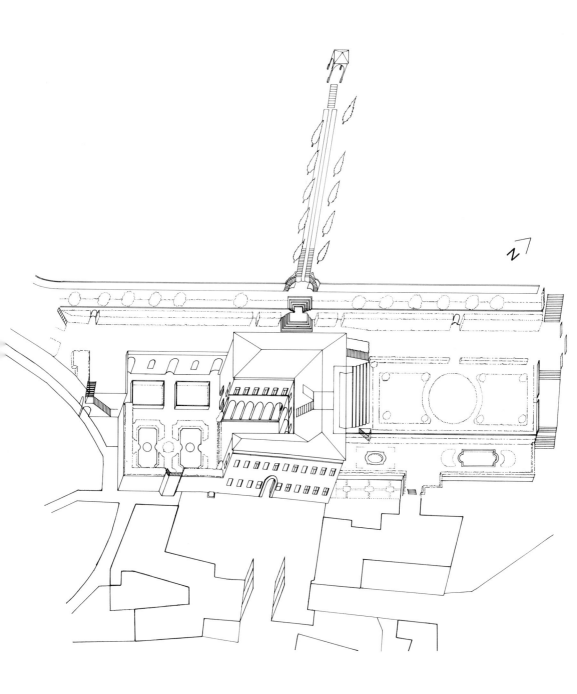

This fifteenth-century villa, situated along the road from Porto Cerésio to Varese, was originally built as a hunting lodge for the Mozzoni family. It is known from archival sources that the Mozzoni entertained Galeazzo Maria Sforza, Duke of Milan, there in 1476. The villa was probably extended to its present size by the brothers Francesco and Maino Mozzoni in the earlier part of the sixteenth century. The first designs for the garden are ascribed to Cecilia Mozzoni, daughter of Francesco, and her husband Asciano. The villa is still in the possession of the Cicogna-Mozzoni family, which, although no longer in residence, maintains the garden in excellent condition.

The village of Bisuschio lies in a valley between two ridges of hills to the west and the east and extends northwards to Lago di Lugano. The villa is situated to the north of the village and is connected to the main road by a drive, ending on the other side of the road in a now neglected pond. The slightly inclined avenue opens on to a square, the entrance of which is marked by two corner buildings which are distinct within the morphological structure of the village. The entrance gate in the east façade of the building is situated on the axis of the drive. This initial centrality appears to be discontinued in a courtyard enclosed on three sides by galleries. Two of the galleries are real and one is an illusionistic painted one. On the fourth side the courtyard opens to the south by means of a garden court which is slightly higher than the *cortile* (fig. 1). This garden is connected to another one on the north side of the house by means of an axis organizing the entrance to the building, the hall and the main staircase leading to the *piano*

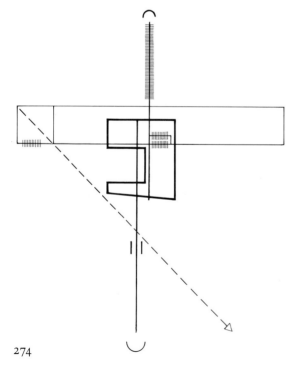

North Italy   *Villa Cicogna*   3

nobile. The landing connects to the higher north garden. On the *piano nobile* the villa appears to be arranged on a cross axis which continues through the french windows into the cascade on the slope, which is crowned by a small summer house. This axis is shifted with respect to the entrance gate and avenue.

The *cortile*, the 'sunken garden', the north garden and the cascade are linked with each other within the geometry of the plan by the ascending route. Along the west façade of the house is a wide gravelled path on the same level as the *piano nobile*. This leads from the *bosco* at its northern end to a terrace at the other end, where the view of the village is related to the receding slopes of the Lombardy hills against which the villa is situated.

A comparison with the Villa Gamberaia is unavoidable. There, too, a similar linear element (the bowling green) is stretched between the wooded slope and the panorama. In both villas the gardens are situated to the sides of the building and the link with the house is made by a cross axis. In the Villa Gamberaia the axis between the patio and the grotto garden runs in the same way as here, where, formed by the cascade and the *tempietto* and at right angles to the gravel path, it continues within the house as the regulating axis. The spatial scheme, however, is more complicated in the Villa Cicogna.

The promenade not only links the slope with the panorama, it also forms the element along which the differences in level of the various elements of the plan are made visible. The retaining wall opposite the house is interrupted only by a set of steps leading to the cascade, connecting the slope to the promenade. The garden court is symmetrically arranged on a cross axis of the promenade and ends in a nymphaeum integrated into the opposite garden wall. This garden wall seems to form a single entity with the projecting eaves of the village buildings. Only on the south terrace is the panorama unfolded in which village and landscape are integrated into the scenery. A concealed set of steps leads back to the sunken garden to reveal the main regulating axis on which these steps, the garden court, and the movement through the house are organized. Thus an axial cross over two levels is created (fig. 2), which orders all the elements of the villa internally, while at three of its extremities the different treatments of the panorama are indicated: *bosco*, summer house and viewing terrace, which are themselves linked by the promenade. At the fourth end of the axial cross is the entrance gate, which itself is finally integrated into the design by the sophisticated movement throughout the plan.

VILLA CICOGNA

Bisuschio

Open Sundays and public holidays:
  April-October 9.00-12.00, 15.00-19.00

LITERATURE

J. Chatfield, *A Tour of Italian Gardens*. New York 1988.
G. Masson, *Italian Gardens*. London 1987.

Villa Crivelli

The Villa Crivelli was once the administrative centre of a vast agricultural area. There are few records surviving concerning the history of the villa. According to Shepherd and Jellicoe, during the seventeenth century the domination of the villa over the farmlands was increased by the construction of the avenues which can still be seen running through the landscape, and by the extensions and modifications made to the service and living quarters. The complex is now in a state of advanced decay.

When the layout of the Villa Crivelli is compared with that of the traditional ceremonial villa, such as those which were built in the Tuscan area, one observes that there is a remarkable difference in the way in which the villa complex was set in the landscape. In the villas whose plans physically extend to their boundaries, the interaction with the landscape is formalized by the *integrazione scenica* of the panorama into the separate parts of the villa within the boundaries of the complex. In those villas in which there is axial development, the axis is fixed within the matrix of the plan or, if the axis is removed from the plan (as at the Villa Bombici), there is a recognizable tension between the axis as a formal component and the composition of other elements within the total plan of the villa. Even the Palladian villas in the Veneto, designed to express the formal control of the agricultural programme, recognized the subordination of the central axis to the rational, agricultural division of the land and served as an armature for the functional organization of the separate elements of villa and landscape,

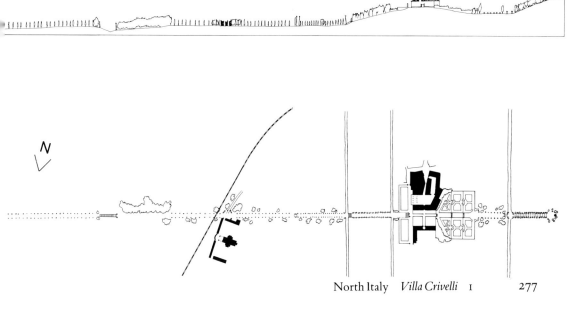

N

expressing the central position of the landowner's residence. With the Villa Crivelli, however, another arrangement has been devised which is best compared with the formal layout of the Villa Cetinale. Both villas took on their final form after Le Nostre had completed his first large gardens in France, and it is obvious that these French gardens have influenced the later Italian villas.

At both the Villa Crivelli and the Villa Cetinale a formal axis is introduced, relating the villa to the horizon and controlling the landscape all the way to the vanishing point. At the Villa Cetinale this point is located in the chapel on top of the hill, and at Crivelli somewhere indeterminate in the hills. The separate parts of the villa and the landscape are arranged and connected with each other, without any suggestion of a hierarchy, along the straight line, stretching for a number of kilometres like a meridian on a map (fig. 1). The plan of the Villa Crivelli is 'infinite'; the panorama is not only 'viewed' but also totally ordered. Herein lies the fundamental difference between these and the French gardens of Le Nostre, where the landscape outside the axially-arranged garden is ignored.

There is a starting point, marked by Il Gigante, a huge statue of Hercules, which, standing on the dividing line between the wood and the open area, surveys the landscape from its lofty position over the axis and is universally visible. From this point the cypress-lined avenue, known as the Scala del Gigante, stretches towards the horizon and apparently beyond (fig. 3). The villa gardens, the stables, the private houses, the barns and, a little further on, the marketplace and a church are grouped along the avenue. At the spot where the avenue is intersected by roads leading to the farmlands, gates, obelisks and other objects mark the centre of the complex. The landscape and the separate parts of the villa are all arranged in the same way along the avenue and become, in relation to a single absolute intervention, equal fragments of an artificially linked cosmos, which can only be surveyed in full by Il Gigante.

The connection between the house and the garden is also broken. The garden, built on three terraces on either side of the avenue, is not accessible from the house and functions as a local intensification of the landscape along the avenue; it is, indeed, intended to be viewed from a distance. In the villa the loggia usually forms the link between the garden and the private house. Here it has become independent, like the other parts, and is placed on the side opposite the house with a direct view of the farmlands. The interaction between landscape and villa does not express anything which is confined to one particular area but here makes a geographically broader statement. Only incidental references are made to the enjoyment of nature, and the worldly power of the landowner is projected on to and taken over by the figure of Hercules emerging from the wood, who, here, plays his divine game of controlling the horizon.

North Italy   *Villa Crivelli*   2, 3

VILLA CRIVELLI

Inverigo

For admission apply at the town hall
or to the owner, Dr Fumagalli,
Via Rillo 89, Meda

House closed owing to its dilapidated
state

LITERATURE

J. Chatfield, *A Tour of Italian Gardens*.
New York 1988.
G. Masson, *Italian Gardens*. London 1987.
J. C. Shepherd & G. A. Jellicoe, *Italian
Gardens of the Renaissance*. London
1986.

Dona dalle Rose / Barbarigo

North Italy *Villa Dona dalle Rose* I

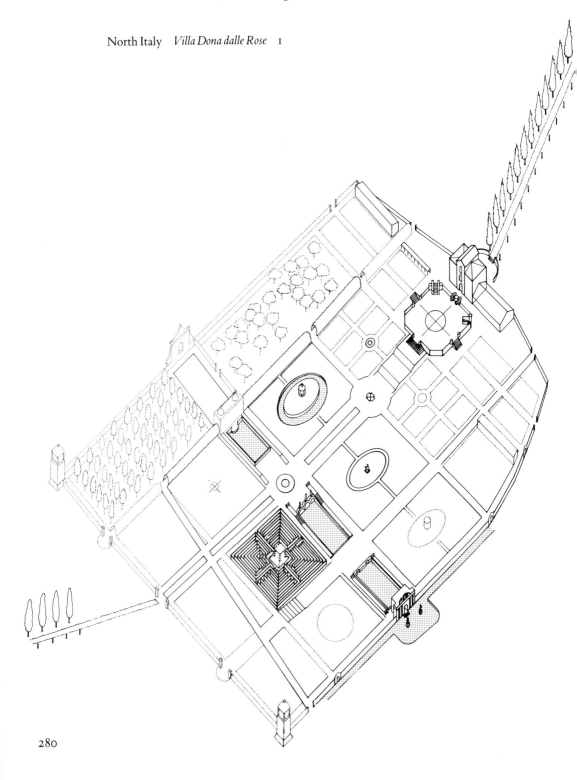

North Italy   *Villa Dona dalle Rose*   2

Antonio Barbarigo, procurator of San Marco in Venice, commissioned the construction of the villa in 1669. The identity of the architect is unknown. Over the years a number of alterations have been made to the original layout. The book *Istoria e coltura delle piante*, written by Paolo Bartolomeo Clarici and published in Venice in 1726, praised the gardens for their range of plant varieties and floriculture. Many of the terraces surrounding the house were arranged as flower gardens. A number of these have now disappeared and other borders were later planted with trees. Some essential components of the garden which were destroyed during the Second World War or fell into disrepair have now been restored. After the Barbarigo family the villa passed successively into the hands of the Dona dalle Rose, the Segré, and finally the Pizzoni Ardemani family, in whose possession the villa still remains.

The Villa Dona dalle Rose lies at the foot of the Eugenian hills. The area is formed by a localized extension of the flat Veneto landscape into these hills, which form a bowl-shaped enclosure around the land, creating a natural amphitheatre. Both house and gardens are placed on the flat portion of the site. The main entrance to the garden was on the eastern side, facing the flat Veneto landscape, and consisted of a water gate, which formed an essential element in all the villas along the Brenta since the principal means of access was by water; important cities like Padua and Venice were reached via the network of canals which spanned the Veneto district. From the water gate a water axis is formed by a series of ponds with cascades and fountains climbing up the gentle slope (fig. 1). Half-way along its length this axis is crossed at right angles by the main axis of the villa, which runs from north to south. On two sides the main orientation is continued by tree-lined avenues which press up the incline. If the villa ever looked as it is represented in an anonymous eighteenth-century painting, it should have been enclosed by a wall in which the ends of both axes were clearly marked by gates. This wall has largely disappeared, however, and the southern and western borders of the garden are blurred.

The house is reminiscent of the Villa Aldobrandini in Frascati, because of the choice of colour, the design of the façades, and the framing of the vertical mid-section of the real façade by the arboreal screens flanking the axis. Likewise, the use of gargoyles hidden in the gravel mosaic in front of the house echoes the villas around Rome, which were renowned for their water theatres. There is, however, an important difference: the opportunity for developing a panorama of the plain by using terracing and placing the house on the hill has been consciously rejected. The house is positioned on the border between the hill and the floor of the valley and the villa thereby remains enclosed within its own domain. This quality is strengthened by a sharp contrast between the horizontal nature of the flat layout and the vertical treatment of the lengthened part of the main axis by the avenues which lead up into the hills. This creates a tension between the arcadian references of the main axis and the reference to the concrete reality of the flat Veneto landscape, formalized by watercourses, in the cross axis.

The panorama bounded on three sides by hills focuses itself at the junction of the axes in the centre of the garden. On the eastern side, where this encirclement is broken, the villa's boundary, the garden wall, is also the horizon, and therefore the panorama is absent. Here the vista is limited to the garden, thus strengthening the enclosure. This motif is repeated throughout. The garden sections which are formed between the crossing axes and the boundary of the villa use tall hedges to surround spaces, where the motif is repeatedly presented in miniature and provided with marginal notes. The rabbit island (*isolotto*) and the labyrinth, diagonally reflected on both sides of the centre, are literally each other's opposites. One is a perfect imitation of the *leporarium* of the Roman Imperial garden, referring in both time and place to the unattainable world of the classical period, while the other is initially a secluded garden stressing extreme intimacy, in which the panoramic view from the elevated midpoint finally resolves the confusion, brings back reality, and turns the villa itself, as it were, inside out.

DONA DALLE ROSE/BARBARIGO

Valsanzibio
Padua

Gardens only: mid-March to mid-
    November 10.00-12.00, 14.00-17.30
Closed Mondays
Fee

LITERATURE

J. Chatfield, *A Tour of Italian Gardens.*
    New York 1988.
G. Masson, *Italian Gardens.* London 1987.
J. C. Shepherd & G. A. Jellicoe, *Italian
    Gardens of the Renaissance.* London
    1986.

Isola Bella

The construction of this villa, squeezed on to a small island, began around 1630. When the land first came into his possession Lancillotto Borromeo had planned to create a quiet and relaxing retreat. The estate comprised several islands and a great portion of the property surrounding the lake, which was then called the Borromean Gulf. His death in 1513 put an end to work on the site. About a century later the then owner, Julius Caesar II Borromeo, revived the idea of building a villa on the island of Isola Inferiore, or Isola di S. Vittore as it was then called. He acquired the grounds, which were distributed among the fishing families, and began the construction of the villa, probably according to the design of Antonio Crivelli. The architect died in 1630 and his client in 1638. The construction of the villa was continued by Julius' brother, Carolus III, who renamed the island Isola Isabella after his wife. The complex was finally completed by his son, Vitalianus VI Borromeo, who had approached several architects. Among them were Francesco Castelli, Francesco Maria Richini and the renowned Carlo Fontana. Filippo Cagnola is also mentioned as having provided a

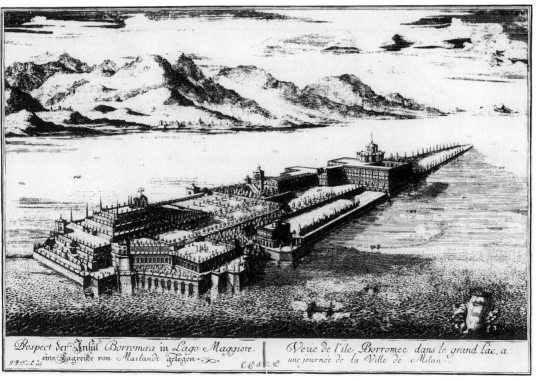

Prospect der Insul Borromäa in Lago Maggiore. eine Tagreise von Mailandt gelegen. *Veüe de l'ile Borromee dans le grand Lac, a une journée de la Ville de Milan.*

new plan at the beginning of the eighteenth century. However, it is more probable that the realization of the villa generally conformed to Crivelli's original design. The garden design was by Gaspare Vismare, although the above-mentioned architects also exercised some influence. The immense reservoir, hidden below the water theatre which was used mainly to supply drinking water for the island, was constructed by the famous Roman hydraulic engineer Mora Torreggia.

With the construction of the villa the island, which originally consisted of bare rocks, underwent a startling transformation. It was extended and terraces were built with rubble carried from the mainland. The existing fishing village remained intact and was even incorporated into the proposed scheme, in which the island was viewed as an immense drifting ship (see the early-eighteenth-century depiction by dal Re, fig. 1). The various parts of the villa were to represent respectively the prow (palazzo), the bridge (water theatre) and the poop (the wide area at the back). This idealized form was eventually modified in the course of construction. An asymmetrical plan came into being which led to the creation of a wedge separating the palazzo and the gardens from each other (fig. 2). Between these two components there was a transitional element which linked both parts of the plan and from which also a connection was made with the mooring in the village. At the entrance square a curious attempt has been made to involve the fishing village in the layout of the palazzo by erecting a false façade. The main entrance to the garden is through the palazzo and the grottoes in the

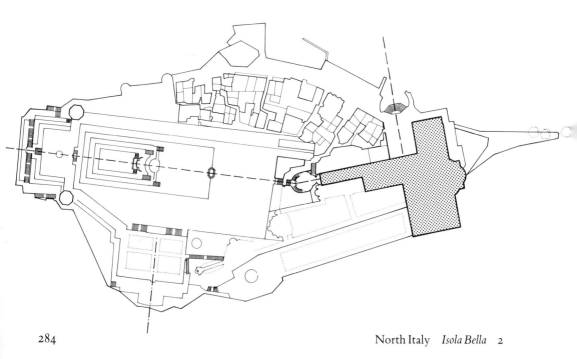

North Italy   *Isola Bella*   3

basement. They form a linked set of bizarre scenes which have a threatening effect when seen in the context of the cruelties which took place at the time of the villa's construction.

Although various authors over time have expressed their admiration for the sublime layout of the Isola Bella, it cannot be denied that such a concentration of individual features takes place that the overall impression is one of a certain pompous tension. It seems as if the component parts of the villa are compressed and an increase has taken place in the scale of the height proportional to its horizontal dimensions. From the water the effect is even stronger. As soon as one lands, however, it is apparent that the surface of the lake plays almost no part in the tension between cosmic stage-management and the lust for enjoyment.

ISOLA BELLA

Lago Maggiore

Access by boat from Stresa, Baveno and
  Pallanza
Open: March–October 9.00–12.00,
  13.30–17.30
Fee

LITERATURE

J. Chatfield, *A Tour of Italian Gardens.*
  New York 1988.
G. Masson, *Italian Gardens.* London 1987.

Villa Pisani / Nazionale

This villa, built for Alvise Pisani, Doge of Venice, was started in 1735 by Girolamo Frigimelica. His work was continued by Francesco Maria Preta and completed in 1756. In 1806 Alvise and Francesco Pisani sold the villa to Napoleon, who gave it to Eugene de Beauharnais, his viceroy in Italy. During this period the design of the garden was drastically altered. The garden was transformed into a park in which only a few of the original features were retained. Most of the sculptures in the garden were removed by Napoleon to Paris, or by Francesco I to Vienna. The villa became a national monument after it had become the property of Victor Emmanuel II.

The villa is situated on a bend of a tributary of the River Brenta, which branches off the canalized main stream at Stra (fig. 1). The building is placed immediately along the road parallel to the water, so that there is a view of the river traffic. As a result of this situation, though, there is hardly any scope

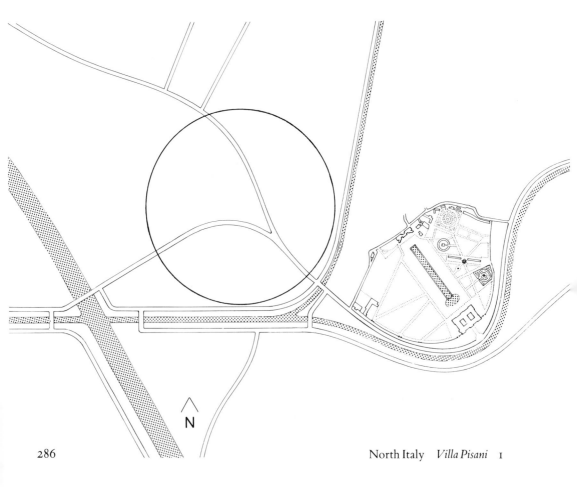

North Italy   *Villa Pisani*   2

for the building of a monumental approach at the front of the building, which, with its 114 rooms, is one of the largest on the Brenta. The building is decorated internally with many *trompe-l'œil* architectural paintings.

The garden is entered through a large atrium. It is laid out in the so-called 'French style'. A broad zone, flanked by two *boschi*, is kept open in the axis of the palace. The linear water element on this axis reminds one of the canals which are characteristic of the region. It is interesting to see how this pool, created in the fairly recent past for the hydraulic experiments of an engineering school, fits remarkably well into the vocabulary of the French style. At the end of the pool are the stables. These are built to resemble a neo-Palladian palazzo; there thus seems to be a second palazzo echoing the first (fig. 3). The monumental character of the façade is reinforced by the water axis and the planting on both sides. The central part of the mock façade, which Girolamo Frigimelica designed for its visual effect, can be seen from the palace on the Brenta, reflected in the water of the linear pool. This compensates, as it were, for the lack of a monumental approach to the real palazzo. Moreover, the location of this imposing mock façade extends, in the imagination, the grounds of the villa; it seems as if there is a further garden behind this façade, while, in reality, it is built exactly on the boundary of the site. A powerful illusion of infinity is evoked by means of this duplication. This illusion also seems to be continued inside the *bosco*. In the east *bosco* are a number of features, including a labyrinth, a summer house and an apparently inaccessible rabbit island. These are visually connected with specific elements – entrance gates in the shape of small towers – on the edge of the west *bosco*. Because the features in the east *bosco* are at its centre, the situation on the other side is assumed to be similar, and the west *bosco* therefore seems more extensive than it really is.

North Italy   *Villa Pisani*   3

VILLA PISANI/NAZIONALE

Stra

Open: 9.00–14.00
Closed Mondays and public holidays
Fee

LITERATURE

M. Faccini, *Guida ai giardini d'Italia*. Milan 1983.
B.M. Nobile, *I giardini d'Italia*. Bologna 1984.

Bibliography

J.S. Ackerman, 'The Belvedere as a Classical Villa', *Journal of the Warburg and Courtauld Institutes* 16 (1951), pp. 78-79.

J.S. Ackerman, *The Cortile del Belvedere.* Vatican City 1954.

J.S. Ackerman, *Palladio.* New York 1986.

H. Acton, *Gamberaia.* Florence 1971.

H. Acton, *The Villas of Tuscany.* London 1984.

L.B. Alberti, *De re aedificatoria.* Florence 1485. Ed. Ticozzi, Milan 1833.

G.M. Andres, *The Villa Medici in Rome,* 2 vols. New York & London 1976.

G.C. Argan, *The Renaissance city.* New York 1969.

M. Bafile, *Villa Giulia, L'architettura – il giardino,* Istituto d'archeologia e storia dell'arte Opera d'arte, Fascicolo 14. Rome 1948.

C. Bargellini & P. de la Ruffinière du Prey, 'Sources for a reconstruction of the Villa Medici, Fiesole', *Burlington Magazine* CXI (799) (1969).

E. Battisti, '*Natura Artificiosa* to *Natura Artificialis*', in D.R. Coffin (ed.), *The Italian Garden.* Washington, DC, & Dumbarton Oaks 1972.

I. Belli Barsali, *Ville di Roma.* Milan 1983.

I. Belli Barsali & M.G. Branchetti, *Ville della Campagna Romana.* Milan 1975.

S. Benedetti, 'Nuovi documenti e qualche ipotesi su Giacomo del Duca', *Palladio* (1970), pp. 3-22.

S. Benedetti, *Giacomo Del Duca e l'architettura del Cinquecento.* Rome 1972.

R. Bentmann & M. Müller, *Die Villa als Herrschaftsarchitektur.* Frankfurt 1970.

A. Berendsen, *Kunstschatten van Rome.* Zeist 1961.

P. Bigot, *Rome Antique au IV Siècle.* Paris 1942.

A. Blunt, *Guide to baroque Rome.* London & New York 1982.

E. Borsook, *The Companion Guide to Florence.* London 1973.

C. Bravero *et al., Florence, guide to the City.* Turin 1979.

H. Bredekamp, *Vicino Orsini und der heilige Wald von Bomarzo,* 2 vols. Worms 1985.

A. Bruschi *et al., Quaderni dell'Istituto di Storia dell'Architettura* 7-9 (1955), pp. 1-76.

A. Bruschi, *Bramante architetto.* Bari 1969.

A. Bruschi, *Bramante.* London 1977.

J.B. Bury, 'Review Essay: Bomarzo Revisited', *Journal of Garden History* 5 (1985), pp. 213-223.

D.R. de Campos, *I palazzi Vaticani.* Bologna 1967.

C. Caneva, *Boboli Gardens.* Florence 1982.

M.W. Casotti, *Il Vignola,* 2 vols. Trieste 1960.

R. Castell, *The villas of the ancients illustrated.* London 1728. Reprinted London & New York 1982.

J. Chatfield, *A Tour of Italian Gardens.* New York 1988.

D.R. Coffin, *The Villa d'Este at Tivoli.* Princeton 1960.

D.R. Coffin, *The Villa in the Life of Renaissance Rome.* Princeton 1979.

F. Colonna (attributed to), *Hypnerotomachia Poliphili.* Venice 1499. London 1904.

T. Comito, *The Idea of the Garden in the Renaissance.* New Brunswick 1978.

H. Conrad-Martius, *Der Raum.* Munich 1958.

C. Constant, 'Mannerist Rome', *A.D. Profiles 20* 49 (1979), pp. 19-22.

C. Constant, *The Palladio Guide.* London 1987.

M.J. Darnall & M.S. Weil, 'Il Sacro Bosco di Bomarzo: Its 16th-Century Literary and Antiquarian Context', *Journal of Garden History* 4 (1984), pp. 1-94.

M. Faccini, *Guida ai giardini d'Italia.* Milan 1983.

M. Fagiolo & A. Rinaldi, 'Artifex et/aut natura', *Lotus International* (1981), pp. 113-127.

G. Fanelli, *Firenze, Architettura e Citta.* Florence 1973.

G. Fanelli, *Brunelleschi*. Florence 1977.

P. Foster, 'Raphael on the Villa Madama: The Text of a Lost Letter', *Römisches Jahrbuch für Kunstgeschichte* (1967-68), pp. 307-312.

P. E. Foster, *A Study of Lorenzo de' Medici's Villa at Poggio a Caiano*. New York & London 1978.

C. Franck, *Die Barock-villen in Frascati*. Munich 1956.

J. Gadol, *Leon Battista Alberti, Universal man of the early Renaissance*. Chicago 1969.

J. Gebser, *Ursprung und Gegenwart*, Bd. 1, *Die Fundamente der aperspektivischen Welt*. Stuttgart 1949.

H. Giess, 'Studien zur Farnese-Villa am Palatin', *Römisches Jahrbuch für Kunstgeschichte* 13 (1971), pp. 179-230.

M. L. Gothein, *A History of Garden Art*. New York 1979.

J. F. Groos, *Villa d'Este*. Delft 1987.

J. Hess, 'Villa Lante di Bagnaia e Giacomo del Duca', *Palatino* 10 (1966), pp. 21-32.

J. Hess, 'Entwürfe von Giovanni Guerra für Villa Lante in Bagnaia (1598)', *Römisches Jahrbuch für Kunstgeschichte* 12 (1969), pp. 195-202.

W. M. Ivins, *On the rationalization of sight, De Artificiali Perspectiva*. New York 1973.

G. Jellicoe & S. Jellicoe, *The Landscape of Man*. London 1975.

G. Jellicoe & S. Jellicoe, *The Oxford Companion to Gardens*. Oxford & New York 1986.

Johannes, Cardinal de Jong, *Handboek der Kerkgeschiedenis*, vol. 3. Utrecht & Antwerp 1948.

P. O. Kristeller, *Eight Philosophers of the Italian Renaissance*. Stanford 1964.

C. Lamb, *Die Villa d'Este in Tivoli*. Munich 1966.

S. Lang, 'Bomarzo', *The Architectural Review* (1957), pp. 427-430.

C. Lazzaro, *The Italian Renaissance Garden*. New Haven & London 1990.

P. Levedan, *et al.*, *L'Urbanisme à l'époque moderne*, XVI-XVIII siècles. Geneva 1982.

P. Ligorio, *L'Antiquità*. Rome c. 1560.

E. MacDougall, 'Ars Hortulorum: Sixteenth Century Garden Iconography and Literary Theory in Italy', in D. R. Coffin (ed.), *The Italian Garden*. Washington, DC, & Dumbarton Oaks 1972.

E. MacDougall, 'The Sleeping Nymph, Origins of a Humanist Fountain Type', *Art Bulletin* 57 (1975), pp. 357-365.

G. Masson, *Italian Gardens*. London 1987.

D. Mignani, *Le ville medicee di Giusto Utens*. Florence 1982.

M. de Montaigne (trans. D. M. Frame), *Montaigne's Travel Journal*. San Francisco 1983.

P. Murray, *The Architecture of the Italian Renaissance*. London 1963.

H. A. Naber, *Van theorama naar sectio divina*. The Hague 1939.

B. M. Nobile, *I giardini d'Italia*. Bologna 1984.

A. Palladio, *The Four Books of Architecture*. London 1965.

E. Panofsky, *Hercules am Scheidewege*. Leipzig 1930.

B. Patzak, *Die Renaissance und Barockvilla in Italien*. Leipzig 1913.

A. Peneira, *American Express Pocket Guide to Rome*. London 1983.

J. Pieper, 'To make landscape visible (Piazza of Pitigliano by Antonio da Sangallo)', *Daidalos* (Dec. 1986), pp. 104-107.

Pliny the Younger (trans. W. Melmoth), *Letters*. Cambridge & London 1961.

P. Portoghesi, 'Nota sulla Villa Orsini di Pitigliano', *Quaderni dell'Istituto di Storia dell'Architettura* 7-9 (1955), pp. 74-76.

P. Portoghesi, *Rome of the Renaissance*. London 1972.

G. Procacci (trans. A. Paul), *History of the Italian people*. N. p. 1978.

L. Puppi, 'The Villa Garden of the Veneto from the Fifteenth to the Eighteenth Century', in D. R. Coffin (ed.), *The Italian Garden*. Washington, DC, & Dumbarton Oaks 1972.

L. Puppi, *Andrea Palladio. Das Gesamtwerk*. Stuttgart 1977.

J. Ross, *Lives of the early Medici as told in their correspondence*. Boston 1911.

H. Saalman, *Filippo Brunelleschi, the cupola of S. M. del Fiore*. N. p. 1980.

C. Scheiberling, *Het leven van de H. Philippus Nerius*. 's-Hertogenbosch 1874.

A. Schiavo, *Villa Doria Pamphili*. Milan 1942.

G. Schöne, *Die Entwicklung der Perspektivbüne von Serlio bis Galli-Bibiena, Theatergeschichtliche Forschungen* No. 43. Nendeln, Liechtenstein, 1977.

G. C. Sciolla, *Ville Medicee*. Novara 1982.

J. C. Shepherd & G. A. Jellicoe, *Italian Gardens of the Renaissance*. London 1986.

M. L. Simo, 'Vincenzo Giustiniani: his Villa at Bassano di Sutri, near Rome, and his « Instructions to a Builder and Gardener »', *Journal of Garden History* 1 (1981), pp. 253-270.

G. Smienk *et al.*, *Architectuur en landschap*. Delft 1985.

C. Stegman & H. Geymüller, *Die Architectur der Renaissance in Toscana*, vol. 2. Munich 1885-93.

O. Stein, *Die architecturtheoretiker der italienischen Renaissance*. Karlsruhe 1914.

H. Tanzer, *The Villas of Pliny the Younger*. New York 1924.

Venturini, *Le fontane del Giardino Estese in Tivoli*. Rome n. d.

A. Vezzosi, *Villa Demidoff, parco di Pratolino*. Florence 1986.

Vitruvius, *The Ten Books on Architecture*. London 1960.

R. Wittkower, *Architectural Principles in the Age of Humanism*. London 1949.

M. Wundram & T. Pape, *Andrea Palladio*. Cologne 1988.

L. Zangheri, *Pratolino, il giardino delle meraviglie*, 2 vols. Florence 1979.

Index

Albani, family: 135
Alberti, L. B.: 15, 19, 20, 21, 22, 23, 61
Aldobrandini, P.: 203
Alexander VII: 51
Algardi, A.: 140, 143
Almerico, P.: 266
Altemps, M. S.: 135, 221, 223
Ammannati, B.: 37, 47, 75, 87, 106, 110,
  124, 164, 166
Anguillara, family: 171
Antoniano, S.: 132
Ariosto, L.: 195
Aristoteles: 22
Azzuri, G.: 90

Bandinelli, B.: 75
Barbarigo, A.: 281
Barbaro, Daniele: 242
Barbaro, Marc'Antonio: 242
Bargellini: 61, 68
Barozzi, G. B.: see Vignola
Barrière, Dom: 204
Bartolani, M.: 252
Battoni, P.: 207
Bazzicchieri, C.: 204
Beauharnais, E. de: 286
Bella, S. della: 77
Benedetti, S.: 135, 155
Bentmann, R.: 7
Bernini, Gian Lorenzo: 148
Bernini, Pietro: 159
Blundell Spence, W.: 61
Boboli Gardens: 31, 33, 34, 36-41, 75, 77
Boccaccio: 18
Bomarzo, Sacro Bosco: 26, 81, 125, 132,
  138, 183, 186, 187-195, 205
Bonani, family: 217
Borghese, family: 190, 203, 223
Borghese, C. S.: 127
Borromeo, Carlo: 95
Borromeo, Carolus III: 283
Borromeo, family: 207, 272
Borromeo, Julius Caesar II: 283
Borromeo, Lancilotto: 283
Borromeo, Vitalianus VI: 283
Borromini, F.: 140, 212
Bourbon, family: 113
Bramante, D.: 89, 97, 99, 101, 102, 123,
  195

Brunelleschi, F.: 33, 39, 40, 69, 73, 89, 191
Buonaiuti: 61
Buontalenti, B.: 37, 47, 73, 75, 77, 126

Cabianca: 252
Cagnola, F.: 283
Camparese, P.: 133
Caneraia, A.: 90
Capello, B.: 75
Capponi, family: 55
Caracci, A.: 217
Carafa, F.: 88
Cardano, G.: 195
Caro, A.: 131, 132
Carpi, Girolamo da: 88
Casino Farnese: 116, 124, 159-162
Casino Gambara: 125, 162, 178, 181
Casino Montalto: 178, 181
Castelli, F.: 283
Cataldi, F.: 133
Cato: 198
Cenzi, F.: 212
Ceri, family: 207
Chigi, Flavio: 51, 133
Chigi, Mariano: 103
Chigi, Agostino: 103, 104
Cicero: 15, 19, 198
Cicogna-Mozzoni, family: 272, 274
Ciocchi del Monte, G. M.: 163
Cioli, V.: 75
Clarici, P. B.: 281
Colonna: 21
Colonna, Filippo I: 95
Colonna, Filippo II: 95
Colonna, Francesco: 195
Contarini, family: 249
Contarini, Francesco: 246
Contarini, Paolo: 246
Conti, Giuseppe Lotario: 131
Conti, Lotario: 131
Conti, Torquato: 131, 132
Contugi, P. A.: 203
Conzaga: 212, 217
Cornaro, Alvisa: 229
Cornaro, Giorgio: 252
Cortile del Belvedere: 89, 97-102, 123,
  124, 164, 195
Crescenzi, family: 106
Crescenzi, P. de: 17, 63, 229

Crivelli, family: 284
Crivelli, A.: 283
Cutting-Scott-Lubbock, Lady: 61

Dali, S.: 190
Danti, V.: 75
Del Duca, G.: 112, 116, 124, 125, 138, 155, 159, 174, 178, 181, 204
Delino, S. F.: 128, 141, 143
Della Porta, G. B.: 203
Demidoff, P.: 77
Dino, A.: 43
Dona della Rose, family: 281
Doni: 250
Dürer, A.: 23

Emo di Alvise, L.: 255
Este II, Ippoloto d': 88, 147, 148
Euclidius: 23

Fagiolo, M.: 80
Falconetto: 229
Falconieri, family: 212
Falda: 204, 224
Farnese I, Alessandro: 153, 198
Farnese II, Alessandro: 104, 112, 113, 132, 139, 147, 153, 159, 162, 178, 187, 190
Farnese, family: 116
Farnese, Ordoardo: 113
Farnese, Ranuccio: 112
Ferri, C.: 213
Ferruzzi: 135
Fichs, G.: 77
Ficino, M.: 15, 16, 19, 61
Filarete: 21
Filipini, family: 113
Foggini, G. B.: 81
Fontaine, P. F. L.: 175, 207
Fontana, C.: 51, 203, 224, 283
Franck, C.: 7, 200, 207, 213
Frigimelica, G.: 286, 287

Gambara, G. G. F.: 159, 178, 187
Garden of Eden: 17
Geymüller: 61
Ghezzi, P. L.: 213
Ghirlandaio, D.: 61
Ghyka, G.: 55
Giambologna: 37, 39, 75

Giusti, G.: 201
Giustiniani, Giuseppe: 171
Giustiniani, Vincenzo: 171
Godi, G. de: 259
Gori, family: 59
Gregory XIII: 99
Grimaldi, G. F.: 140
Gualtiero: 259

Hadrian: 122, 147

Innocent VIII: 86
Isola Bella: 272, 283-285

Jellico, G.: 277
Julius II: 124, 164
Julius III: 99, 153, 163, 168

Lambardi, C.: 171
Lancelotti, family: 217
Lante, family: 190
Lapi, Z.: 55
Laurentiis, D. de: 131
Letarouilly, P.: 115
Ligorio, P.: 11, 88, 99, 102, 115, 124, 147, 169
Lippi: 106
Loos, A.: 237
Lorenzo di Pierfranceso: 47
Lorenzo the Magnificent: 19
Lucullus: 198
Lunghi, M.: 221

Maccarone, C.: 88
Machiavelli: 16
Maderno, C.: 171, 178, 203
Madruzzo, C.: 135, 139, 187, 190
Maratta, C.: 213
Marchi, family: 43, 55
Martinus V: 95
Mattei, family: 217
Mazzini, A. 61
Mazzuoli, B.: 53
Medici, Alessandro de: 73
Medici, Cosimo I de: 15, 31, 37, 47, 61, 63, 73
Medici, Cosimo III: 39
Medici, family: 11, 31
Medici, Ferdinando: 73, 75, 106, 108, 110

Medici, Franceso I: 31, 37, 75, 77
Medici, Giovanni: 61
Medici, Lorenzo de: 31, 75
Meneghini, J.: 164
Michelangelo: 43, 105, 138, 164
Michelozzi, M.: 31, 61, 70
Michiel, G.: 106
Mirandola, G.P. della: 19
Monaldi: 133
Montaigne: 48, 77, 81
Montalto, A.P.: 101, 178
Montelupo, Raffaello da: 195
Moore, J.: 128
Moschino, S.: 195
Mozzi, G.: 61
Mozzoni, Cecilia: 274
Mozzoni, family: 274
Mozzoni, Francesco: 274
Mozzoni, Maino: 274
Müller, M.: 7
Muttoni, F.: 263

Napoleon I: 286
Nicolas III: 135
Nicolas V: 135
Nubale, F.: 133

Odescalchi, family: 171
Olivieri, O.: 203
Orsini, Pier Francesco I see Vicino
    Orsini
Orsini, Vicino: 124, 125, 131, 132, 139,
    181, 184, 186, 187, 190, 192, 193, 194
Orsini, Niccolò: 124, 125, 183
Orti Farnesiani: 87, 111-119, 124, 159, 181
Ovid: 16

Palazzo del Tè: 123
Palladio, A.: 7, 11, 21, 26, 51, 201, 223, 225,
    227-270
Pallavicini, family: 207
Pamphili, Andrea Doria: 141
Pamphili, family: 203
Pamphili, Giambattista: 140
Parigi, Alfonso: 37
Parigi, Giulio: 37, 74
Passignano, Domenic da: 203
Patzak: 61
Paul I of Sforza: 212

Paul III: see A. Farnese I
Pedemuro: 259
Pélerin, J.: 23
Penazzi: 135
Percier, C.: 175, 207
Peruzzi, B.: 87, 99, 103, 104, 105, 122, 153
Petrarch: 16, 23, 24, 179
Piccolomini, family: 217
Piovene, Antonio: 263
Piovene, Tomasso: 263
Piranesi, G.: 88, 89, 108
Pisani, Alvise: 286
Pisani, Franceso: 286
Pitti, L.: 37
Pius IV: 99, 124, 169
Pius V: 99
Pius VI: 169
Pius VII: 101
Pizzoni Ardemani, family: 281
Plato: 18, 19
Pliny the Younger: 10, 15, 33, 70
Plotinus: 19
Poliziano, A.: 61
Ponzio, F.: 127, 223
Pozzichelli, P.: 171
Praz, M.: 190
Preta, F.M.: 286
Pythagoras: 19

Quintilius: 147, 221

Rabelais, F.: 195
Rainaldi, G.: 113, 128, 140, 159, 171
Raphael: 103, 105, 123
Re, M. dal: 284
Ricci, Giovanni: 106
Ricci, Giulio: 106
Richini, F.M.: 283
Romano, G.: 123
Rosso, Zanobi del: 39
Rubin, G.: 133
Ruffino, A.: 212

Sacro Bosco: see Bomarzo
Sangallo, Giuliano da: 31, 75, 99, 122, 153
Sanmicheli, M.: 229
Sansovino, J.: 229, 255
Santen, J. van: see Vasanzio, G.
Scalza, I.: 139

Scamozzi, Bertotti: 263
Scamozzi, Vincenzo: 266
Segré, family: 281
Seneca: 15
Serlio, S.: 124, 155
Sgrilli, B.S.: 77
Shepherd, J.C.: 277
Sixtus V: *see* Montalto, A.P.
Specchi: 204
St Augustine: 19
Strozzi, family: 73

Telesio, B.: 19, 22
Toledo, Eleonora di : 37
Torreggia, M.: 284
Toti, F.: 139, 195
Tribolo, Niccolò: 37, 47, 73

Utens, G.: 31, 47, 73, 75

Vanvitelli, L.: 128
Varro: 115, 147
Vasanzio, G.: 127, 223
Vasari, G.: 37, 61, 87, 163
Vasi: 48, 95
Veronese: 242
Vestri, O.: 207
Viato: 23
Vicentino, L.: 266
Victor Emmanuel II: 286
Vignola: 11, 112, 116, 124, 125, 135, 153,
    155, 156, 162, 164, 174, 178, 181, 204, 221
Villa Abamelek: 89
Villa Albani: 110
Villa l'Albergaccio: 16
Villa Aldobrandini: 25, 26, 200, 201,
    202-206, 209, 214, 282
Villa Artimino: 31
Villa Barbaro: 201, 228, 240, 242-245, 259
Villa Barberini: 87
Villa Belpoggio: 25, 26, 205, 207-210
Villa Belvedere: 86, 89, 97, 99
Villa Bombici: 42-45, 51, 277
Villa Borghese: 85, 89, 107, 127-129, 141,
    223
Villa Bosco Parrasio: 87, 90-93
Villa Buoncompagni: 102
Villa Cafaggiolo: 31
Villa Careggi: 15, 16, 31

Villa Castello: 31, 34, 37, 46-48, 73, 123
Villa Catena: 126, 130-132
Villa dei Cavalieri di Malta: 87, 88
Villa Cetinale: 26, 27, 34, 49-53, 278
Villa Chigi: 103, 104, 133-134
Villa Chigi-Albani: 135-139
Villa Cicogna-Mozzoni: 272, 273-276
Villa Colonna: 87, 94-96
Villa Contarini: 228, 246-250
Villa Cornaro: 223, 228, 251-254
Villa Corsini: 89, 141, 145
Villa Crivelli: 26, 272, 277-279
Villa Demidoff: 77
Villa Dona dalle Rose: 272, 280-282
Villa Doria Pamphili: 25, 85, 89, 126,
    140-145
Villa Emo: 228, 237, 255-258, 263
Villa d'Este: 25, 81, 122, 126, 146-152, 181
Villa Falconieri: 211-214, 221, 223
Villa Farnese: 81, 112, 126, 132,
    135, 139, 147, 153-158, 162, 174, 181, 204
Villa Farnesina: 87, 103-105
Villa Gamberaia: 33, 34, 54-58, 275
Villa Garzoni: 255
Villa Giulia: 25, 26, 116, 124, 153, 163-
    169, 181
Villa Giustiniani: 89, 170-176
Villa Godi: 228, 242, 257, 259-261, 264
Villa Gori: 51, 59-60
Villa Grazioli: 205
Villa Hadriana: 39, 113, 122, 147
Villa Lancelotti: 201, 214, 215-219
Villa Lante (Rome): 87
Villa Lante (Bagnaia): 25, 26, 81, 116, 125,
    126, 158, 159, 161, 177-182, 225
Villa Lapeggi: 31
Villa Ludovisi: 87
Villa Madama: 87, 123, 164
Villa Mandosi: 89
Villa Marignolle: 31
Villa Mattei: 87
Villa Medici (Rome): 86, 87, 89, 106-110
Villa Medici (Fiesole): 25, 31, 33, 55, 58,
    61-70
Villa Mondragone: 200, 209, 213, 220-
    225
Villa Montalto: 86, 87
Villa Montevettolini: 31
Villa Muti: 205

Villa Orsini: 125, 183-186
Villa Patrizi: 110
Villa Petraia: 31, 48, 71-74
Villa la Pietra: 51
Villa Piovene: 228, 257, 260, 262-264
Villa Pisani (Montagnana): 252
Villa Pisani (Stra): 126, 272, 286-288
Villa Pisari La Rocca: 266
Villa Poggio a Caiano: 31, 75, 77
Villa Poggio Imperiale: 31
Villa Poggio Torcelli
Villa Pratolino: 31, 34, 75-81, 126
Villa Quirinale: 87, 88, 89, 102
Villa Rotonda: 228, 244, 257, 265-269
Villa Ruffinella: 217
Villa Sciarra: 87
Villa Torlonia: 205
Villa del Trebbio: 31

Villa Tuscum: 10
Villa Vecchia: 112, 125, 162, 181, 221, 223, 225
Villani, G.: 31
Vincenzo, G.: 176
Vinci, Leonardo da: 19, 23
Virgil: 16
Visconti, family: 207
Vismare, G.: 284
Vitruvius: 20, 242
Volterrano: 73

Wittkower, R.: 7, 237

Zelotti, G.: 255, 259
Zocchi: 61, 77
Zuccari: 153, 203
Zucchi, J.: 106